SHARPENING THE SWORD OF STATE

BUILDING EXECUTIVE CAPACITIES IN THE PUBLIC SERVICES OF THE ASIA-PACIFIC

SHARPENING THE SWORD OF STATE

BUILDING EXECUTIVE CAPACITIES IN THE PUBLIC SERVICES OF THE ASIA-PACIFIC

Edited by Andrew Podger and John Wanna

Australian
National
University

PRESS

ANU PRESS

School of Government the Australia and New Zealand

Published by ANU Press
The Australian National University
Acton ACT 2601, Australia
Email: anupress@anu.edu.au
This title is also available online at press.anu.edu.au

National Library of Australia Cataloguing-in-Publication entry

Title:	Sharpening the sword of state : building executive capacities in the public services of the Asia-Pacific / editors: Andrew Podger, John Wanna.
ISBN:	9781760460723 (paperback) 9781760460730 (ebook)
Series:	ANZSOG series.
Subjects:	Public officers--Training of--Pacific Area. Civil service--Pacific Area--Personnel management. Public administration--Pacific Area. Pacific Area--Officials and employees. Pacific Area--Politics and government.

Other Creators/Contributors:

Podger, A. S. (Andrew Stuart), editor.
Wanna, John, editor.

Dewey Number: 352.669

Cover design and layout by ANU Press. Cover photograph adapted from: 'staples' by jar [], flic.kr/p/97PjUh.

Contents

Figures

Tables

Abbreviations

4GP	Four General Principles
AASC	Australian Administrative Staff College
AIM	Australian Institute of Management
ANZSOG	Australia and New Zealand School of Government
AOs	Administrative Service Officers
APS	Australian Public Service
APSC	Australian Public Service Commission
ASEAN	Association of Southeast Asian Nations
ATS	Administrative Trainee Scheme
AusAID	Australian Agency for International Development
BCG	Boston Consulting Group
BCS	Bureau of Civil Service
CCP	Chinese Communist Party
CELAP	China Executive Leadership Academy Pudong
CEO	chief executive officer
CES	Career Executive Service
CES-TLC	Career Executive Service Thought Leadership Congress
CESB	Career Executive Service Board
CESDP	Career Executive Service Development Program
CESOs	career executive service officers
CESPES	Career Executive Service Performance Evaluation System
CET	cadre education and training
CFAP	Centre of Training for Public Administration
CFJ	Legal and Judicial Training Centre (Macau)

CIPD	Chartered Institute of Personnel and Development
CIRCLE	Creative Innovations and Reforms for Committed Leadership and Effectiveness
COAM	Community-Organisational Attachment Module
COTI	Central Officials Training Institute
CPDS-CES	*Omnibus Rules, Guidelines and Standards on the Continuing Professional Development System for the Career Executive Service*
CPM	Centre for Public Management
CSC	Civil Service Commission (Philippines)
CSC	Civil Service College (Singapore)
CSDI	Civil Service Development Institute
CSPTC	Civil Service Protection and Training Commission
CSTDI	Civil Service Training and Development Institute
DAP	Development Academy of the Philippines
DFAT	Department of Foreign Affairs and Trade
DGPA	Directorate-General of Personnel Administration
DGs	Directors-General
DOO	Department of Organisation
DOP	Department of Propaganda
DPJ	Democratic Party of Japan
DSP	Deputy Secretary Program
EFP	Executive Fellows Program
ELM	Executive Leadership Management
ELP	Executive Leadership Program
EMPA	Executive Master of Public Administration
ENA	Ecole Nationale d'Administration (National School of Administration)
FASID	Foundation for Advanced Studies on International Development
FC	Foundation Course
FEI	Federal Executive Institute
GDP	gross domestic product
GE	General Electric

HKPF	Hong Kong Police Force
HKSARG	Hong Kong Special Administrative Region Government
HKUPOP	Public Opinion Programme of the University of Hong Kong
HRD	human resource development
HRM	human resource management
HURIS	Human Resource Innovations and Solutions
ICAC	Independent Commission Against Corruption
ICC	Intermediate Command Course
ICT	information and communication technology
ILS	Integrated Leadership System
INTAN	National Institute of Public Administration (Malaysia)
IPAM	Institute of Public Administration and Management
IPD	Institute of Policy Development
JAPSTC	Joint Australian Public Service Training Council
JCC	Junior Command Course
KMT	Kuomintang
KSAVA	knowledge, skills, ability, values and attitude
LAFIA	Leading Australia's Future in the Asia-Pacific
LAP	Leadership in Administration Program
LATI	Local Administration Training Institute
LDP	Leadership Development Program
LDP	Liberal Democratic Party
LEAP	Leader's Enterprise Attachment Program
LI	*Leading and Innovating*
LOGODI	Local Government Officials Development Institute
MAP	Management Apprenticeship Program
MAP-CPEP	Management Apprenticeship Program Continuing Professional Education Program
MAP-FCS	Management Apprenticeship Program Foundation Course Series
MATB	Management Aptitude Test Battery
MBA	Master of Business Administration
MBO	management by objectives

MBTI	Myers-Briggs Type Indicator
MDT	Mainland Development Training
MNSA	Master of National Security Administration
MOGAHA	Ministry of Government Administration and Home Affairs
MOPAS	Ministry of Public Administration and Security
MPA	Master of Public Administration
MPM	Master of Public Management
MPP	Master of Public Policy
MPSA	Master of Public Safety Administration
NACS	National Academy of Civil Service
NCCESO	National Council of Career Executive Service Organizations
NCSI	National Civil Service Institute
NOTI	National Officials Training Institute
NPA	National Personnel Authority
NSG	National School of Government
NUCESO	National Union of Career Executive Service Officers
O&M	operation and maintenance
ODT	Overseas Development Training
OECD	Organisation for Economic Co-operation and Development
OJT	on-the-job training
OMDT	Overseas and Mainland Development Training
OVT	Overseas Vocational Training
PACE	Pacific Executive Program
PAP	People's Action Party
PC	performance contract
PCAR	Provisional Commission for Administrative Reform
PPP	public–private partnership
PS21 Office	Public Service for the 21st Century Office
PSB	Public Service Board
PSD	Public Service Division
PSMC	Public Sector Management Course

ROI	return on investment
RR	*Regular or Routine*
RRF	Recruitment and Training Department
SAFP	Serviços de Administração e Função Publica (Public Administration and Civil Service Bureau)
SARS	Severe Acute Respiratory Syndrome
SCC	Senior Command Course
SCS	senior civil servants
SCSSMS	Senior Civil Service Special Management System
SDG	Senior Directorate Group
SELCF	Senior Executive Leadership Capability Framework
SES	Senior Executive Service
SLT	Social Learning Theory
SMCPS	Shanghai Municipal Committee Party School
SMP	Senior Management Program
SOE	state-owned enterprise
STM	senior training manager
T&D	training and development
TAFE	technical and further education
TDI	Trainers and Development Institute
UNPAN	United Nations Public Administration Network
VUW	Victoria University of Wellington

Contributors

Peter Allen

Peter Allen is the former deputy dean of the Australia and New Zealand School of Government (ANZSOG) and Victoria's Public Sector Standards Commissioner. He joined ANZSOG after more than 20 years in the Victorian Public Service during which time he held several positions, including under secretary in the Department of Human Services, chief drug strategy officer, secretary of the Department of Tourism, Sport and the Commonwealth Games, secretary of the Department of Education, director of Schools and deputy secretary of Community Services.

Alex B. Brillantes Jr

Alex B. Brillantes Jr is Professor and former dean of the National College of Public Administration and Governance of the University of the Philippines and is currently on secondment as Commissioner of the Commission on Higher Education. He earlier served as chairman of the Philippine Social Science Council and executive director of the Local Government Academy of the Department of Interior and Local Government. He obtained his PhD from the University of Hawai'i. He has published locally and internationally and received the International Publications Award of the University of the Philippines for several years up to 2014. His areas of research and expertise are local governance, institutional development and reform and poverty.

Hon S. Chan

Hon S. Chan has worked at City University of Hong Kong since 1989 and was head of its Department of Public and Social Administration from 2005 to 2011. He has served as a member of a number of key committees and boards at the departmental, faculty and university levels. Professor Chan specialises in public policy and administration.

His major teaching and research interests cover public sector personnel management, performance measurement, civil service reforms, comparative institutional and policy capacity studies and environmental policies.

Maricel T. Fernandez-Carag

Maricel T. Fernandez-Carag is currently with the United Nations Educational, Scientific and Cultural Organization (UNESCO) Doha office, working in the education sector. She was a recipient of the 2013 International Publications Awardee (IPA) of the University of the Philippines (UP). She was a senior researcher at the UP National College of Public Administration and Governance from 2006 to 2014. Her fields of specialisation are public administration theory, local governance, volunteerism and human rights education.

Yijia Jing

Yijia Jing is Professor in Public Administration and Associate Director of Foreign Affairs at Fudan University, China. He is the Editor-in-Chief of *Fudan Public Administration Review* and serves as the Vice-President of its International Research Society for Public Management. Jing is Associate Editor of *Public Administration Review* and Co-Editor of *International Public Management Journal*. He is also the founding co-editor of a Palgrave book series, *Governing China in the 21st Century*.

Pan Suk Kim

Pan Suk Kim is Professor of Public Administration in the College of Government and Business at Yonsei University in South Korea. He is currently President of the Asian Association for Public Administration (AAPA) and a Lifetime Fellow of the National Academy of Public Administration (NAPA) in Washington, DC. He has broad experience as an expert in governmental affairs from both academic and policy-practitioner perspectives, and was dean of the College of Government and Business at Yonsei University and president of the International Institute of Administrative Sciences (IIAS) in Brussels from 2010 to 2013.

Hiroko Kudo

Hiroko Kudo is Professor of Public Policy and Public Management at the Faculty of Law of Chuo University, Japan, and Senior Visiting Research Fellow at the Policy Research Institute of the Japanese

Ministry of Finance. Her research interests include: governance theory, performance measurement and policy evaluation; human resource management and capacity development; decentralisation and local government; e-government; information and communication technology and innovation; cultural and sport policy; and public administration reform.

Liu Kun-I

Liu Kun-I is Chairman of the Research and Evaluation Commission, Taoyuan City, and an Associate Professor in the Department of Public Administration and Policy at the National Taipei University. He received his PhD from National Chengchi University and focused his research on public management, personnel administration and organisational theory. Dr Liu has served as a policy advisor and board member for many government agencies and non-profit organisations, including the Examination Yuan, Directorate-General of Personnel Administration, National Development Council and Taiwan Transparency International.

Pauline Lai Pou San

Pauline Lai Pou San is Principal Consultant and Senior Technician in the Financial Services Bureau of Macau Special Administrative Region. She has a keen interest in government integrity and the quality of government services, and is an active researcher of Macau's public administration.

James Low

James Low completed his PhD in political science and international relations at The Australian National University in 2014. A Singaporean national, his thesis topic was an administrative history of training schools in the Singapore Civil Service between 1959 and 2001. He is a senior researcher in the Civil Service College Singapore.

Andrew Podger

Andrew Podger is honorary Professor of Public Policy at The Australian National University, Adjunct Professor at Xi'an Jiao Tong University and Visiting Professor at Zhejiang University. A former Australian Public Service commissioner and secretary of the departments of Health and Aged Care, Housing and Regional Development, and Administrative Services, he retired from the public service in 2004.

He was national president of the Institute of Public Administration Australia from 2004 to 2010, and a member of the foundation board of the Australian and New Zealand School of Government.

Su Tsai-Tsu

Su Tsai-Tsu is Professor of Political Science and Director of the Graduate Institute of Public Affairs, National Taiwan University, where her teaching and research are focused on fiscal administration, administrative reforms and policy analysis. She was the head of the Department of Political Science at National Taiwan University from 2005 to 2009, and has served as a policy advisor or board member for numerous Taiwanese Government agencies, including as a member of the Central Government Reform Committee. Professor Su received a PhD from Carnegie Mellon University and taught at the State University of New York at Stony Brook before returning to Taiwan in 1991.

John Wanna

John Wanna is the Sir John Bunting Chair of Public Administration in the Australia and New Zealand School of Government and Professor in the School of Politics and International Relations, College of Arts and Social Sciences, at The Australian National University.

Joseph Wong Wing-ping

Joseph Wong Wing-ping is Adjunct Professor at the Department of Government and Public Administration of the Chinese University of Hong Kong. He joined the Administrative Service of the Hong Kong Government in 1973 and, in a career spanning four decades, held a variety of senior positions including assistant director and later deputy director of Trade, deputy secretary for the Civil Service, deputy secretary for Trade and Industry, Hong Kong's permanent representative to GATT (now the World Trade Organization), director of Home Affairs, secretary for Education and Manpower and secretary for the Civil Service. Wong's last Administrative Service appointment was as secretary for Commerce, Industry and Technology.

1

Public sector executive development in the Asia-Pacific: Different contexts but similar challenges

Andrew Podger

Governments around the world invest considerable resources in enhancing the capabilities of their civil service administrations with the intention of improving the quality and effectiveness of public administration. While most developed and many developing nations have established professional bureaucracies that are, in Weberian terms, strong on procedural operations (consistency, routine, compliance and due diligence), they are also now facing huge challenges as governments increasingly require their administrative organs to be more managerial, perhaps more business-like, externally oriented and client-focused, and responsive to changing needs and priorities of government and society. Governments are also acutely aware that they now operate in a rapidly changing world, a globalised environment, where nations are increasingly interconnected and impacting upon each other in various ways. In these turbulent and uncertain times, governments have realised that they require higher level leadership, strategic and analytical skills within their bureaucracies to better steer the ship of state.

This present volume, *Sharpening the Sword of State,* explores in detail the various ways in which 10 jurisdictions around the East Asia-Pacific region enhance their administrative capabilities through training and executive development. It traces how modern governments across this region look to develop their public services and public sector organisations in the face of rapid global change. For many governments there is a delicate balance between the public interest in promoting change and capacity enhancement across the public service, and the temptation to micro-manage agencies and make political appointments. There is a recognition in the country case studies that training and executive development is a crucial investment in human capital but is also couched in a much wider context of public service recruitment, patterns of entry and retention, promotion, executive appointment and career development. The various expert contributors with proximate knowledge of their jurisdictions find that there is a richness of historical traditions and administrative cultures that still informs and structures much of the training and development agendas *in situ*, although many nations are increasingly experimenting with newer and more innovative executive development programs.

The focus on East Asia-Pacific was intentional. This is one of the fastest growing areas of the globe in terms of economic activity, trade, population density and rapid modernisation. It also includes nations with long-established traditions of governance as well as newer nations and jurisdictions still experimenting with governance structures. It is to be appreciated that many of the jurisdictions included in this volume have used public service training and executive development explicitly as a means of nation-building and to pursue a broader set of strategies aimed at reforming government to promote integrity and accountability, and reduce corruption. Rarely have we had assembled such an interesting and detailed account of executive development strategies and capabilities for the Asia-Pacific region.

The nine country contributions in this publication expand on and update papers discussed at an international conference held in Taipei on 'Building Executive Capacity in the Public Sector for Better Governance' (2011). They describe contemporary arrangements for developing public sector leaders in the context of major political, economic and social change, both within each of the countries concerned and across the region and globally. They encompass a range of countries across Asia and the Pacific with very different norms and cultures, different sizes (both geographically and in terms of population), different histories and different stages of development. Not surprisingly, therefore, their approaches to public sector executive development differ; clearly, there is no universal model. Yet there are common challenges, and lessons that each country can draw from others' experiences or, at the very least, experiences elsewhere that can trigger valuable reflection on each country's approach. These challenges and lessons are relevant also to other countries in the region and beyond.

Contributors were asked to address a series of common questions. First, there were questions about context: political institution arrangements and the relationship between politics and administration, which can frame the responsibilities of public sector leaders and the skills and capabilities they need to have to be effective in their environment, and also the administrative culture of each country's public sector. Second, a set of questions was posed relating to what might be considered the 'demand' side of public sector executive development: the specific skills and capabilities that effective leaders should have, the level of investment in development and the processes for ensuring training and development deliver what is required. A third set of questions related to the 'supply' side: how are training and development provided and by whom, and how is the capacity of those providing such support maintained and enhanced?

These questions have helped to address the requirement for all cross-border learning: the need to 'learn about' before we can 'learn from' (Klein 1997; Marmor et al. 2005). Not surprisingly, in addressing these questions, the contributors raise further important questions about what they mean precisely when describing their countries' approaches to executive leadership. These papers could not possibly cover all such questions but, as Evan Berman commented at the conference, they can certainly provide an important first step towards learning from each other. There is also, of course, a further big step to adapt any lesson to the context of one's own country.

Contexts

Differences

Some differences in context do not need any explanation: Singapore, Hong Kong and Macau, as city-states, differ enormously from the geographic scales of China and Australia. China's population is at least one if not two or more orders of magnitude bigger than the others (Japan, Philippines and South Korea coming next, followed by Australia and Taiwan; Hong Kong, Singapore and Macau are substantially smaller again).

The political frameworks differ substantially. The majority have explicitly democratic processes with elected political leaders, but institutional arrangements even among these vary widely, with practice also varying with regard to the relationship between politics and administration. Some, such as Australia and Singapore, have a history of a clear distinction between elected politicians and professional non-partisan public servants, while others, such as Japan and the Philippines, have a more blurred distinction. China is the main outlier, without a democratic tradition and where, formally, there is no distinction between politics and administration.

Most chapters describe the way administrative or non-political professional leaders in the public sector are developed. In China's case, however, the processes described relate mostly to leaders who in the other countries would be described as political. Leadership development in China's case therefore has a dual emphasis on political skills and authority and on capacity to manage the public sector and solve public problems. Yijia Jing's Chapter 3 describes the increasing emphasis on knowledge and professionalism among China's leaders and their executive training and development, while still retaining a focus on Communist Party loyalty in the face of the country's marketisation and opening up. To a degree, I suspect, this represents some emerging de facto distinction between politics and administration as more emphasis is given to 'merit' in senior appointments and more formal approaches are introduced to manage individual performance in the public sector (Chen et al. 2015).

Even where clear separation between politics and administration appears to exist, different political traditions affect approaches towards public service leadership and leadership development. Singapore's long tradition of a single party in power may well have contributed to its capacity to invest so heavily in the recruitment and career development of its leaders, as described by James Low (Chapter 9). Equally, perhaps, Su Tsai-Tsu and Liu Kun-I (Chapter 10) suggest that Taiwan's more recent democratisation has contributed to a degeneration of its civil service, which has become more passive and no longer insulated from electoral politics. Alex Brillantes Jr and Maricel T. Fernandez-Carag (Chapter 8) also report problems with the lack of political support for civil service professionalism in the Philippines, and Hon S. Chan and Joseph Wong Wing-ping (Chapter 4) highlight the challenge facing the Hong Kong Police Force in maintaining its political neutrality.

Administrative norms and cultures evidently vary, with important implications for how leadership development is pursued, and even for the objectives of leadership development. Singapore, for example, has a more directed career management tradition than Australia, where there is a more laissez-faire tradition, with individuals deciding which positions to apply for and promotion decisions being made on the basis of competition among those choosing to apply. Accordingly, Singapore's leadership development process is aimed more explicitly at succession management, though there are signs of Australia also looking to improve career management, particularly with its ageing public sector workforce and impending changing of the guard.

Associated with these variations in norms and culture are the differences across countries over the extent to which staffing decisions are centralised or devolved, and the extent to which there is a whole-of-public sector executive cadre rather than separate agency-based leadership teams. Despite its generally laissez-faire approach to career management and its devolved human resource management system, Australia has had a Senior Executive Service (SES) for more than 30 years and is looking to strengthen the role of the SES as a government-wide leadership cadre. This reflects a British-born tradition, shared with Singapore (and to some extent with Hong Kong), of a generalist administrative elite with broad experience across government functions and skills that can be easily transferred. The Philippines and Korea also have long emphasised service-wide executive development within a centralised framework.

The challenges the nine countries' governments face in serving their peoples vary. Some have highly developed economies while others, like China, are still very much in the developing stage (though growing very rapidly). Japan has been addressing the challenge of an ageing workforce for some years now—a problem of growing importance now to Australia and of inevitable concern to China in about 20 years. Others, like the Philippines, face the no less challenging problem of an oversupply of young people seeking work and improved wellbeing; China is also currently in this position, pending its future challenge of an ageing population.

More general training and education arrangements also vary across countries, some involving highly sophisticated and mature public and private institutions well able to serve both the public and the private sectors, others less developed, meaning that public sector executive development must rely on especially created civil service training organisations. In some cases, such as Singapore and the Philippines, dedicated civil service organisations established in the past, when wider education and training capacity was less developed, have adapted and flourished and continue to offer high-quality services. In other countries, there is increasing use of external education and training service providers with the public sector taking advantage of competition to gain the services it wants at an acceptable price.

Some convergence?

Despite these wide differences in the context in which countries are addressing their executive development needs, the country chapters reveal some interesting common challenges from shared pressures.

All the country chapters refer to globalisation and the increasing international agendas their governments must address. Executive development must recognise these agendas and prepare leaders to manage them.

These agendas, as well as the varying domestic ones, also seem increasingly to demand capacity to work across government and more closely with the community and business. This adds to demands for whole-of-government executive development approaches with perhaps stronger central direction than some have applied in the past.

All the countries have been experiencing changes in the role of the state, whether through marketisation in China and democratisation in South Korea, the Philippines and Taiwan, or through new public management and more recent public sector reforms not only in Australia, Singapore and Japan but also across all the countries covered in this volume, which have led to increased opening up of public services and greater involvement by the private and not-for-profit sectors in the provision of public services and in the policy process.

The increasing demands on government in all countries, whatever their stage of economic development, are also placing more pressure on the professional skills and capacities in the public sector, particularly among the executive leadership. This in turn is leading to the need to invest more in development and, perhaps, to be more demanding about the formal levels of education and competence of leaders and to rely less on informal on-the-job training gained solely through experience. On-the-job training remains critical, but it is becoming more carefully planned and managed and integrated with formal training activities.

A possible consequence of these common challenges is that, notwithstanding the wide differences in political–administrative relationships, improved executive development with increased investment requires commitment from the political leadership. Many countries, including Korea, Singapore and Taiwan, have already demonstrated strong interest from political leaders (including the President, in Korea's case) in administrative leadership development but, even in Australia, political engagement has proven to be critical to such initiatives.

Demand-side arrangements

Who sets the objectives and determines the content?

The objectives of executive development are set explicitly or implicitly by those most concerned about the performance of current and future public sector leaders. Singapore's tightly managed career system is closely controlled from the centre. Its determination to attract and retain the very best and brightest from Singapore's universities is reflected not only in its executive development but also in its elite selection and promotion management and its highly generous remuneration policies (extraordinarily so relative to the other nations). China's unique party framework also involves close control from the centre.

Countries with less tightly managed career systems still have centrally or collectively set requirements for executive development and selection and some centrally determined programs and activities for senior-level staff identified as having potential for top positions. But to varying degrees these are complemented by agency-level policies for other staff and by agency-level programs aimed to complement the executive skills development offered across government to those with potential for the top positions.

This attempt to balance central and agency-level requirements may be illustrated best by the Australian approach. Despite its devolved authority to make employment decisions, the Public Service Commissioner must 'certify' SES appointments. There is also a service-wide approach to executive development for the SES, which all agencies have been encouraged to adopt, though they often complement this with their own leadership programs and activities. The Centre for Leadership and Learning has been established in the Australian Public Service Commission (APSC) to offer and regularly update a suite of programs based on the earlier 'Integrated Leadership System' that was developed cooperatively with agencies to guide middle-level and senior executive development across the APS (APSC 2004; Podger 2004).

The Philippines' framework, developed by the Career Executive Service Board, would seem to provide guidance to Philippines' agencies that is similar to that provided by the APSC, though perhaps with a somewhat firmer hand.

The Hong Kong Police Force's arrangements represent an exemplar of a comprehensive agency-based approach. While Hong Kong also has a civil service-wide approach to executive training and development, the police force has responded not only to its own technical and professional requirements but also to its broader leadership and personnel management requirements, consistent with whole-of-government approaches. In this way, it ensures training and development of Hong Kong police are much more closely tied to its own workforce planning requirements and to the culture of professionalism and shared learning it is looking to promote across the police force.

The Australia and New Zealand School of Government (ANZSOG), described by Peter Allen and John Wanna (Chapter 2), represents an important further advancement in shared leadership development, not only across agencies within a jurisdiction but also across jurisdictions. Two national governments and eight sub-national governments own ANZSOG and, through its board, determine the programs and their content. Participating universities are also represented on the board. While ANZSOG focuses on an elite group of current and emerging leaders, and provides only a limited range of programs, it is influencing the wider range of leadership activities of all 10 jurisdictions.

Who pays? How much?

Responsibility for funding executive development activity corresponds very broadly with the extent to which the requirements are set centrally or distributed. In Singapore, half the funding is provided centrally. In Australia, very little is funded centrally, although the national and state/territory governments have injected substantial capital into ANZSOG and each government has made a centralised commitment to participant numbers. Nonetheless, almost all the costs of training and development—whether through ANZSOG or the wide range of other programs provided through the APSC and other jurisdictions' central personnel agencies—are met by each agency for its employees.

In some countries, the centrally provided funds are directed to the government supplier of training programs, while in others the funds support the participants. In China, there is a mix, with the centre subsidising participants and trainers, while agencies are responsible for meeting the remaining costs of their participating staff. The benefits of funding via participants and their agencies include placing competitive pressure on service providers and requiring providers to respond more carefully to the demands of participants and their agencies (that is, 'customer focus'). Funding direct to the supplier, however, may better ensure investment in research and trainer development and thereby lead to better-quality programs in the future, despite the danger of complacency arising from having a monopoly supplier. It would be interesting to test further the experience countries have had in these respects.

While it is hard to be sure about the definitions involved, there appear to be wide variations in the levels of investment in executive development. Several countries, such as Korea, Singapore and Taiwan, the Hong Kong Police Force and Macau, appear to be investing about 3 per cent or more in training and development programs (in terms of total administrative expenses and days or hours dedicated to development activities, which is often referred to as a 'good practice' benchmark). Others—for example, Australia—seem to be spending nearer to 1 per cent, although there are suggestions this is increasing as Australia's tradition of career public servants learning constantly on the job (like lifetime apprentices) has been shifting, with greater mobility and advances in technology and knowledge requiring more formal education and training.

What is the content?

It is hard to draw comparisons of content as different countries describe their programs using their own terminology and without any common definitions. The Taiwan chapter, for example, refers to a progression from 'management capabilities' to 'leadership development' and then 'strategy development', linked to 'core competencies'; the chapter on the Hong Kong Police Force refers to a progression from 'vocational skills' to 'professional development' and on to 'executive development'.

Australian distinctions and definitions, while not fully explained in Chapter 2, might provide a useful framework for further international comparisons. The Integrated Leadership System distinguishes between leadership, management and technical skills, suggesting that the importance of technical skills generally declines at executive levels while the importance of leadership and management skills increases. It also implies that the development of technical skills is the responsibility of individual agencies but, as the management and leadership responsibilities increase, a stronger role in executive development needs to be played by the centre.

The precise balance between these three sets of skills or capabilities will depend on the precise responsibilities of the (executive) position, as technical or particular professional skills may still be critical for top executives in some agencies (for example, police, Treasury, attorney-general's) or particular executive positions in other agencies (for example, chief medical officer, chief scientist, chief economist).

Nevertheless, as people rise up the ranks, their sphere of control tends to widen, their budget responsibilities increase, their time horizon lengthens, their breadth of critical relationships broadens and the impact of their decisions increases. Accordingly, their management responsibilities increase and the management skills they require change—from supervising small numbers of staff and managing a number of tasks, to managing small budgets and planning projects and activities, to broader business planning and program management and to strategic planning and capability building. Similarly, leadership capabilities become more important and shift—from being a productive member of a team, to leading small teams and to leading and positioning agencies and achieving whole-of-government outcomes or even multi-jurisdictional ones.

A distinction between management and leadership has been emphasised in the leadership literature of the past 30 years or more (see, for example, Burns 1978; Kotter 1996), with that on leadership focusing, for example, on collaboration and empowerment rather than direction, and relating more to a changing rather than a static environment. The capabilities required for leadership have been articulated in the Australian model as:

- achieving results
- communicating with influence
- cultivating effective working relationships
- shaping strategic directions
- exemplifying personal integrity and commitment.

As a person takes on a more senior role, the specific skill requirements for each of these capabilities change and deepen. Behind these capabilities there is also the theme of constant learning and building 'learning organisations'.

More recently, Australia has also begun to draw on Harvard's 'Knowing, Doing, Being Framework' (Nohria and Khurana 2010) focusing on, respectively, learning specific management and technical skills, applying them in the public sector environment to build leadership capabilities (identified above) and to strengthen self-awareness, social skills and situational awareness.

The various chapters in this volume reflect strong interest in developing similar leadership capabilities and management skills among their public sector executives, and to building learning organisations. Pan Suk Kim (Chapter 6) refers to the Korean competency framework that emphasises 'thinking, working and building relationships'. The Philippines chapter describes its programs for Career Executive Service Officers, with its foundation program focusing on 'knowing oneself', 'relating to others' and 'leading the organisation' and its specific leadership and management competencies including communication, networking, leadership, change management, performance management and strategic thinking. Taiwan also emphasises communication skills.

Many of the capabilities and skills involved are sometimes called 'soft skills' but they are anything but 'soft', and developing them requires careful effort. There is a danger in the leadership rhetoric, however, that it becomes too generic and loses its sharpness and hardness. The Singapore approach described here has a hard edge throughout. The Senior Management Program includes translating policy intent into implementation, public consultation and public communications; the Leadership in Administration Program for top executives involves thinking critically about the future of Singapore and how the public service should respond, and also includes policy implementation, specific management skills and organisational leadership and learning about political, economic and social developments in Singapore and across the region.

It would be useful therefore to consider in more detail the content of the programs and measures identified by governments and agencies as likely to develop their future executives. Most are looking to a mix of activities, not relying solely on education and training programs. The Hong Kong Police Force devotes only one-quarter of its effort to formal education and training programs, placing much more emphasis on mentoring, coaching and careful career management. Australia is now utilising a 10:20:70 template for its development activities: 10 per cent in the classroom, 20 per cent in structured self-learning and 70 per cent on the job. Singapore and Australia are also encouraging mobility to widen the experience of future leaders, testing individuals in challenging projects and programs, placing some in jobs outside the public service and complementing education and training programs.

The content of the education and training programs is also focused on practical skills. A number of countries emphasise their practical or case management style; the Hong Kong chapter refers to its 'problem-based' approach as distinct from a 'curriculum-based' approach. Hiroko Kudo (Chapter 5) refers to Japan's emphasis on shared learning and participant-led training with a practical orientation. ANZSOG also makes much use of case studies and group learning, though it also tries to explore theory as well as practice to ensure participants are trained for the challenges they may face in the future and not just learning the experience of past challenges.

While there are slightly different emphases, all are pursuing content-rich programs. ANZSOG's Executive Master of Public Administration (EMPA) curriculum, for example, includes: delivering public value, managing public sector organisations, designing public policies and programs, leading public sector change, governing by the rules, decision-making under uncertainty and government in a market economy.

A common theme for nearly all the countries is the need to ensure future public sector executives are globally aware. Some, such as Singapore, Hong Kong and Macau, provide some or all senior executives with study trips, while others are offering positions in other countries' executive development programs. All ensure within their training and development programs some exposure to international developments, using educators and trainers from elsewhere to complement homegrown teachers. As a conference participant noted, the costs of sending executives to Harvard may be prohibitive, but it may be possible to bring some Harvard or similar international experts home for a visit.

Who, if anyone, evaluates and how?

Most countries have been reviewing their executive development programs, mostly through central agencies working with the training and development providers. The Taiwan chapter highlights the use of scientific methods to evaluate its programs. ANZSOG, with a board of senior jurisdiction representatives and university leaders, also uses formal evaluation processes. The board has called for formal reviews of its EMPA program and its research activity, each time establishing a small team of independent experts who have surveyed and consulted widely with practitioners, academics and program participants before providing reports later made public on ANZSOG's website.

A challenge for any review or evaluation is whether the performance of those who undertake executive development has been improved by the experience and whether the performance of their agencies in delivering public services has materially improved as a result. Intermediate results are more easily measured, such as the promotion success of participants, the views of their supervisors on the extent and usefulness of the knowledge and skills gained and the views of participants. The ANZSOG review in 2007 of its EMPA program warned against relying too heavily on participants' views, as there is a risk they reflect the 'entertainment' value of the program rather than its usefulness and effectiveness.

Trends

All the countries are looking to increase investment in executive development and to ensure greater end-user control. Despite the wide variation in extent of centralisation or devolution in their public administration culture, all are ensuring a significant whole-of-government approach and, within the different content of the programs, all are giving more emphasis to leadership capabilities and are looking to ensure senior executives are well exposed to international developments and thinking and that they learn about working across borders. There is also increasing recognition that executive development requires much more than education and training programs.

Supply-side arrangements

Most of the countries concerned have a major government-owned provider of training and development services though many are increasingly using other service providers as well, particularly for more specialist training. In most cases, the government-owned provider receives some funding directly from government.

Australia (and New Zealand) is the main exception to this. ANZSOG, while owned jointly by the participating jurisdictions, does not itself deliver the training but works through a network of participating universities with some core components of the training provided centrally through contracted staff from Australia and New Zealand and elsewhere. As explained in the Australian chapter, ANZSOG is also only one part of the system of executive development training, with the remainder provided by a range of education institutions and private sector training organisations operating strictly on a fee-for-service basis, sometimes based on panel contracts negotiated by the APSC and similar bodies in other jurisdictions.

The formality of the training varies. Some, such as in Taiwan and for the Hong Kong Police Force, requires accredited training to support the competency-based occupational structure. Executive training and development similarly may have a formal, competency-based style although this is often complemented by an array of less formal short-course training programs provided by various public and private suppliers. Again, Australia is somewhat of an outlier with its more devolved and laissez-faire approach to human resource management, traditionally giving less emphasis to formal, accredited training, but that has been changing over the past decade or two. Partly tied to the increasing reliance on a graduate workforce, there has been a steady increase in postgraduate certificates and degrees, and training that is recognised towards such certificates and degrees.

An important by-product of more accredited training is the discipline education institutions themselves place on the quality of the courses and the assessment of the participants. The participants also value the accreditation, seeing the benefits attached for future job prospects. On the other hand, control by the education institutions can limit end-user influence and make modifications for changing requirements harder to achieve.

Several chapters, including those on Taiwan and South Korea, express concern about the quality of the executive development effort by education and training providers, particularly where the trainers are poorly paid. Enhancing the capability of the providers is seen as a priority, but the budgetary implications will be difficult to overcome. Differentiating programs targeted towards the high fliers, as is done in Singapore and Australia, can limit the costs involved but requires acceptance of this elite approach. The approach may not disadvantage others if, as seems to have happened in Australia, the elite programs have influenced a wider array of other executive training and development, increasing demand, the resources available and the quality of the teaching.

Another important factor in ensuring the capability of training and development providers is to fund research linked to the training. Most countries surveyed in this volume have been building up case studies that can be widely drawn on. Others, such as ANZSOG, go substantially further to support research into areas of public administration that can be drawn on in teaching, and to encourage practitioners to conduct and use research. These keep the teaching programs up-to-date both with current practice and with developments in public administration theory.

Trends

There seem to be several common trends and issues. As mentioned earlier, there is more emphasis on ensuring suppliers of executive development services are meeting the demands of the market— the requirements of top management in the government.

There appears to be a breaking down of monopoly suppliers so that, even where there remains a dominant government supplier, it is complemented by other organisations including higher education institutions and private companies and is thereby subject to some competitive pressures.

If not already doing so, countries appear to be giving more weight to accredited education and training organisations, and are increasingly concerned about the capability of the training providers and looking for ways to review the quality and effectiveness of learning programs and methods.

Conclusion

Constant themes throughout this volume include not only the importance of public sector executive development but also the desire for executives to have an international focus and to be 'world-class' leaders able to deal with and influence international agendas.

All the countries recognise the need to invest in executive development but the costs are high, particularly if the training includes international engagement, and more effort is required to ensure value for money.

A common theme is the need to ensure the supply of executive development services is responsive to the demands of top management and the government, and to ensure these demands are carefully developed and analysed and constantly reviewed.

The skills and capabilities being developed vary, but it seems that all are giving more emphasis to leadership and management skills—the 'soft' skills concerned with effective working relationships within agencies, across government, across jurisdictions and beyond government—and in shaping rather than directing strategic change. They also rely heavily on public service values and integrity. Complementing these are more specific management and technical or professional skills. Encompassing them all is an attitude of continuous learning and the capacity to build learning organisations.

Such executive development requires a mix of strategies, with increasing emphasis on learning through experience to complement formal education and training programs. A challenge for all countries is how to assess the effectiveness of the learning methods used and how to build capacity among those responsible for providing education and training services.

References

Australian Public Service Commission (APSC) 2004. *Integrated Leadership System*. Canberra: APSC.

Burns, J. M. 1978. *Leadership*. New York: Harper & Row.

Chen, L., Chan, H. and Yu, J. 2015. Party management of talent: Building a party-led, merit-based talent market in China. *Australian Journal of Public Administration* 74(5): 298–311.

Klein, R. 1997. Learning from others: Shall the last be the first? *Journal of Health Politics, Policy and Law* 22(5): 1267–78.

Kotter, J. 1996. *Leading Change*. Boston: Harvard Business School Press.

Marmor, T., Freeman, R. and Okma, K. 2005. Comparative perspectives and policy learning in the world of healthcare. *Journal of Comparative Policy Analysis* 7(4): 331–48.

Nohria, N. and Khurana, R. (eds) 2010. *Handbook of Leadership Theory and Practice*. Boston: Harvard Business School Press.

Podger, A. 2004. Innovation with integrity: The public sector leadership imperative to 2020. *Australian Journal of Public Administration* 63(1): 11–21.

2

Developing leadership and building executive capacity in the Australian public services for better governance

Peter Allen and John Wanna

Introduction

Australian governments have invested in public sector training and development since the pre-Federation decades in the last quarter of the nineteenth century. Dedicated training to impart basic skills and routines in the embryonic public services of colonial times was immediately recognised as a necessity across all the established Australian jurisdictions—first, the colonial states, then the Federal Government and subsequently in the territories and at local government levels—with each conducting their own training programs to suit their own needs and requirements. Historically, various central oversight bodies (such as public service boards and commissions with statutory independence) were charged explicitly with responsibility for ensuring training and development in departments and agencies, with official reports and commissions of inquiry charting progress, highlighting problems and recommending courses of action (Parker 1993; Caiden 1967; Spann 1973).

In this chapter, we suggest that public sector training in Australia has evolved from informal on-the-job training supported by 'in-service' programs aimed at conveying basic administrative requirements, functional tasks and operating procedures to more formalised, externally provided, qualification-based educational development and training. The latter tended to take one of two directions: professional education involving specialist forms of expertise and technical skilling; or the inculcation of more generically inspired managerial capabilities and familiarisation with emerging organisational and work perspectives—operation and maintenance (O&M), management by objectives (MBO), financial and human resource skills, computing and technology, as well as fashionable managerial philosophies such as 'new public management' or 'public value' approaches. In recent years, Australian governments have focused on developing strategic leadership skills and building executive capacities in and across public organisations and their network partners or service providers.

This chapter locates public sector training within Australia's traditions of governance. It briefly explores the historical development and increasing importance of educational qualifications and formalised training programs. It then reviews the changing patterns of demand for types of training and skills development, the evolving curricula and professional orientation of training and the changing composition and roles of training providers (the supply side), going from 'in-house' training units to generalist educational institutions and eventually to specialist consultant providers. In the Australian context, executive development programs have increasingly become integrated within formal staff appraisal processes and performance review systems, while at the same time such philosophies have shifted from transmitting basic technical skills to thinking about developing organisational human resource capabilities, and eventually to the encouragement of team-based problem-solving leadership potentialities (AIM 2013). The chapter finishes with a case study of the Australia and New Zealand School of Government (ANZSOG), a unique interjurisdictional and intervarsity executive development institution dedicated to growing executive capabilities not only among its Australasian members but also in the wider Pacific region.[1]

---

1   The authors would like to thank Professors Gary Banks and Andrew Podger for comments and suggestions on earlier drafts.

Public services shaped by Australian traditions of governance

Australia, like New Zealand, inherited its main political traditions in the nineteenth century from its colonial power, the United Kingdom, including ideas about the formation of governments, election systems, political parties and the nature of its public services across the various self-governing colonies. Westminster-derived notions of 'responsible government' (with an elected executive responsible to parliament under a constitutional monarchy with vestiges of crown privilege) were transplanted to Australian shores from the British motherland along with the desire to populate the 'New World' with white settlers comprising deported convicts and free-settler émigrés (see Patapan et al. 2005). British traditions of small 'c' constitutionality (*Magna Carta*, *habeas corpus*, parliamentary sovereignty, the rule of law, consent and tolerance, and so on) underscored the main Westminster political traditions involving a reliance on pragmatic political conventions, majoritarianism, a strong executive held 'responsible' to parliament, competing political parties and loyal opposition. These were foundational principles, with some local adaptations, in the Australian colonies and in the new federal administration after 1901.

These governing traditions also informed notions about the nature of public administration and the institution of the public service— particularly the 'fused' but subservient relationship with formal politics (the elected executive)—as well as its normative roles and responsibilities, hierarchical structure and organisation, composition and skill base, recruitment and promotion and internal administrative cultures (see Podger 2003). To outsiders, the British character of public administration has often been categorised as dilettantish or amateurish, fundamentally class-ridden and too reliant on its reputed 'good chap' sensibilities towards serving in public office (Hennessy 1988). Australia and New Zealand followed the United Kingdom in establishing a permanent civil service, which in the Antipodes enjoyed a formal statutory status that codified an observed separation (and protection) from politics (essentially eschewing ministerial involvement in senior appointments). Australian public services were conceived as permanent apparatuses of state, loyal and obedient to the government of the day, but apolitical, neutral and anonymous (Crisp 1972; Spann 1973). Public service organisations (ministerial departments and statutory authorities) were administratively interdependent with government, having professionally to work closely with cabinet and its ministers and so become to some extent politically savvy without being politically active. Over time, public servants developed considerable administrative expertise, advisory skills and effective relations with elected (and frequently changing) ministries. If politicians became regarded as the temporal and alternating rulers of government, public officials were often conceived of as permanent institutions of the state imbued with the techniques of statecraft— at least until the 1970s and 1980s, when some of their privileges were withdrawn and contestability for advice became more commonplace (Davis and Rhodes 2000).

State-level public services generally date from the mid-1850s, with the federal administrative institutions now approaching 115 years of age—previously called the Commonwealth Public Service but now known as the Australian Public Service (APS). These public services (now nine separate jurisdictions) all became career services, generally unified as a jurisdictional workforce, enshrining the principles of continuity, neutrality, anonymity and largely internal notions of merit (Caiden 1965). They typically recruited from school-leaver entrants who saw public service as their sole vocation, closed off from the wider labour market, offering internal promotion opportunities and providing lifetime employment (historically this was primarily open only to males, because various prohibitions on married women removed them from the service and allowed career employment only to non-married women, until the bar on married women was lifted from the 1960s). The various services were staffed by a combination of predominantly generalist administrators with some specialist professions. They were highly insular and not open to 'strangers' (very little lateral recruitment or 'lateral entry' from outside), and increasingly became bureaucratically industrial in their employment orientations (with strong public sector unions organised by administrative categories). For decades, governments and their central personnel management agencies (the public service boards) were preoccupied with improving the quality and reliability of administration, including economy and efficiency, routinisation and consistency of administrative practice, due diligence, compliance accountability and ethics (PSMPC 2001). More recently, these perennial bureaucratic issues have tended to be overshadowed (but not totally displaced) by the imperatives of improved management, greater reliance on business techniques and conceptual skills, performance and program effectiveness over results and outcomes, capacity building, developing outward-oriented cultures of responsiveness and client-focused forms of service delivery, and consultative practices and public engagement.

Australia's 'training-for-purpose' approach to public service training and executive development

There are some standard features of Australia's approach to training and development in the public service that have not changed unduly over time. Australian public services remain career services, with the majority of officials enjoying continuing employment (through to the most senior Band 3–level Senior Executive Service (SES) appointments with reversionary employment rights even if they are serving on more lucrative three to five-year contracts). Entering administrative recruits generally start at the bottom (base-grade clerical) and progress through the service via internal promotion routes not usually open to outside competition as they accumulate on-the-job experience and achieve competencies. Training and development for public servants were not a statutory requirement (and are not mentioned in older or newer versions of the various *Public Service Acts*), but service-wide bodies and individual agencies maintained an enduring interest in 'training for purpose'. Most of the larger agencies tended to operate their own training activities (and could contract external providers for specific workshops), while central agencies (public service boards or commissions) retained some overall service-wide responsibilities, including coordination and ensuring agencies fulfilled their training and executive development obligations. Accordingly, most training and development were fragmented and conducted at the individual agency level, with considerable in-service delivery and customised on-the-job training. Taken together, these training regimes formed a matrix of self-administered, 'job-focused' training, generally characterised by piecemeal provision, internally provided with short-term focuses, stop-start in delivery and 'not for credit'—that is, they did not count as upper secondary or tertiary qualifications.

These in-service offerings—resourced primarily at the individual agency level—could be supplemented at the individual officer level with formal 'out-service' instruction 'for credit' (qualification-based programs delivered by business and secretarial colleges, night schools and further education colleges, dedicated training institutes and universities).

Significantly, however, no Australian or New Zealand jurisdiction has invested in a single monopoly provider of training services. There has never been an equivalent in Australia or New Zealand of the central civil service colleges, such as the centrally funded Singapore Civil Service College or the Taiwanese National Academy of the Civil Service, with service-wide responsibilities for training and development. This is not to say that there have not been constant tensions between and debates over the merits of agency-specific 'training for purpose' and the 'holy grail' of devising centrally coordinated generic training regimes.[2]

The evolution of public service training and development

Gerard Caiden once wrote that 'the traditional approach to public service careers in Australia has stressed the recruitment of young school-leavers who could be trained on the job and promoted according to promise and performance' (1967: 217). But this was not the full picture as, even at the time he was writing, about half the Commonwealth and state public services comprised returned servicemen who were given preferred employment status and who had relatively limited schooling. Returned servicemen, with limited educational levels and policy capabilities, posed a major dilemma for the public service because by the time these officials had reached their 40s and 50s, further training was of questionable value and few were likely to volunteer for (or be accepted in) formal courses in tertiary institutions. Central personnel agency control and direction of training were most pronounced between the 1940s and the 1980s (with some centrally designed and delivered generic courses, although

---

2   For example, the Public Service Board established the Central Training Section in 1947 to plan and coordinate training activities, especially systematic training of clerical and administrative staff.

there were debates about whether the board should seek to provide training that was available through external providers; see Caiden 1967). Before and after these decades, line agencies themselves tended to take responsibility for their own training needs or, in the later period, looked to the market.

Service-wide interest in training began in the late 1930s, mainly encouraging job rotation in departments and supporting external studies by individual officers (see Appendix 2.1 for key milestone dates of training provision). By the late 1940s, routine in-service training consisted of induction sessions for new recruits (new entrant schools), procedural training related to compliance and specific administrative tasks (claims handling, benefit assessments, investigation procedures, safety and maintenance work, machine operation, technician training) and refresher courses to ensure better performance and reliability (correspondence and report writing, dictation and typing, improved reading, work simplification, bookkeeping, and so on) (Betts 1949; Caiden 1967: 219). Even from the late 1920s and early 1930s there was some scope for recruiting a handful of graduates for non-professional clerical divisions, and some encouragement for public servants to undertake 'outside studies' at night schools or colleges of further education. From the 1950s, public services gradually (and sometimes reluctantly) tried to make themselves more attractive employers, recruiting graduate intakes (still in very limited numbers), cadet entrants and from administrative trainee schemes.[3] By the 1960s greater emphasis was placed on professional skills and data analysis (administrative data processing), usually as an investment in potential human capital (and university cadetships that 'bonded' the individual recipients for up to five years with the public service). As well, jurisdictions paid particular attention to entry-level training, new entrant induction programs and professional skills development directly linked to merit and promotion (not organisational seniority). Senior administrative staff and professional grades were given their own selective training—from senior management conferences to executive development programs and mentoring/coaching schemes.

3   In 1962 the Public Service Board (PSB) celebrated the recruitment of 93 graduates into the clerical division, commenting that the figure was the 'highest for many years' (Caiden 1965). The 44th PSB *Annual Report*, for 1968, listed the annual intake of graduate appointments from 1933 to 1967; the intake ranged from none or one or two to 200 or 300 with the main growth only occurring from the mid-1960s.

However, much in-service training remained experience-related, where the twin objectives were 'to see that an individual knows what to do without being told and to see that he is more receptive when he is told' (Spann 1973: 84). There is little evidence that training needs were closely aligned with 'manpower planning' or with thinking about future workplace human resource needs.

In the 1970s as policy work expanded, the number of graduates entering the various services increased. While most of those in the higher grades (first and second divisions) were graduates by the late 1970s, only 1,748 new graduates were appointed into the clerical division in 1975—up from 884 in 1969 and only 212 in 1959. By 1978 quota limits on the number of entering graduates were abolished and, gradually, as they rose through the ranks, these more educated public servants stressed the importance of knowledge and intellectual and analytical abilities. Yet although the numbers of graduates increased significantly (rising to almost 4,000 per annum by the early 1980s), very few had any formal tertiary training in public administration (but more would have had social science training, including government or political science degrees). By the 1980s, the focus had shifted to middle-management training and business and management training, often with graduates undertaking subsequent graduate diplomas and master's courses in professional areas, including Master of Business Administration (MBA), law and accounting masters. Internal training tended then to focus on competency-based training, gap analysis for required skills and selective recruitment. A frequent structure for courses was based on three themes: technical skills, interpersonal skills and self-management skills (PSC 1992: 37–8). A government-mandated training guarantee program in the early 1990s requiring agencies to spend 2 per cent of their budgets on training saw the proliferation of many private-sector training organisations and providers of organised conferences on work-related topics under the banner of training. In addition, a number of senior executive services (SESs) had been created by the early 1990s across the jurisdictions, and specialist development programs were devised for this cohort, including a dedicated induction program called SEMP. Executive development relied on a formal leadership capability framework to broaden capabilities and develop high-performance leadership (by encouraging people to develop executive capabilities to shape strategic thinking, cultivate productive working relations, communicate with influence, exemplify personal drive and integrity and achieve results) (see APSC 2004). At the same time, a 'cooperative venture' between all the Australian jurisdictions and a consortium of universities provided middle-management development courses with formal university qualifications (graduate certificate), called the public sector management course (PSMPC 2001: 191). As the 2000s progressed, many jurisdictions adopted forms of an 'integrated leadership framework' applying to their SES and other executive levels (see APSC 2004; Chapter 1, this volume).

Changing dynamics of demand

Demands for training were historically decentralised in origin, driven by agency needs and often provided by agencies themselves. In the APS, training was historically seen as a means of transmitting departmental cultures, norms and procedures as well as administrative capabilities. Usually the agencies employing the staff chose the course topics and types of training provided and the quantum of attendees. Individual agencies also funded the training they provided themselves or paid for outside providers from within their budgets (and accepted the costs associated with deploying staff away from normal duties). Agencies naturally focused on their own immediate needs and purposes, and the training was not particularly anticipatory or strategic in content. Some agencies developed extensive in-house training programs, some of which were compulsory for new recruits and middle-level officials. But in-house training with its focus on agency-specific vocational on-the-job experience had its limitations, which were gradually apparent across the public services from the 1960s.

Government departments and individual public servants both energised the demand for formal qualifications (tertiary degrees, advanced diplomas, graduate diplomas, masters by coursework) as endemic 'credentialism' manifested itself in the public service. Almost all new recruits possessed graduate qualifications (or were close to graduating), and many were sponsored to undertake (relevant) higher-level studies, especially vocationally oriented masters courses—for example, public policy, policy studies, public management, accounting or generic business studies. Universities and technical and further education (TAFE) colleges expanded their vocational offerings as well as beginning to tap the part-time student and distance-education markets. But, at the same time, traditional courses in the building blocks of public administration tended to decline as an academic specialisation, replaced with more generic courses in business techniques, organisational design, human resource management, computing studies and information technology (Davis and Wanna 1997). The number of institutions offering postgraduate MBAs increased from two in the 1970s to more than 30 by the late 2000s, and these business-oriented higher degrees were, for a while, remarkably popular with public servants and their departmental supervisors. Eventually rivalling this development of generic business credentialism was the establishment of a number of dedicated public policy tertiary courses (some offered at the undergraduate level but most provided at the masters level to graduates) (see the survey of Australian university public policy/public management centres/ degrees by Di Francesco 2015). Enrolments across tertiary institutions increased from 200,000 in 1985 to 600,000 by 2014, forming a huge pool of educated jobseekers from which to recruit staff.

Australia also saw the growth of specialist professional institutions delivering executive education. Along with the Workers' Education Association (dating back to the nineteenth century with mechanics' institutes), there arose dedicated training centres such as the Australian Administrative Staff College (AASC, a residential executive college established in 1954), which later became the Mount Eliza Business School, and then merged in 2004 with the Melbourne Business School of the University of Melbourne. There was also increased provision from various professional bodies such as the various public service commissions, the Australian Institute of Management (AIM) and the Institute of Public Administration of Australia (see AIM 2013). These professional bodies tended to provide professionally oriented and vocational training, stressing 'learning and development' and often concentrated on some generic capabilities—for example, public policy skills, business and management techniques, accounting and specialist law programs and health and safety training. Learning and development were typically based on a 70:20:10 pedagogic model, with 70 per cent related to on-the-job training, 20 per cent learnt through networks and relations and 10 per cent through formal education programs. A host of private sector training and executive development providers also sprang up from the 1980s, often headed by former top executives from the public and private sectors—for example, the Centre for Public Management (CPM), YellowEdge and Timmins & Stewart Consulting.

Within government, attention to high-level specialised executive development became a focus from the 1950s, and various programs succeeded one another to target and prepare future leaders from among the most talented in the public service—for instance, an annual conference of second-division officers began in 1954, emphasising special skills for senior administrators. Initially, programs such as the Deputy Secretary Program (DSP)—identifying potential next-generation leaders—provided tailored individual plans including career placements or secondments, orchestrated workplace experience, senior shadowing, senior expertise in policy development as well as managing technical and functional areas of government. The DSP was essentially a nurturing program for identified senior executives with a largely domestic focus. Such programs were typically run by the relevant public service boards for cohorts of internal participants who had seniority and/or were deemed to have leadership potential—although there was some scepticism about whether such headstart/elite programs were actually successful and whether the next generation of leaders actually emerged from these identified cohorts. The federal DSP gradually gave way to more international/comparative leadership programs, such as the annual Leading Australia's Future in the Asia-Pacific (LAFIA) study tour program, which was established in 2000 and provided senior executives with a greater understanding of Asia's economic growth and political regimes to encourage greater engagement with Asia and the Pacific. LAFIA was a contractual program undertaken as a joint initiative between the Australian Public Service Commission (APSC) and The Australian National University (Crawford School) and, by 2015, it had trained more than 300 senior executives. Elsewhere across the public service, senior executive development was also promoted by deputies' forums such as the APS200 group (a deliberative/shared learning exchange) plus various learning centres and talent management exercises. Other international-focused dialogue events/forums include the Harvard Club of Australia, the Australian American Leadership Dialogue, the Greater China Australia Dialogue, the Indonesia–Australia Dialogue, as well as domestic bodies such as the Lowy Institute and the Grattan Institute.

Recent evaluations of Australia's commitment to training and executive development

In March 2010 a new blueprint for the reform of Australian government administration, entitled *Ahead of the Game*, was publicly released. While it noted that the existing performance of the APS could be assessed overall as comparable with some of the world's best public services, the case for further reform was strongly supported. One of its major findings was that the APS was underinvesting in its talent, particularly in comparison with the private sector, where estimates were that as much as 80 per cent of a company's worth could be tied up in its employees and their human capital. Across Australia's private sector, average expenditure on employee development floated at about 4 per cent of their total budgets. In comparison, almost half of APS agencies reported spending less than 1 per cent of their budget on staff development. Only a small proportion reported spending amounts comparable with the best private sector organisations. In addition, the quality of learning and development was identified as a problem, with fewer than one in three APS employees rating the effectiveness of their learning and development program as high or very high in terms of helping them improve performance.

The *Ahead of the Game* report identified significant challenges faced by government in respect of executive development, which were that:

- a generational shift was occurring in the leadership group
- there was a shallow pool of successor talent
- there were real difficulties in delivering a breadth of experience to future leaders
- governments had made low investment (compared with best-practice corporations) in the development of executive talent
- there was difficulty in giving senior executives 'time out' to refresh and reflect
- there was a pressing need to attract high-potential graduates to public sector careers.

In response, reforms recommended in *Ahead of the Game*—and unanimously endorsed by the Australian Government—aimed to enhance agency agility, capability and effectiveness, and expand and strengthen learning and development. Consultations with stakeholders identified the need to improve leadership and management across the APS. Specific gaps in performance and capability were identified as people management skills, the capacity to steer and implement change and the capacity to think strategically. Specific recommendations included:

- strengthening the role of the APSC to drive the reform strategy
- establishing a leadership development centre that utilises best-practice talent development from the public and private sectors.

Recommendations also required the APSC to develop a stronger relationship with specialist providers of leadership development programs across Australia to ensure 'capacity exists to meet increased demand for high quality professional development' (Australian Government 2010: 60). The report called for more political and executive 'buy-in' for dedicated training, more robust engagement with the contours of supply and demand in training markets and the development of more structured or segmented markets and accredited providers. It also noted that many traditional issues of concern were still relevant today—namely: the relevance of training, its applicability or operability to those undertaking training and whether agencies were making best use of innovation strategies and were open to new ideas and management practices.

The Australia and New Zealand School of Government: A unique response to building executive capabilities

A significant innovation in the Australian context is the formation of a dedicated executive development institution, the ANZSOG. In its promotional material, the school committed itself to become:

> [A] world-class centre providing cutting-edge research and tailored learning opportunities for future leaders of the public sector. ANZSOG's purpose is to encourage improved public sector leadership, decision-making, policy outcomes and performance for the benefit of the community. ANZSOG plays a crucial role in promoting public service as a vocational profession of great social value to the public interest. (ANZSOG n.d.)

To achieve these ambitious objectives, ANZSOG concentrated on three core functions:

1. To provide executive education development including the Executive Fellows Program for senior executives and the Executive Master of Public Administration degree for mid-career government officials.
2. To produce a high-quality teaching case study collection available for training and executive development (currently about 220 cases are available for use).
3. To undertake an active research program investigating topics of immediate relevance to public sector managers 'to deepen knowledge and understanding of government and to disseminate that understanding throughout the community' (ANZSOG n.d.).[4]

While these lofty intentions would seem logical and far-sighted, the creation of ANZSOG was actually brought about because other specialist or tertiary institutions were not providing these functions, or not providing them to the satisfaction of key public sector leaders. ANZSOG was the response to the perception of various Australian governments that there was a 'market failure' in the provision and quality of training and development programs available for public sector executives, especially focused on public leadership and management. Governments therefore took the initiative and made the necessary investments to create, with the collaboration and support of leading universities across the two nations, their own multi-jurisdictional school of government to which they could send their mid-senior executives identified as likely future leaders.

Establishment of the school in 2002

The establishment of ANZSOG about the turn of this century reflected a proactive recognition that the task of designing, delivering and maintaining the quality of professional development for future public

---

4   These objectives have changed only slightly since 2002–03. The most recent statement of the school's objectives claim its purpose is 'dedicated to creating value for citizens by providing world-class education for public sector leaders, conducting research and facilitating informed discussion on issues that matter for public sector performance, and promoting and supporting innovation in the public sector' (ANZSOG 2014). Only the last phrase is an augmentation of earlier statements.

sector leaders is challenging governments and specialist educational providers across the world. Existing approaches range from reliance on dedicated government-owned institutions (such as the Singapore Civil Service College and the French National School of Administration) to specialist institutes attached to leading universities. In this latter category the United States, for example, has a number of world-class providers such as Harvard's John F. Kennedy School of Government, the Brookings Institution, the Woodrow Wilson School of Public and International Affairs (Princeton) and the Goldman School of Public Policy at the University of California, Berkeley. Recent UK experience has witnessed the demise of the government-owned National School of Government in 2012 (Civil Service College and Cabinet Office), although new initiatives have emerged as replacements, such as the Oxford University Blavatnik School of Government, as well as continuing roles for established providers such as the London School of Economics and Warwick University.

Against this background, Australian and New Zealand public sector leaders determined to pursue a distinctively different approach to executive development, one that attempted to harmonise and build on the respective capacities of governments and universities across the two nations. Their innovative vision and subsequent work resulted in the creation of ANZSOG, founded in 2002.

The history of the school and how it came to be established in the form in which it has operated continuously since its formation can be traced back to the mid-1990s, especially to public debates about how Australia could best build a world-class graduate school to train senior business executives in the private sector. The initial focus of these debates was on developing elite business schools to encourage entrepreneurial skills in the next generation of business leaders. An influential report to the Australian Government in 1995 by the Industry Task Force on Leadership and Management Skills, chaired by David Karpin and known as the Karpin Report, found:

> One of the principal criticisms of Australian management schools
> … is that, while individual academics and departments within
> some schools are world class, it is unlikely that there is a world
> class management school in Australia. The principal issue is one of
> scale, in that none of Australia's leading schools approaches the size

the Task Force considers necessary to provide the infrastructure most likely to support world class quality in teaching and research. A world class school is vital to provide leadership to the rest of the postgraduate management sector and to assist Australian enterprises by promoting the latest management thinking. (Karpin 1995: 41)

While the focus of the Karpin Report was explicitly on the development of private sector executive leadership, its conclusion was equally apposite to Australia's public sector, where, arguably, the problems were more pronounced. While many universities had graduate programs aimed at public officials, they were all constrained by limited demand, comparatively small and regionally focused academies and limited and highly conditional support from public service leaders. There was also a growing concern that the executive development of public executives was becoming a case of market failure: a dissipated and fragmented pattern of tertiary education institutions not investing sufficient resources to produce the required specialist courses and training opportunities that governments needed and requested. There was a view across the public sector that universities at the time were not providing the required intellectual perspectives or teaching expertise necessary to meet governments' needs. And, accordingly, a new consolidated model was needed to provide world-class public sector executive education.

The release of the Karpin Report stimulated renewed discussion among public sector leaders about whether a similar case should be made for the development of public sector management and leadership capability. While there was endorsement of the need, exploratory discussions with Federal Government department heads and some scoping research, the idea did not gain sufficient traction through the 1990s to establish a critical mass of government support.

Exploratory discussions resumed again in 2001 when then secretary of the Victorian Premier's Department, Terry Moran, established a working group to consider whether there was sufficient interest in and a credible business case for a world-class 'school of government'. Soundings were taken from public sector, private sector, university and business school leaders, with a consistent message that any proposed development would need to be underpinned by a well-researched business plan and strong support from both government and universities.

To investigate potential demand and develop a credible business case, the Boston Consulting Group (BCG) was engaged. BCG's November 2001 report concluded that across Australian governments there were market demand and strong support for a national school of government. BCG's (2001) advice, however, was that:

- implementation of the proposed school would require a comprehensive communication campaign to broaden the basis of support and translate 'in-principle support' to 'actual support', as well as firm commitments to student numbers
- across government, chief executive officers (CEOs) and senior line management should be targeted in a face-to-face communication campaign because key stakeholder support for the new school was essential.

BCG's work also concluded that there were sufficient expertise and sufficient teaching staff (academics and practitioners) to establish a world-class faculty but the expertise was dispersed across the nation. Their conclusion was that the new school would need to draw on faculty from around Australia and include practitioners among its teaching staff. The new school's faculty staff would need to be regarded by governments as outstanding and be accomplished teachers as well as renowned academics, and able to draw extensively on practical experience. Overall, BCG's conclusion was that there was market demand for the proposed offerings of a new school and a good basis of support on which to build.

The majority of preparatory work during the balance of 2001 and much of 2002 focused on securing the necessary support from governments and universities, including some early curriculum discussions involving practitioners and academics. One unexpected but particularly opportune development was the high level of interest expressed by the New Zealand Government and Victoria University of Wellington (VUW) in joining the new school. In many ways, this unplanned support crystallised the opportunity and benefits of collaborative action across government and universities.

By mid-2002, the five 'foundation members' had been identified with commitments to fund the agreed intake for both ANZSOG's Executive Master of Public Administration (EMPA) and Executive Fellows Program (EFP) for at least the first three years. Governments emphasised that support beyond this initial commitment was dependent on ANZSOG's performance. In November 2002, the founding government and university members signed an agreement. In early 2003, the appointment of the inaugural dean was announced (Professor Allan Fels), key staff were recruited and work was completed on detailing the EMPA curriculum, accredited as a new master's degree by the academic boards in each of the nine founding member universities.[5]

Enrolment of the initial 130 public sector managers in the inaugural EMPA was completed and delivery of the week-long course on 'Delivering Public Value' occurred in May 2003, with the balance of the 10-course master's program delivered through 2003 and 2004. The inaugural delivery of the EFP occurred across October and November 2003, with an enrolment of 80 senior public officials from across Australia and New Zealand, and a faculty drawn from Australian, New Zealand, US and UK universities, and Australian and New Zealand public sector leaders.

Since 2003 the EMPA and EFP have been delivered each year, with more than 2,295 public servants completing one of the two programs by 2015. ANZSOG programs also have expanded to include a program for public sector managers making the transition from operational to strategic leadership roles ('Towards Strategic Leadership'), an extensive range of executive education short courses, programs aimed at building public sector capability in the Asia-Pacific, a leadership development program for local government and an increasingly active research program (see ANZSOG 2013, 2016). By 2015 there was a total of 3,393 alumni across all programs (but not including executive education short courses).

Important features distinguishing ANZSOG from other international public service training institutes, such as the former UK National School of Government, are the role of and investment in research—research that underpins the core curriculum and informs and supports teaching. In this domain, a key initiative of the Australian Government was its agreement to fund, with matching support from

---

5   The five original jurisdictional members were the governments of the Commonwealth of Australia, New Zealand, Victoria, Queensland and New South Wales. The nine founding university members were The Australian National University, University of Canberra, Victoria University of Wellington, Monash University, Melbourne Business School, Griffith University, University of Queensland, Sydney University and the University of New South Wales.

The Australian National University, the Sir John Bunting Chair of Public Administration. Professor John Wanna was the inaugural appointment to the chair and led an extensive research and publications program, including supervision of doctoral students, some of whom may develop as future teachers of ANZSOG programs. This was followed by a series of other government-sponsored senior academic research posts in other member jurisdictions, as well as joint teaching–research appointments. ANZSOG has also invested heavily in the development of executive-level teaching cases, overseen initially by Professor John Alford and Janet Tyson, with an available library now of more than 200 written case studies. In addition, under the guidance of a research committee chaired initially by the head of the Australian Treasury, Ken Henry, and then by the second Dean, Professor Gary Banks, ANZSOG provides modest project funds on a contestable basis for research that meets the priority needs of government and that supports and informs future teaching.

While ANZSOG naturally shares many characteristics with other schools of government, it also has several distinctive features. These can be summarised by the following:

- ANZSOG is a consortium of stakeholder governments and universities designed to achieve economies of scale and scope addressing the needs of government.
- It is a collaborative partnership between multiple jurisdictions across two closely related nations (Australia and New Zealand).
- Government identifies its emerging leaders from around Australia and New Zealand, and supports them financially during their engagement with ANZSOG.
- The school has the capacity to attract first-class teachers from Australia, New Zealand and overseas.
- Its rigorous EMPA is accredited by Australian and New Zealand universities.
- The school offers a research-driven, practitioner-oriented curriculum.
- Its pedagogic philosophy stresses innovative and engaging program delivery.
- It has strategic linkages with other prestigious international schools of government in Europe, America and Asia.

With aspirations to be recognised as a significant school of government within the Asia-Pacific region, ANZSOG has also designed and delivered a range of programs for public officials working in other countries. Sponsored places in ANZSOG core programs were offered through scholarships provided by prime ministers Howard and Clark from 2003. Each year a small number of senior leaders from South-East Asian nations attend the three-week EFP, establishing lasting relationships with Australian and New Zealand public sector leaders. Between 2007 and 2013, with the support of the Australian Agency for International Development (AusAID) and the Department of Foreign Affairs and Trade (DFAT), ANZSOG delivered a senior leadership program to public officials from 10 Pacific nations (the Pacific Executive Program, or PACE). It has also delivered a series of capacity-building programs—again, with AusAID support—to emerging public sector leaders in Indonesia. ANZSOG's priority focus on senior leadership development was also reflected in delivery of the China Advanced Leadership Program and Indian Advanced Leadership Program from 2011. And it has provided input to DFAT's sponsored 'leadership precinct' in Papua New Guinea.

ANZSOG's journey to date has maintained, and broadened, strong high-level support from its 10 governments and 15 university owners. Over the 12 years to date, delivery of ANZSOG programs has seen the following:

- 1,383 Australian and New Zealand 'high potentials' complete or completing the EMPA. The average overall participant rating for the program is 4.0 (on a five-point scale). Follow-up surveys of alumni indicate more than 60 per cent of graduates have been promoted since completing the program.
- 912 Australian, New Zealand, Chinese Singaporean, Canadian and Indian public sector leaders have completed the EFP, with an average overall participant evaluation of 4.24.
- There are now more than 200 heads of department and agencies in Australia and New Zealand who have completed ANZSOG's CEO forum, led by Professor Mark Moore from the Harvard Kennedy School.
- 186 public sector leaders from Pacific Island nations have completed or are completing the PACE program, with an average participant rating of 4.8.

- More than 200 teaching case studies have been researched and written, drawn from Australian and New Zealand public sector agencies and now accessed worldwide by teachers, plus more than 50 research monographs produced through ANU Press, together with various occasional paper series available on the ANZSOG website.

- Alongside these core programs, between 30 and 50 specialised executive education workshops have been delivered each year for public officials working for ANZSOG's member governments.

- The past few years have seen an increased emphasis on 'policy roundtables' devoted to issues of concern to member governments and conducted under Chatham House rules.

When examining the factors that appear to have contributed to ANZSOG's progress and the continuing high level of support it enjoys from both its government and its university owners, six factors stand out. First, the school prioritises a continuing focus on meeting governments' needs in senior executive development, with the corollary that continuing support from government stakeholders requires maintaining relevance and high levels of customer satisfaction. Second, it has invested in a significant commitment to research that informs teaching and learning, often hosting pro bono forums and workshops for stakeholder governments. Third, it demonstrates a commitment to teacher development focused on effective postgraduate/mid-career teaching and learning. Fourth, it actively utilises an extensive network of scholars and practitioners, across Australia and New Zealand and internationally, to provide input into programs and courses. Fifth, the school maintains an active engagement with and support from alumni, including providing ongoing educational refreshers and network opportunities. And, finally, the school operates with a robust business model designed to maximise its effectiveness and influence, while providing value for money for governments and participants.

Cumulatively, these factors have generated and sustained ANZSOG's development to date and provide a robust foundation on which further development can be built. Future development will need to address the ongoing challenges of ANZSOG's comparatively small scale and related traditional reliance on a comparatively small number of academics able to teach successfully in its programs. As most of these have been guest presenters and adjunct staff, a continuing challenge is sustaining a strong sense of collective ownership of key programs. Periodic reviews by independent experts of teaching quality and pedagogies, as well as research agendas and published contributions, will continue to be important to the school's ongoing contribution.

Conclusion

Australia has relied on a fragmented matrix of training and educational providers, combining in-house on-the-job training for staff with more technical and intellectual education available across the public sector. At times, such training needs have been coordinated by central agencies, which also tended to provide some basic and specialist courses within their jurisdictions. Historically, training was often loaded towards the induction stages of employment with sporadic training offered towards mid-career grades. In the past five decades, training and development philosophies have been oriented towards developing managerial skills and encouraging the inculcation of leadership qualities. The marketplace for educational and training providers has proliferated and deepened, not only through the provision of tertiary courses (addressing different levels of demand) but also through the growth of private sector providers offering relatively specialised training and development. The experiment with ANZSOG is unique in that it provides an interjurisdictional locus for executive development, working closely with expert scholars and practitioners, but 'owned' by the stakeholder governments themselves.

References

Australia and New Zealand School of Government (ANZSOG) n.d. *The Establishment of the School*. Melbourne: ANZSOG.

Australia and New Zealand School of Government (ANZSOG) 2013. *Annual Report 2012*. Melbourne: ANZSOG.

Australia and New Zealand School of Government (ANZSOG) 2014. *Annual Report 2013*. Melbourne: ANZSOG.

Australia and New Zealand School of Government (ANZSOG) 2016. *Annual Report 2015*. Melbourne: ANZSOG.

Australian Government 2010. *Ahead of the Game*. Canberra: Australian Government.

Australian Institute of Management (AIM) 2013. *Learning and Development in the Public Sector*. August. Sydney: AIM.

Australian Public Service Commission (APSC) 2004. *Integrated Leadership Capability Framework*. Canberra: APSC.

Betts, J. J. 1949. The training of Commonwealth public servants. *Public Administration (AJPA)* 8(2–3) (June–September).

Boston Consulting Group (BCG) 2001. *Australian Graduate School of Government: Development of a business model*. Final report, November. Melbourne: BCG.

Caiden, G. 1965. *Career Service: Introduction to the history of personnel administration in the Commonwealth Public Service of Australia 1901–1961*. Melbourne: Melbourne University Press.

Caiden, G. 1967. *The Commonwealth Bureaucracy*. Melbourne: Melbourne University Press.

Crisp, L. F. 1972. Politics and the Commonwealth Public Service. Australian Journal of Public Administration 31(4): 287–309.

Crisp, L. F. 1978. *Australian National Government*. 4th edn. Melbourne: Longman Cheshire.

Davis, G. and Rhodes, R. A. W. 2000. From hierarchy to contracts and back again: Reforming the Australian Public Service. In M. Keating, J. Wanna and P. Weller (eds), *Institutions on the Edge?* Sydney: Allen & Unwin.

Davis, G. and Wanna, J. 1997. Does the teaching of public administration have a future?' *Australian Journal of Public Administration* 56(4): 1–5.

Di Francesco, M. 2015. Policy analysis instruction in Australia. In B. Head and K. Crowley (eds), *Policy Analysis in Australia*. Bristol: Policy Press.

Fels, A. 2003. The Australian and New Zealand School of Government. *Canberra Journal of Public Administration* (108) (June).

Hennessy, P. 1988. *Whitehall*. London: Secker & Warburg.

Karpin, D. 1995. *Industry Taskforce on Leadership and Management Skills*. [Karpin Report]. Canberra: AGPS.

Parker, R. 1993. *The Administrative Vocation*. Sydney: Hale & Iremonger.

Patapan, H., Wanna, J. and Weller, P. (eds) 2005. *Westminster Legacies*. Sydney: UNSW Press.

Podger, A. 2003. Trends in the Australian Public Service, 1953–2003. *Canberra Bulletin of Public Administration* (109) (September).

Public Service & Merit Protection Commission (PSMPC) 2001. *Serving the Nation: 100 years of public service*. Canberra: PSMPC.

Public Service Commission (PSC) 1992. *Accounting for Your Training Dollar*. Canberra: PSC.

Spann, R. N. 1973. *Government Administration in Australia*. Sydney: George Allen & Unwin.

Appendix 2.1

Key milestones in executive development and staff training in the Australian Public Service

1933	A new section (36A) was inserted into the *Commonwealth Public Service Act 1933* to provide for the appointment of university graduates to the service, as base-grade clerks.
1937	The Department of External Affairs began to recruit a small number of clerks (above base grade) with qualifications and knowledge, oriented particularly to the department's international activities.
1943	Introduction of a more formal cadetship scheme in the Department of External Affairs; 12 cadets were selected and sent to the University of Sydney for full-time intensive training and study in selected subjects.

1947	Provision for the Public Service Board to grant extended unpaid leave (up to three years) to allow officers to undertake courses of study relevant to the duties of their respective offices and to meet postwar reconstruction needs. Establishment of Central Training Section to coordinate service-wide training.
1950	Board Personnel Cadet Scheme provided cadets with a combination of part-time academic studies and departmental training in all phases of service personnel work, followed by examinations, over four years (later four and a half years). The academic training component included eight university courses/subjects in designated areas (generally English, a psychology 'major' of three units, political science or public administration and three other units from economics, history and philosophy).
Early 1950s	Australian Administrative Staff College established (it later became the Mount Eliza Business School and then merged with the Melbourne Business School).
1957	Abolition of the diplomatic cadetship scheme instituted in 1943. The original short, intensive period of training at the University of Sydney was superseded by a two-year course at the then Canberra University College (linked to the University of Melbourne), where a special postgraduate School of Diplomatic Studies had been established.
1958	In Canberra, the Brassey House training centre was opened as a service residential training centre in December 1958, for use both by the Board and by departments. Its facilities were expanded in 1964–65.
1959	The Boyer Report into recruitment and training was released, stressing the employment of more graduates.
Early – mid-1960s	Central training in new technologies and statistical packages, automatic data processing.

1963	Board intensive training scheme for its own graduate recruits, which evolved into the wider-ranging Administrative Trainee Scheme (ATS), with consistent annual intakes of between 20 and 35 graduates from 1965 onwards. This was a one-year highly integrated training scheme with some 11 weeks of course work and, normally, three different, carefully selected work placements.
1966	New graduate recruitment procedures were introduced, with upgraded selection techniques and significantly improved induction and training arrangements.
Early 1970s	Increased numbers of graduate entrants and agencies increased the number of staff undertaking part-time university studies (including some fee reimbursement and provision of study time in work hours).
1974–76	The Coombs Royal Commission was critical of public service training, saying much was not linked to the objectives of the organisation. The Royal Commission supported more emphasis on tertiary education supplemented with specialist courses and on-the-job training. It argued the Public Service Board should act as a 'resource bank' for improving the quality and delivery in departments and agencies.
Late 1970s	Greater emphasis focused on executive development schemes, interchange programs and senior women in management programs.
1981	Suspension of the ATS due to costs and in recognition of the progressive improvement that had occurred in APS graduate recruitment generally, with better provision by departments of induction arrangements and development opportunities.
1984	Senior Executive Service established as a dedicated leadership group, beginning to address leadership and development needs of this group.
1985	Reintroduction of the ATS.

1989 The ATS finally discontinued, with training and development of graduate recruits to become solely a departmental responsibility.

1989 Establishment of the Joint APS Training Council (JAPSTC)—a direct consequence of award restructuring under the Industrial Relations Commission's Structural Efficiency Principle. The government also allocated A$10 million per annum for the Middle Management Development Program, which included:

- the subsidisation of middle-management development activities
- and, importantly, the development of the Public Sector Management Course (PSMC) for middle managers in both the Commonwealth and the state public sectors, created by government but delivered by external university providers.

1990s JAPSTC sponsored curriculum development and training courses, including to SES level. The Commonwealth Government introduced the Training Guarantee Scheme requiring employers (including public sector agencies) to allocate funding to training needs.

1991–92 Development of a PSMC curriculum was undertaken by the University of Wollongong (then revised extensively on two occasions by Griffith University academics), with course materials then trialled in the Australian Capital Territory and four states; external providers along with staff from Griffith and Flinders universities and Queensland University of Technology were involved in delivery and quality assurance.

1992 SES development programs launched by the Public Service Commission, using the Senior Executive Leadership Capability Framework (SELCF), emphasising the critical success factors for improved organisational performance.

1993	Strategic Planning for Training & Development (MAB) report, which led to the National Training Reform Agenda embracing competency-based training and identification of skills needed in the workforce.
1993	PSMC middle-management course started with more than 600 Commonwealth and state participants in the first year, undertaking 170 hours of course contact time and a 40-hour work-based project. The first graduates received their certificates in May 1993.
1993	Endorsement of the ABS core competencies by the National Training Board.
1994–95	JAPSTC developing a framework for implementing competency-based training for APS entry levels through to middle management, using both external educational institutions and in-service resources.
	Establishment of the National Public Administration Training Advisory Board, with the conversion of APS-endorsed standards to national standards passed to that body.
1999–2000	The PSMC program was successfully delivered in Fiji and also piloted to other Pacific countries.
2000	Public Services Training Package directed towards providing individuals with clear skill and career pathways, through attainment of recognised qualifications from nationally recognised training providers.
2002	Five government jurisdictions (Australia, New Zealand, Victoria, New South Wales and Queensland) collaborate with nine universities to establish ANZSOG, which takes its first intake of 130 students in 2003.
2004	The Integrated Leadership System (ILS) program adopted by the APS (from the previous SELCF); the ILS uses five clusters of executive leadership capabilities (achieve results, cultivate productive workplace relations, communicate with influence, exemplify personal drive and integrity, and drive strategic thinking).

2006+   The ILS stimulates agencies to customise and adapt the frameworks to suit agency needs; meanwhile, the framework is gradually incorporated into departmental staff appraisal and performance management systems.

2010   The *Ahead of the Game* report finds the APS is underinvesting in training and executive development and recommends renewed efforts to expand learning and development and enhance its quality to achieve high-quality professional leadership.

3

Civil service executive development in China: An overview

Yijia Jing

Civil service executive development has become increasingly important for China since it began market reform in the late 1970s. As society becomes more complex, diverse and open, and as citizen expectations of the government become more demanding, the professional training of public managers has become indispensable. To reduce gaps in executive capacity created by rapid development and a relatively stable bureaucracy, the Chinese Government has launched ambitious efforts to modernise its civil service, focusing on staff in leading positions. Like many other countries, China faces the task of designing and organising executive development programs to make governmental officials more efficient, accountable and clean.

China's efforts in civil service executive development have been a result of both its modernisation and its institutional environment. Executive development in China's civil service takes the form of cadre education and training (CET). Under the political leadership of the Chinese Communist Party (CCP), the Western practice of a 'neutral' civil service does not exist. Civil servants in China are still treated as cadres who, according to the Civil Service Law of 2005, are supervised by the party. The CCP's political, ideological and organisational leadership over the public sector has set parameters over the relatively young Chinese Civil Service by specifying the fundamental values of civil service (Jing and Zhu 2012). In fact, civil service development has been embedded into the old cadre personnel system (Chan and Li 2007). The party's organisational system is directly in charge of CET, particularly for cadres at or beyond county/division level. Training of entry-level civil servants is left to governmental organisations. One of the CCP's rebuilding efforts in recent years, CET has come to play an increasingly important role (Shambaugh 2008). CET features a peculiarly Chinese approach to shaping the civil service, especially its high-ranking officials, and achieving the necessary executive capacities for the country.

This chapter seeks to provide a better understanding of Chinese CET. The chapter will first offer an overview of CET including its historical development, major institutions and training system, and then discuss the functions of CET in China's governing system. A case study of the Shanghai Municipal Committee Party School will illustrate CET activities.

The historical development of cadre education and training in China

CET can be traced to the CCP's infancy. Effective training of cadres was deemed essential during the revolutionary periods. Although early CET was far from systematic, it was an integral part of the party's core political and ideological work. Marxist–Leninist theories and Mao Zedong's thoughts were used to train cadres, soldiers and the working classes to unify their thoughts and actions. The focus was to mobilise their loyalty to the party and the revolutionary cause, and there was an overwhelming emphasis on the party's desire for capable cadres to make revolutionary ideals a reality. As Mao Zedong emphasised, 'after political routes are set, cadres determine their implementation'. He further identified unified frontlines, military struggle and party development as the three keys to the success of the Chinese revolution, with the last the most important (Mao 1968: 569). In 1939, the CCP established the Department of Cadre Education, which was later absorbed into the Department of Propaganda (DOP), which took responsibility for cadre education before 1949 (DOO of the

CCP 1989: 312). In general, in-class training was difficult to organise, with the exception of training for high-ranking officials. CET was often carried out through studies organised by the party and governmental agencies, and was practised and strengthened in cadres' daily work. In times of war and vast change, political work including CET guaranteed the political quality and solidarity of cadres and created a strong fighting team, in comparison with the Kuomintang (KMT) government, which the communists saw as corrupt and factional.

CET in the early years of the People's Republic of China inherited the traditions established in the revolutionary period. Before the completion of the socialist transformation in 1956,[1] which was defined as China's shift from a period of socialist revolution to one of socialist construction, the CCP's major task was to consolidate its political leadership and restructure society. Yet although CET maintained its focus on political work, it had to adjust to the increasing demands of socialist construction by improving the capacity of revolutionary cadres. The training system was gradually established, enriched and institutionalised. External training institutes, especially the party school system, were systematically established. The DOP and the Department of Organisation (DOO) were two major party agencies in charge of CET. Categories of CET included political theory education, professional education and cultural education,[2] which could be delivered through on-the-job study or full-time study in schools (requiring leave from work). As China entered the 10-year Proletarian Cultural Revolution that returned the party's focus from construction to revolution, political movements were relied on to purify the cadre team and CET was paralysed.

From 1978, CET began a stage of restoration and rapid development as the CCP shifted its focus to economic market reform and globalisation. In 1980, Deng Xiaoping proposed 'Four General Principles' (4GP) of cadre team building: revolutionary spirit, youth, knowledge and professionalism. In the same year, the DOP and the DOO jointly issued the *Opinion to Strengthen Cadre Education Work* and decided to establish a network of cadre education comprising party schools

---

1   The period from September 1949 to December 1956 is known as the period of 'Socialist Transformation', during which the state nationalised private capital and established an economic system based on public ownership.

2   Professional education trained cadres in knowledge and skills for dealing with their work. Cultural education was to improve cadres' general level of education.

and professional cadre schools. In 1984, the Central Leading Team on Cadre Education was established within the DOO. Provincial counterparts were also established. Since then, the DOO and its local branches have been entrusted with the responsibility of coordinating cadre education issues.

Post-1978 developments in CET are reflected in the following aspects of the program.

Management system

Although many agencies at multiple levels of the hierarchy have various types of authority in relation to the management of CET, the DOO plays a leading and coordinating role. At the central level, DOO is responsible for major directions, policies and plans for CET. It monitors CET at central and provincial agencies and organises CET for centrally supervised cadres. The DOP is responsible for directing theoretical studies and organising CET for cadres in propaganda and culture systems. The Ministry of Personnel directs and coordinates the training of civil servants and professional technical personnel. The state-owned Asset Supervision and Management Commission directs the training of cadres in state-owned enterprises (SOEs). The State Development and Reform Commission approves central CET bases and projects. The Ministry of Finance makes financing policies for CET. Other party and governmental agencies are also involved.

Three characteristics can be identified. First, while both party and governmental agencies are involved, party agencies play a dominant role. Second, the authority to organise CET involves a relatively centralised cadre management. The DOO may organise CET not only for cadres that it directly supervises but also for cadres one or two ranks lower.[3] Third, across-the-board management is applied as party cadres, administrative cadres, SOE cadres and professional-technical cadres are all covered by CET and are expected to receive synchronised education and training.

---

3   For example, Central DOO organises CET for both provincial-level and bureau-level officials. It also trains county mayors and party secretaries.

Training system

The training system comprises party schools, administrative schools, cadre schools and cadre training centres, university training programs and social training programs.[4] At the central level are the Central Party School, the National School of Government, three Cadre Schools (Pudong, Yan'an and Jinggangshan) and Dalian Senior Manager School. Of these, party schools are the major channels of CET. In 2009, there were 4,501 training bases at or beyond county level, including 3,115 party schools, 295 administrative schools, 424 cadre schools and 667 training centres, with a maximum capacity to accommodate 1.32 million students at any given time. The number of employees in these institutes reached 184,000, including 108,000 faculty members, 6,034 full professors or researchers and 27,000 associate professors or researchers (Zheng 2010: 166). In addition, these institutes have adjunct faculty members including leading party and governmental cadres, external experts and professors and entrepreneurs.

Targeted cadres

Cadres at all levels and in all categories are targeted by CET, although party-governmental officials at or beyond county level and their deputies form the core focus of CET. In 2004, China had more than 40 million cadres, including more than 500,000 cadres at or beyond county/division level; about 40,000 at or beyond the municipal/bureau level; several thousand high-ranking officials (provincial/ministry level); and about 200 central committee members (Wei 2004: 3). Cadres are classified into several major categories with corresponding CET programs. These categories include party-governmental leading cadres, young cadres, civil servants, SOE managers, professional technical staff, judges, procurators, police and other political legal cadres, grassroots cadres, ethnic minority cadres, non-CCP cadres, female cadres and West Region cadres.[5] Corresponding to the career stages of officials, CET programs are generally classified as pre-promotion training, post-promotion training, positional training and specialised training.

---

4   In addition to this domestic training system, a substantial number of middle- and senior-ranking Chinese public servants are sent abroad for executive development.
5   Refer to the *2001–2005 National Plan of Cadre Education and Training*, issued in January 2001 by the Central Committee of the CCP.

Cadres are required to participate in full-time study, central team study of affiliated party committees and on-the-job self-study. Off-work study has been the core and is also the focus of this chapter. According to the *Implementation Opinion to Train Cadres between 2008 and 2012*, the central committee organises annual seminars for provincial/ministry leading cadres while the central DOO organises annual seminars for major leaders of centrally supervised SOEs and financial agencies and for major leaders of centrally supervised universities. Every year, DOO also organises off-work CET in Beijing for 130 leading municipal cadres and 1,100 leading county cadres and expects to cover all cadres within five years. These cadres are required to have no less than 100 study hours of annual off-the-job training and no less than 550 cumulative study hours within five years.

Training content

Degree education was popular for CET in the 1980s as the general educational level of cadres was low at that time. The urgency for such education gradually disappeared.[6] Currently, major categories of training content include political theory, knowledge and capacity, and party spirit (*dang xing*). Political theory education aims to consolidate cadres' political orthodoxy and their loyalty to the socialist cause. It is founded on Marxist–Leninist and Maoist thinking, and focuses on the socialist theoretical system with Chinese characteristics—for example, the 'Outlook of Scientific Development'. Knowledge and capacity education tends to improve cadres' knowledge of economic, political, cultural and social construction, and their leadership and technical capacities in handling pragmatic issues. Party spirit education aims to purify the officials as moral citizens committed to the people and their work. Morality, the party's revolutionary history, devotion to work and resistance to corruption are emphasised. Notwithstanding, content may vary according to the different focuses of the training programs, and training agencies may exercise discretion in determining the exact courses and lectures.

---

6   The proportion of civil servants with a college diploma or superior qualification rose from 30 per cent to 86 per cent between 1992 and 2007. These data are taken from a talk given by Yin Weimin, the Minister for Human Resources and Social Security, on 3 March 2009.

Institutionalisation

There have been efforts to institutionalise CET as part of regular party-governmental work. Legal, administrative and party documents were approved to guide and regulate its development. Both the *Provisional Regulation on State Civil Service of 2003* and the *Civil Service Law of 2005* stipulate training as part of the rights and obligations of civil servants. Basic training plans were determined by the party, which since the 1980s has continuously made five-year plans for CET. In 2006, the party enacted the *Provisional Ordinances on Cadre Education and Training*. After that, the Central Committee of the CCP and the State Council issued, respectively, *Work Ordinances of Party Schools of the Chinese Communist Party* and *Work Ordinances of Administrative Schools*. Basically, leading cadres at or beyond county level are required to undergo three months of CET including one month of study outside work every five years. These policy developments have created stable and ample resources for CET-affiliated agencies, especially the party schools.

Functions of CET in China's governance system

The functions of CET—explicit or implicit—have to be understood in the context in which they evolved. In the light of the CCP's continuing transformation from a revolutionary party to a ruling party, the many challenges it faces are to be tackled by its leading cadres. The design of CET reflects the party's desire to better cope with environmental challenges and rebuild itself. Meanwhile, informal roles are also played by CET that serve to reduce the gap between formal institutions and everyday life. The formal functions of CET, which correspond directly with the party's and the government's demands for loyal as well as technically competent officials, are addressed first.

Political (re-)engineering

CET demonstrates a repeated and limited politicisation effort on the cadre personnel system in order to create political loyalty and activeness. As the party has rejected social movements in mobilising and refreshing itself, indoctrination through CET is one major way to create consistent actions and avoid internal conflicts. This is especially important as the government has basically made economic construction its highest priority, and as society is becoming increasingly liberal and open. CET features regular reminders of the leading cadres' role as agents of the party and the people, and functions as a preventative mechanism against distrust of the party and its political authority. It also strengthens psychological acceptance of an integrated party–state system. Pieke (2009) argues that the main mission of training remains Leninist 'unification of thought'; yet to overcome the rigidity of indoctrination, political learning in CET combines classic Marxist–Leninist theories and their recent local developments such as the 'Deng Xiaoping Theory', 'Three Representatives' and 'Outlook of Scientific Development'. Although CET produces high compliance with these principles, the party is aware of the gap between ideology and reality and has been trying to reduce it through efforts to adapt Marxism to the Chinese context.

Political engineering is also crucial because 'united thought' is especially important for China with its large population and regional diversity. The Central Government needs a strong hand to guarantee effective implementation of its policies across very long chains of command. Concentrated study provides an opportunity to directly convey the central authority's political intentions and policy objectives, mobilise compliant actions and impose accountability. For example, to push forward the New Village Construction policy, the Central Committee in 2006 organised 50 seminars on this topic for county mayors and party secretaries across the nation, and trained 5,740 such cadres. In 2008, to disseminate the spirit of the third plenary of the Seventeenth Party Congress, more than 2,000 party secretaries of Chinese counties were trained.[7]

Capacity and knowledge building

Besides the emphasis on improving the political quality of cadres, CET is also expected to create and maintain talent and intellectual capacity for economic modernisation. While pre-promotion training, post-promotion training and positional training share a relative focus on theories and 'party spirit', specialised training tends to have

---

7   In 2008, there were 2,862 counties in China.

a greater emphasis on leadership and specialised knowledge. General management, public administration theories, leadership skills, economic theories, philosophy, finance, social management, history, communication skills and many specialised seminars are offered. The training system, including party schools, is making efforts to modernise its faculty team and introduce new elements of training. In her study of the Shanghai Party School, Tran (2003: 15) argues that the school is being gradually turned 'into a modern institute of public administration, where the teaching has a direct application to the management of the city'. This may be a slight exaggeration, but it reflects the fact that party schools have been trying to increase their attractiveness by offering useful training.

While CET's formal functions are directly emphasised and pursued, some informal functions are also created as by-products. These functions are far from unimportant.

Collective as well as stratified identity

CET gathers cadres of comparable age and rank to study together. A strong sense of mission is created as peers, either leading cadres or their deputies, are learning the skills of governance together. This easily builds a collective identity among the elite who were previously the proletarian vanguards and are now the country's decision-makers. Such an identity helps to differentiate the cadres from directionless bureaucrats. Meanwhile, the ranking-based training system creates an internally stratified identity as officials tend to identify more with peers of the same rank.

Social connections

Related to collective identity are the social connections that can benefit officials in handling public and private issues (Tran 2003; Pieke 2009). Chinese society has continued to rely heavily on interpersonal relations (*guan xi*), which are a form of social capital with both positive and negative effects. Seminars, classes and extracurricular activities create lasting networks characterised by a common identity, trust and reciprocity.

The case of the Shanghai Municipal Committee Party School

As the designated principal channel of CET, party schools offer the best lens through which to observe the evolving trends of CET. In the following sections of this chapter, the Shanghai Municipal Committee Party School (SMCPS) is used as a case study to illustrate trends in CET. The SMCPS was established in June 1949, one month after Shanghai was taken over by the People's Liberation Army. Since then, the SMCPS has been responsible for training leading cadres. As in the majority of China's provinces, the SMCPS is integrated with the Shanghai School of Government. We rely heavily on information on the SMCPS website for this analysis (now discontinued).

Educational programs

The educational programs of the SMCPS include degree education and non-degree CET. Degree education has been diminishing due to competition from ordinary universities. The SMCPS stopped its distance-learning program in 2010, and will gradually stop recruiting undergraduate students who are jointly educated by the Shanghai Normal University and the SMCPS. The core of degree education in the future will be its masters program.

CET constitutes the focus of the SMCPS. In recent years, 10,000 students have been trained annually, divided more or less equally between planned programs (*ji hua nei pei xun ban*) and ad hoc programs (*ji hua wai pei xun ban*). Planned programs are regular programs provided for local cadres, with a certificate issued by the SMCPS; unplanned programs are for cadres outside Shanghai and even for officials in Hong Kong and Macau according to the requests of their supervisory agencies, with a certificate issued by the Training Centre of the SMCPS. The latter is mostly a response to market demand. In general, a program accommodates about 50 students. The future plan of the SMCPS is to train 15,000 students annually.[8]

---

8   This goal was in fact achieved in 2010, in time for the Shanghai Expo.

Planned programs

Planned programs are the core competency of the SMCPS and are designed and operated by its Education Department. In 2010, the SMCPS offered 86 planned programs (58 types of programs) and trained 5,808 students. Table 3.1 shows the structure of the training programs. These programs in general last between several days and several weeks.

Table 3.1: Planned programs offered by the SMCPS

Main programs (zhu ti ban)	Leading cadre programs (1)	Post-promotion training of cadres promoted to vice bureau-level positions.
	Leading cadre programs (2)	Positional training of bureau-level cadres.
	Division-level cadre programs	Positional training of full division-level cadres.
	Middle-aged and young cadre programs	Pre-promotion training of backup cadres to be promoted to vice bureau-level positions.
	Non-CCP middle-aged and young cadre programs	Pre-promotion training of backup cadres without a CCP membership who are to be promoted to vice bureau-level positions.
	Young cadre programs	Pre-promotion training of deputy cadres to be promoted to vice division-level positions.
	Leading division-level civil servant programs	Post-promotion training of backup cadres to be promoted to division-level positions.
	Specialised topic programs	Specialised topics for officials at or beyond vice division level.
Other programs	Assigned programs (Wei tuo he zuo ban)	All kinds of general or special training on the request of party-governmental agencies. In general, for cadres at or below division level.
	Self-sponsored programs	Programs developed by the SMCPS. Information is disseminated to organisational and personnel departments of party-governmental agencies who may voluntarily send their cadres to participate.
	Faculty training programs	Programs to train the faculty members of party schools in Shanghai.

Source: Shanghai Municipal Committee Party School (internal planning document).

Different programs target different cadres and have different training content. The *main programs* are the most important for the SMCPS as they reflect the basic CET mandates. The Organisational Department of the Shanghai Municipal Committee of the CCP and the Civil Servant Bureau of the Shanghai Municipal Government are responsible for assigning students to these programs. Consequently, students are of high rank—in general, beyond the vice division level. *Assigned programs* are joint programs between the SMCPS and party-governmental agencies (which send students to the programs). *Self-sponsored programs* depend on the SMCPS's judgement of current demands for training; these programs may be increased or closed according to the 'market' response. The above three categories account for about one-third of the programs. *Faculty training programs* serve to enhance the human capital of faculty members in Shanghai's party school system and the number of programs is small.

Content of training

Despite a general emphasis on theories and 'party spirit', there is significant variation in training content across the programs. The *main programs* have demonstrated a consistent commitment to political and ideological training. For example, the 76th positional training of bureau-level leading cadres, held over one month in 2011, had four teaching units: including 'In-Depth Study of Socialist Theoretical System with Chinese Characteristics', 'Major Theories and Practices in Reform and Development', 'Carry Out the 12th Five-Year Plan and Push Forward Shanghai's Socioeconomic Development' and 'Party Spirit Analysis'. The first unit was part of theoretical studies, the second and third were part of capacity and knowledge training and the last unit was part of party spirit training. Of the 22.5 study days, the first and fourth units accounted for 10.5 days (46.7 per cent). Such a proportion has been consistent across the main programs, with the exception of specialised topic programs. This coincides with Liu's (2009: 106) observation that the curriculum of the Central Party School is 'infused with the values and political culture (including belief conflicts) of the national elites in the Party centre'.

There are two main types of *specialised topic programs*. One is to train general leadership capacities. For example, the Twenty-Sixth Specialised Topic Program on Essential Comprehensive Capacities of Cadres, held in 2010, had seminars on the following topics:

- study and practice of the Outlook of Scientific Development
- writing official documents
- making speeches

- innovative thinking
- modern social intercourse and etiquette
- psychological adaptive capacity
- coping with complex international situations
- the China model from a global perspective.

The other kind of *specialised topic program* focuses on knowledge and capacity in specialised areas. For example, the Second Specialised Topic Program on Social Organisation Construction and Management, held in 2010, had seminars on the following topics:

- current situations and tasks of social construction
- new thoughts on the development of social organisations in China
- comparison of the development and management of non-governmental organisations (NGOs) in China and foreign countries
- innovations in philanthropic services
- a case study of the practices of social organisations
- on-the-spot teaching of the cultivation and development of community organisations
- teaching the survival strategies and values of social organisations
- the building of collaboration between governments and social organisations.

Although *specialised topic programs* tend to be pragmatic and technical, the seminars have been designed to ensure they are consistent with socialist theories and party spirit.

The design of *entrusted programs* and *self-sponsored programs* is similar to the above three kinds of programs. For *unplanned programs*, socioeconomic development in Shanghai and leadership and management are two major themes of training. While the *main programs* have to be approved by the Shanghai Department of Organisation, the SMCPS enjoys some discretion in designing other programs.

Trainers

In 2011, the SMCPS had 92 full faculty members, including 65 professors or associate professors. They were under a management and evaluation system similar to that of university faculty members, although their work emphasised applied research and training.

In recent years, the SMCPS has intensified its efforts to modernise its personnel by recruiting recent PhD graduates and established scholars from elite universities. However, its focus on training still makes it difficult to attract good researchers, who prefer universities with more academic breadth and freedom. The SMCPS has established incentives for faculty members to offer new courses, apply new methods of teaching and pay attention to student feedback. The SMCPS also sends them to the Central Party School or other institutes for training or degree studies, and provides opportunities for them to work in governmental agencies temporarily or to study abroad.

To enrich SMCPS's teaching resources, it has more than 30 experts and scholars as guest professors or researchers, and more than 20 leading cadres as adjunct professors. A teaching database has been established with more than 100 external experts and scholars and the courses they can offer. Currently, an external faculty teaches about 30 per cent of the courses. It is especially important for the SMCPS to offer specialised topic programs. It has been found that as the rank of students increases, the demand on external teaching tends to increase. In general, 70 to 80 per cent of CET programs for bureau-level officials involve external faculty teaching; the figure is 40 per cent for CET programs for deputy officials of bureau-level positions, 20 per cent for division-level officials and 10 per cent for lower-ranking officials. The reason is that higher-ranking officials tend to demand more specialised and more practical knowledge. It has also been found that more senior officials tend to prefer traditional methods of teaching while young cadres tend to accept new methods such as case studies, contextual teaching and on-the-spot teaching.

Local leading cadres are playing an important role in offering capacity and knowledge training. Major party-governmental leaders of Shanghai take turns to offer the first lecture at the beginning of every semester for the main program students. The Municipal Party Committee made a by-law in 2009 requiring leading cadres in Shanghai to do some teaching at the SMCPS. The SMCPS also collaborates with overseas institutes such as Oxford University and the John F. Kennedy School of Government at Harvard University to offer short-term training.

Financing

The 2006 *Provisional Ordinances on Cadre Education and Training* stipulate that CET expenses should be listed as public expenditure in government budgets. In general, departments of organisation at different levels have funding for basic CET they directly supervise, while every party-governmental agency has some CET funding for their employees. In 2011, the Department of Organisation of Minhang District in Shanghai had a CET budget expenditure of RMB9.4 million (A\$1.6 million), accounting for 32 per cent of the total budgeted expenditure of that agency.[9]

The SMCPS charges all its students, though at present fees are charged to and covered by sending agencies. Since expenditure is fully covered by public finance, training revenue is submitted to the Treasury. The school's budget is also linked to the training fees it collects so there is a financial incentive for the SMCPS to expand training and attract more students. If market reform were ever introduced to the SMCPS, the ability to meet demand would be crucial in building its money-making capacity. The training fees from *planned programs* average RMB200 (A\$35) per person per day, not including textbook and accommodation fees. For *self-sponsored programs* and *unplanned programs*, fees are generally charged at the market level.

Quality assurance

The SMCPS has no real competitor in the training market as its *main programs* have a monopoly and create a unique platform from which to extend the value chain by developing other programs. Nonetheless, quality assurance has been receiving more attention due to some indirect competition and widespread cynicism among students. The establishment of the China Executive Leadership Academy Pudong (CELAP) in 2005 has challenged the SMCPS's leadership in setting benchmarks for CET even in Shanghai. Many universities and training enterprises are expanding their share in the CET market. For example, Fudan University, under the support of the Shanghai Department of Organisation, offers a specialised topic program (Public Management Capacity and Leadership Quality Program) to train bureau and division-level officials. On the other hand, the formal goals

---

9   Available from: shmh.gov.cn/xxgk/Content.aspx?Id=89714 (accessed 2011) (site discontinued).

of CET are often only achieved to a limited extent as the courses can be old-fashioned, far removed from reality or authoritative rather than analytical, and this affects the enthusiasm of students to participate. These are issues faced across the board by the party schools and they put pressure on schools to seek feedback from and meet the demands of individual cadres.

Quality assurance at the SMCPS has multiple aspects. First, the SMCPS established a consultative team for the design and planning of training programs in 2009. The team comprises 12 members including the vice-chancellor, the provost, the chief officials of the educational, student and research departments, and officials from the Municipal Department of Organisation and the Municipal Bureau of Civil Servants. This team examines the main programs and decides on their appropriateness. Second, the SMCPS has been active in developing new programs and new courses. In 2007, it offered 17 new programs, accounting for 16.5 per cent of the programs offered in that year and 33.8 per cent of the students trained. In 2008, it offered 20 new programs. The new programs tend to keep pace with the fast-changing national and local socioeconomic conditions. For new courses, programs need to pass a two-stage review. Third, the SMCPS has used multiple methods to discover and respond to the demands of cadres. Since the spring of 2008, it has carried out an annual questionnaire survey of the training demands of its main program students. In October of the same year, it cooperated with five district party schools and the Party School of Municipal Construction Commission to survey students about training demands for 2009, obtaining 705 responses from students in these schools. Fourth, choice and evaluation have been introduced. For example, the second of the four study units of the positional training of bureau-level leading cadres comprises seminars on economic, administrative and social issues. Given the required number of credits, students can decide what to study by themselves. Further, the SMCPS has improved student evaluation of program design, program operation and teaching quality by making the evaluation process, standards and reward–punishment measures more sophisticated. Seminars that on two consecutive training sessions cannot achieve 70 per cent student satisfaction[10] will be suspended.

---

10   A student is considered satisfied if he or she assigns a general evaluation score of no less than 80 to a seminar.

Conclusion

CET in China has evolved over time, adapting to new demands and expectations, and keeping pace with the goals and missions of the CCP. Consequently, the changes and challenges faced by the CCP in governing the country are also reflected in the evolution of CET. CET has been strengthened in recent decades to enhance the capacity of the party and the government to identify and address governance issues. In that process, CET has shifted from training cadres with revolutionary thoughts to developing cadres with political loyalty and the capacity to manage a complex society. CET also has a secure, institutionalised source of funding. The whole system of CET is very different to executive development in Western countries, although CET continues to learn and adapt from overseas practices.

In the preceding discussion, some basic characteristics of CET can be identified. First, CET features highly centralised, rigorous and authoritative planning and operation by the Department of Organisation. CET is organised according to party directives rather than legal or administrative guidelines. Such a top-down model emphasises the demands and concerns of the party. Meanwhile, market elements and greater choice are gradually being introduced into CET.

Second, political engineering remains a fundamental goal of CET. In accordance with the exclusive leadership role of the party, the content of CET focuses on political learning and analysis of party spirit. Virtues of civil service neutrality are not recognised. CET also functions as an important form of policy mobilisation. Due to the rapid growth of a complex society, more attention has been paid to the practical usefulness of CET, even as the party explores ways to modernise, seeking a strategic response to a rapidly globalising world.

Third, CET features the comprehensive management of cadres. It covers not just party-governmental officials with party membership, but also officials of minor parties or those without any party affiliation, and officials of the People's Congress, SOEs, public service organisations such as universities, and social organisations. While officials with different occupational backgrounds may be matched with specialised training programs, pre-promotion, post-promotion and positional training programs are essentially the same for all.

References

Central Department of Organisation of the Chinese Communist Party (DOO of the CCP) 1989. *Cadre Education Work under Reform.* Beijing: The Central Party School Press.

Chan, H. S. and Li, S. 2007. Civil Service Law in the PRC: A return to cadre personnel management. *Public Administration Review* 67(3): 383–98.

Jing, Y. and Zhu, Q. 2012. Civil service reform in China: An unfinished task of value balancing. *Review of Public Personnel Administration* 32(2): 134–48.

Liu, A. 2009. Rebirth and secularization of the Central Party School in China. *The China Journal* 62: 105–25.

Mao, Z. 1968. Foreward to Communist periodical. In *Selected Papers of Mao Zedong. Volume Two.* Beijing: People's Press.

Pieke, F. 2009. The production of rulers: Communist party schools and the transition to neo-socialism in contemporary China. *Social Anthropology* 17(1): 25–39.

Shambaugh, D. 2008. Training China's political elite: The party school system. *The China Quarterly* 196: 827–44.

Tran, E. 2003. From senior official to top civil servant: An enquiry into the Shanghai Party School. *China Perspective* [Online] 46: 1–19.

Wei, M. 2004. Foreword. In M. Wei and S. Wang (eds), *General Situations of Cadre Education in the New Era.* Beijing: The Central Party School Press.

Zheng, J. 2010. Historical development, reforms and innovations in the Party's cadre education and training. In J. Feng (ed.), *Research of the Reforms and Innovations in Cadre Education and Training.* Beijing: People's Press.

4

Building capacity: A framework for managing learning and development in the Hong Kong Police Force[1]

Hon S. Chan and Joseph Wong Wing-ping

Transforming a government agency into an efficient and effective entity requires a systematic management approach to learning and development as an integral part of workforce planning. The Hong Kong Police Force (HKPF) is regarded as the most efficient and effective civil service unit in the Hong Kong Special Administrative Region Government (HKSARG). This chapter discusses the context and examines the historical evolution of executive development programs in the HKPF.[2] The prime objective of this chapter is to identify the distinctive training and executive development strategies utilised in the HKPF over the years and to study the way it has transformed itself into a modern and professional police force.

---

1   The authors are grateful for the generous support from the Hong Kong Police Force in providing all related information and arranging interviews with several senior police officers. Any errors and omissions, however, remain the authors'.
2   While this case study specifically highlights police training in Honk Kong, it is representative of the broader approach to civil service development in the territory.

While this chapter looks at the training framework of the HKPF, it is appropriate to place this within the context of the overall training policy and strategy of the HKSARG. The objective of the training and development laid down by HKSARG is to enhance individual and organisational performance to maintain and enhance the provision of quality public services. It adopts a two-pronged strategy in the training and development of senior civil servants. At a central level, the Civil Service Bureau, the ministry responsible for the overall management and performance of the civil service, provides high-level and holistic leadership and management training for senior civil servants across bureaus and departments, through the Civil Service Training and Development Institute (CSTDI). For example, the CSTDI organises leadership programs with renowned local and overseas institutions, sponsors high-ranking civil servants to attend courses at reputable universities such as the John F. Kennedy School of Government at Harvard, the London Business School and INSEAD, and also arranges study courses in China. The CSTDI also provides consultancy and advisory services to departments through its team of training officers.

At departmental level, heads of departments are responsible for training and developing their senior civil servants so they have the necessary, and constantly improving, executive capacity for leadership. Given its background and unique position in Hong Kong—as the largest department and one that is always well funded and resourced—the HKPF offers the best example of building executive capacity through a sustainable program of learning and training within a department.

History and development of the Hong Kong Police Force

Established in 1844, the HKPF has always played an important role in the governance of Hong Kong. Early efforts to build its policing capacities were launched in the 1920s with the creation of the Criminal Investigation Department. In 1930, the HKPF spearheaded the formation of the Emergency Unit, which was designed chiefly to deal with serious crimes and minor disturbances. After World War II, the HKPF reorganised itself by recruiting ex-servicemen from abroad and at home. After the 1956 riots, the Police Tactical Unit was formed and given responsibility for maintaining internal security. This enabled the HKPF to develop a permanent reserve for emergencies.

The British Government attached great importance to the development of a quality police force in Hong Kong. In 1893, Francis May, who headed the police force, insisted that every new recruit should go through training in a police college. In 1912, he became governor and ensured that during his term of office, which ended in 1919, the HKPF continued to develop and improve its services.

Half a century later, the paramilitary strength of the HKPF was tested during the riots of 1967, which were a spillover from the Cultural Revolution in Mainland China. For almost a year, handmade bombs were planted throughout the streets of Hong Kong. One day Chinese soldiers opened fire from the border; five Hong Kong policemen were killed in the incident. But the determination of the HKPF and the overwhelming support of the Hong Kong Chinese who chose freedom over nationalism helped put an end to the riots. In 1969, in recognition of the loyalty and outstanding performance of the Hong Kong police, Queen Elizabeth II conferred the title 'Royal' on the force.

The respect the police earned during the riots soon gave way to rampant corruption, which became widespread throughout the HKPF in the late 1960s and early 1970s. This led to the establishment of the Independent Commission Against Corruption (ICAC) in 1974. The government managed to win the war on police corruption not only because of the outstanding and sometimes ruthless job of the ICAC, but also as a result of two significant developments. First, the government raised—substantially—the pay of police officers so they could afford to live comfortably without having to resort to seeking benefits from outside. This policy of paying police officers generously and better than other civil servants has continued to the present day. Second, there was a sense of awakening in the management of the HKPF, which felt the need to inculcate a sense of pride among police officers in their service to the public. Externally, the HKPF has since reached out to various sectors of the community, attended district meetings and set up Junior Police Calls. Internally, the management has been promoting healthy living among its officers and a high standard of honesty and integrity as part of its development programs.

Within a short span of 20 years, the HKPF became the most respected government department. In July 1997, a month after China's resumption of sovereignty over Hong Kong, according to an opinion poll conducted by the Public Opinion Programme of the University of Hong Kong (HKUPOP), 79.4 per cent of respondents were satisfied with the performance of the police. By comparison, only 44.3 per cent of respondents were satisfied with the overall performance of the HKSARG during the first three months of its establishment.

The new public management trend did not make much of an impact on the civil service sector in Hong Kong. Major management reforms gained momentum mainly with the arrival in 1992 of Christopher Patten, the last Governor of Hong Kong. He brought with him the UK 'citizens' charter' concept of administrative responsiveness and quality service delivery. In response to Patten's initiative, the Service Quality Wing was established within the HKPF in 1994. The Living-the-Values Workshops, organised mainly for uniformed officers, are the most recent manifestation of the service quality culture. Under this initiative, work improvement teams, station improvement projects and staff suggestion schemes are instituted to drive continuous improvement in service delivery.

Importantly, the handover of Hong Kong to the Mainland did not make much change to the policing system. The Basic Law, which is Hong Kong's constitution, stipulates that the central authorities are responsible for defence and foreign affairs, while the HKSARG is responsible for the maintenance of law and order. Under the principle of 'one country, two systems', the HKPF retains its own policing system, is not connected hierarchically or organisationally with—and, in this sense, is separate from—the Mainland Public Security Ministry or any geographically close divisions (for example, the Guangdong Public Security Bureau).[3] Since the introduction of this law, HKPF training and development have been set within a professional, organisational and societal context. The force incorporates a number of dynamic driving factors into its training and executive development plan, including

---

3   This information was provided by a senior police officer in the Hong Kong Police College. We also conducted interviews with several senior police officers in October 2011. Subsequent phone communications were made to either gather additional information or make inquiries about the information provided. To provide an accurate picture of the HKPF's development, this chapter uses the database, documents, reports, statistics and figures given by the HKPF; these sources are quoted directly or paraphrased in some of the discussions in this chapter.

the volatility of the external environment (the increasing complexity of policing and the policing landscape), HKPF developments (such as the improved calibre of recruits in recent years and, as a result, the increased expectations on training and development) and customer and government expectations (rising demands for a responsive and responsible police service) (see Hong Kong Police College 2008b).

Force management structure

The HKPF is a large organisation with more than 27,700 uniformed staff in 12 different ranks.[4] Because of Hong Kong's history—as a colony of the United Kingdom and, since 1997, a Special Administrative Region of the People's Republic of China—the HKPF is the principal law enforcement agency as well as the agency of first response and last resort. Its portfolio of duties covers a wide spectrum including crime-fighting, public order maintenance and internal security.

There are two entry-level ranks in the force: constable and inspector. New recruits normally join the force between the ages of 18 and 23. The normal retirement age is 55, or 57 for those in the senior directorate. As is the case in other metropolitan police forces, here there are different career streams such as frontline policing, special operations, criminal investigation and administrative and management-related duties.

The Commissioner of Police is charged with the supreme direction and administration of the police force under Section 4 of the *Police Force Ordinance*, Chapter 232. The commissioner is subject to the orders and control of the Chief Executive of the HKSARG. Under his administration, there were 433 gazetted officers, 2,159 inspectorate officers and 25,323 junior police officers, with 3,858 civilian staff in 2010 (see Table 4.1, the headline figures represent total staff including officers on pre-retirement leave, while figures in brackets indicate actual staff numbers of police at each level).

---

4   The most up-to-date figure is 27,700, provided by another senior police officer in our interview conducted on 4 October 2011. The figures in the following discussion were drawn from the *Hong Kong Police Review 2010* (HKPF 2010); they are therefore 2010 figures.

The Senior Directorate Group (SDG) is the executive body of the HKPF. It comprises two deputy commissioners of police (operations and management), four senior assistant commissioners of police and one civilian officer of equivalent rank. The last five SDG members mentioned are program directors of operations, crime and security, personnel and training, management services, and the civilian director of finance, administration and planning. Fourteen assistant commissioners, one police civil secretary (a general civil service grade with the rank of senior principal executive officer) and one financial controller (a departmental civil service grade with the rank of assistant director of the treasury department) assist the commissioner and his SDG members. Another 401 gazetted officers variously hold the ranks of chief, senior superintendent and superintendent. This group of gazetted officers is the core executive group of the HKPF.

In brief, the governance of the force starts with the commissioner and the SDG. Policy direction cascades down to frontline commanders and officers through various schemes including the *Hong Kong Police Force Vision and Statement of Common Purpose and Values*, the Controlling Officer's Report, the Strategic Action Plan and the Commissioner's Operational Priorities. Daily policing activities follow the HKPF's policy direction in the form of regional, district and divisional plans.

Table 4.1: Establishment and actual strength of the Hong Kong Police Force, 2005–10

	2010	2009	2008	2007	2006	2005
Gazetted officer	433 (422)	430 (426)	423 (418)	422 (411)	401 (419)	411 (412)
Inspectorate	2,159 (2,230)	2,162 (2,218)	2,145 (2,176)	2,138 (2,139)	2,101 (2,142)	2,132 (2,161)
Junior police officer	25,323 (25,466)	25,142 (25,334)	24,770 (25,216)	24,779 (25,001)	24,419 (24,813)	23,969 (24,831)
Total (strength)	27,915 (28,118)	27,734 (27,978)	27,338 (27,810)	27,339 (27,551)	26,921 (27,374)	26,512 (27,404)

Source: HKPF (2010).

HKPF Steering Committee on Human Resource Management

The HKPF Steering Committee on Human Resource Management (and its predecessor, the Policy and Coordinating Committee on Force Training and Development) is the main human resource management (HRM) body in the HKPF. The terms of reference for the steering committee outline its main tasks:

- To steer and monitor the implementation of established HRM policies in support of the Force Vision, Common Purpose and Values.
- To consider proposed policies on HRM to ensure alignment with HKPF objectives and strategic directions.
- To review and update HRM policies to ensure they meet the changing needs of the HKPF and the community it serves.
- To oversee new HRM-related initiatives to ensure alignment with the HKPF's strategic framework.
- To oversee new course/development initiatives and, where appropriate, make recommendations to ensure alignment with HKPF objectives and strategic directions.
- To recommend, where appropriate, the allocation of resources for local/overseas training courses for vocational/development purposes and to ensure the principle of value for money is applied.[5]

The steering committee has 12 members and is chaired by the Director of Personnel and Training—a senior assistant commissioner position. The personnel wing of the HKPF and the police college are the executive arms of the steering committee. With a uniformed staff of 27,770, the HKPF has 729 training staff. There are 509 officers working in the Hong Kong Police College, 135 in the Police Tactical Unit Headquarters, 57 in the Training and Staff Relations Office and 27 in the Marine Police Training School. Together they provide expert assistance in training and development policies to major formation commanders as required, coordinate the Force Training and Development Plan and report on and maintain the Force Training

---

5   Information provided by the HKPF on 11 October 2011.

Directory, evaluate feedback from major formation commanders on training and development needs and perform environmental scans to select topical training subjects (see Hong Kong Police College 2009).

Methodology of training and development

The 'learning trio'

As shown in the *Training and Development Plan 2006–08* formulated by the then Policy and Coordinating Committee on Force Training and Development, the prevailing training philosophy of the HKPF is that 'effective training and development can foster a continuous learning culture and realise the potential of its officers to meet the needs of the Force and the community it serves' (Hong Kong Police College 2006: 8). Promoting the 'learning trio' within the HKPF reinforces this continuous—that is, lifelong—learning culture (see Figure 4.1). Three key components underline this training trio. Induction training, which, together with other mid-career programs, is perceived as formal training, is the first component. About 25 per cent of all police officers' learning is acquired through formal training.

Formal training

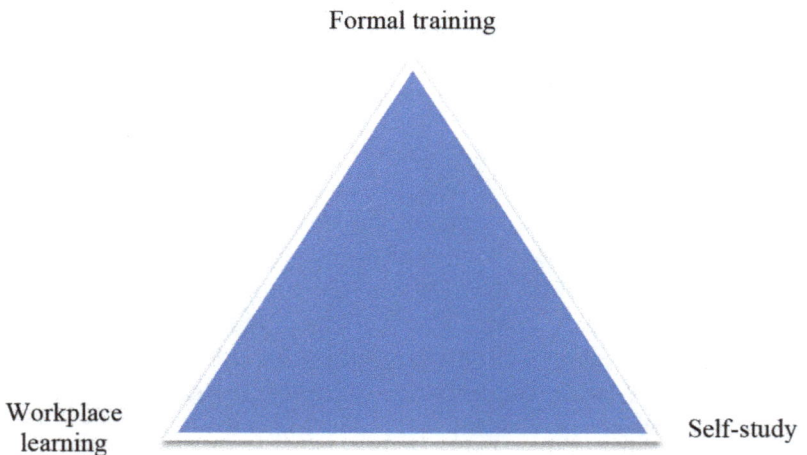

Workplace learning

Self-study

Figure 4.1: The 'learning trio'
Source: Created by the authors.

Apart from organising formal structural programs, the police college helps to support workplace learning and self-study. Learning takes place not only within the formal classroom setting; police officers gain workplace learning from work experience, interaction with peers and job assignments.

In relation to job assignments, the HKPF has stepped up measures to carry out a comprehensive program of training and executive development for all police officers. Police officers will take up mandatory or structured postings as assigned to ensure full exposure to the various aspects of workplace experience in the force. Police officers are encouraged to indicate their preferences for postings at a certain point in their career. The HKPF has also identified police officers with potential—that is, those who demonstrate excellent performance in formal training and receive an outstanding performance rating—for various ranks and has tailored their career advancement accordingly. On the job, officers receive ample coaching and mentoring from their supervisors. To facilitate quality peer coaching, the police college implements training of junior police officers for supervisory roles. Other HKPF initiatives include schemes for mentoring potential officers and tutoring police constables.

Self-study is regarded as being as important as following a structured curriculum. Learning is both an organisational and a personal responsibility. Given this understanding, the police college works on the principle that police officers must function as active knowledge promoters and learning facilitators. All police officers are required to share their experiences with other members and coach subordinates and peers within their areas of expertise. In short, they must not only learn, but also help other police officers learn. Apart from adopting a self-study approach for individual development in the HKPF, the police college supports continuous learning through organising formal seminars and providing financial subsidies. Many such ad hoc learning programs are scheduled outside office hours so that interested officers attend these programs in their own time. Reimbursement of course fees for short local courses helps police officers, particularly junior officers and junior inspectors, to engage in learning mostly by way of completing a bachelor or master's degree in their own time. Academic accreditation of training from local as well as overseas tertiary institutions is a further step to encourage officers to pursue higher university qualifications in policing and other related disciplines.[6]

Training hierarchy

A senior police officer explained, in an interview with the authors conducted on 4 October 2011, a strategy to groom future leaders within the force by developing the skills and competencies of staff through a tiered hierarchical approach to training and development, which is another important methodology in training and executive development of the HKPF (see Figure 4.2).

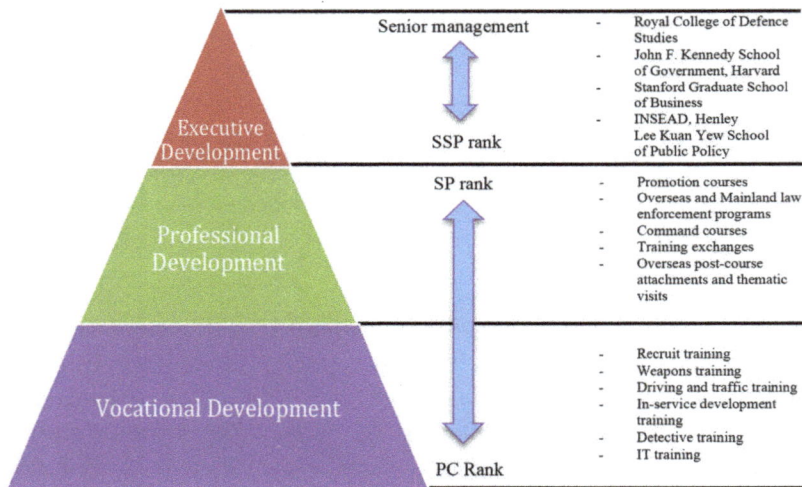

Figure 4.2: The police training hierarchy
Source: Created by the authors. PC = police constables; SP = senior police officers; and SSP = senior superintendent police officers.

The first tier emphasises vocational training, which begins with induction or foundation courses on appointment to the HKPF. These courses provide officers with the practical job-based skills to prepare their career. The force also arranges specialist and mid-career training programs that are open to all ranks of police officers throughout their service. In alignment with the 'learning trio' concept (illustrated in

---

6   Information gathered from interviews with senior police officers on 3 October 2011.

Figure 4.1), the HKPF has developed a workplace learning strategy to encourage personal development through job rotations, mandatory or structured career paths, mentoring and coaching. The HKPF rotates officers on a regular basis—normally every two to three years—to enable them to experience a broad range of police duties in regional units as well as at police headquarters. To supplement this policy, the force has introduced career paths for junior inspectors so they can indicate their preferred posting and gain exposure to the full range of core police functions at an early stage. Mentoring and coaching both on a formal and an informal basis are crucial for passing on institutional culture and learning experience. On a day-to-day basis, this primarily involves line supervisors and colleagues at two levels in the hierarchy. On a more formal basis, the HKPF has created a peer advisory scheme accessible via the police intranet, whereby staff can consult a group of experts in areas such as public order policing and crime investigation.

The second tier of professional development refers to training and development in generic competencies such as police management and leadership skills. This is pursued both internally through promotion and command courses and externally by sending officers on overseas training attachments, to international conferences or accompanying senior directorate officers to international conferences. All newly promoted officers will be required to attend command courses at their respective levels, to equip them with updated professional knowledge, leadership and management skills, as well as knowledge of the political, economic and social matters important to the service delivery of the HKPF. Supplementing the learning experience from vocational and professional development, the HKPF arranges for officers to attach themselves to overseas and Chinese provincial police forces for experience sharing, updating professional knowledge, developing an international perspective and networking. The force also regularly dispatches teams of officers of different ranks to visit overseas police forces to broaden their vision and engage in international dialogue. Locally, the HKPF has seconded officers to government departments and related educational establishments. For example, in recent times the HKPF has seconded officers ranging from the rank of constable to senior superintendent to the Security Bureau, Department of Health and Hong Kong International Airport Authority. International secondments have included postings to the

Interpol General Secretariat in Lyon, France, the Interpol Liaison Office in Bangkok, the UK National Policing Improvement Agency and the Chinese People's Public Security University in Beijing.

The third tier of executive development gives emphasis to areas such as strategic planning, policy analysis and development of strategic vision. Newly promoted senior superintendents and above are required to attend the Management Development Program, which is designed internally and comprises regular seminars and modular training workshops for the sharing of strategies to meet challenges in the HKPF and the civil service, the development of more advanced management skills and broadening horizons on contemporary issues. Externally, the HKPF tailors the executive development programs and sends senior police officers to courses through its Overseas Development Training (ODT) and Mainland Development Training (MDT) programs organised by institutions in the United Kingdom, the United States, Australia, Austria, Canada, Germany, Indonesia, Malaysia, the Netherlands, Singapore, Sweden, Switzerland, Thailand and Mainland China. These programs help to develop the critical thinking skills and global perspectives required of a future leader of the HKPF.[7] The HKPF planned to expand ODT places from 121 in 2010–11 to 142 in 2011–12, and MDT places from 252 in 2010–11 to 366 in 2011–12, representing an increase from 373 places to 508 (a 27 per cent increase) across the two programs.[8]

Key components of training and development in the HKPF: Command courses

Three types of command courses make up the three key components of training and executive development of the HKPF. These courses are run by the Hong Kong Police College. The paper *A Conceptual Framework for Command Courses*, developed by the police college in 2011, clearly spells out the pedagogy, the conceptual framework, the course design and other related aspects of the three command courses (Hong Kong Police College 2011a). In the interests of space, this chapter addresses the conceptual framework, course design and the tentative schedule of the three command courses to be offered in

---

7   Information from an interview with a senior police officer on 4 October 2011.
8   Information given by the HKPF on 12 October 2011. Figures in 2010–11 are current, while those for 2011–12 are estimates.

2011–12, to put the discussion in perspective. Before going further, it is important to note that the three command courses are designed to cater for the training and development needs of police officers in their respective ranks. The Junior Command Course (JCC) is designed mainly for junior police officers. The Intermediate Command Course (ICC) is for police officers holding a rank of chief inspector or above. The Senior Command Course (SCC) is for police officers of a rank of superintendent or above.

Conceptual framework

For many years, the HKPF has been moving away from a curriculum-centred approach towards a more problem-based approach (see Figure 4.3). In shifting the emphasis, there is a need to balance actual workplace experience with theoretical knowledge. Traditional classroom face-to-face learning, while remaining useful for experience sharing and learning theoretical knowledge, tends to give a rather restricted perspective on work in a police setting. Hence classroom learning has to be supplemented with hands-on, job-based practice and problem-motivated learning in policing. It is believed this helps build confidence and competence in problem-solving among police officers.

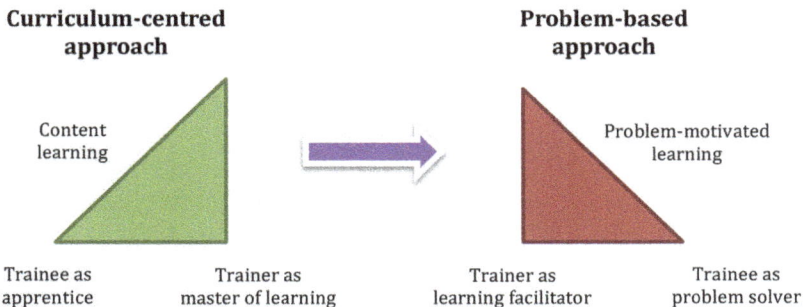

Curriculum-centred approach		Problem-based approach	
Content learning		Problem-motivated learning	
Trainee as apprentice	Trainer as master of learning	Trainer as learning facilitator	Trainee as problem solver

Figure 4.3: From a curriculum-centred approach to a problem-based approach
Source: Created by the authors.

Problem-based learning seeks to develop officers' analytical powers, critical thinking and decision-making skills while simultaneously giving them real-life situations and a safe environment in which to learn by trial and error. Learners are required to apply problem-solving skills to identify the problem and assess the time, information and resources needed for its solution.

There are many adult-learning theories that have been incorporated by the HKPF in the development of these three command courses. Some learning theories are presented in the conceptual paper. The first example is the *transformative learning* theory. Research has shown that transformative learning produces different individual, interpersonal and organisational outcomes. Transformative learning involves questioning assumptions as well as unlearning habits, behaviours and beliefs that are either outdated or no longer useful. Hence, the command courses must provide participants with the ability to question existing beliefs and the skills necessary to assess the validity of these assumptions.

The other examples of learning theories are *action learning* and *action research*. Action learning requires the learners to discuss real-world problems. They are then asked to apply both critical thinking and communication skills that assist in the transfer of learning into the workplace beyond the confines of the teaching environment. Action research as a requisite tool for action learning has gained increasing popularity in the HKPF as a way of contributing to ongoing professional development. This theory emphasises self-reflection and self-evaluation during and after problem-solving episodes. This learning style maintains that the individual is fully aware of their responsibility for their own actions. With this awareness, individuals will presumably improve their self-management as well as professional skills (see Hong Kong Police College 2011a: 2–3).

Design of command courses

The focus of each level of command course will differ substantially. The HKPF has sought to provide a continuum as officers advance through each command course with promotion. There are two ways to explain the differences. Since different stakeholders naturally hold different views about what is worthy of inclusion in the curriculum, the HKPF proposes a broad focus for each level of command course, as follows:

- JCC: Broad introduction to all three modules (leadership and self, context of policing and organisational effectiveness) with an emphasis on operational issues.
- ICC: Refresher on three modules with focus on staff issues including motivation, team building and translating organisational strategies into practical and effective activities.

- SCC: Refresher on three modules with a focus on creating public value through strategic planning and the implementation process (see Hong Kong Police College 2011a: 4).

A different way to illustrate the difference is by comparing the degrees of emphasis each command course puts on *personal development, professional development* and *vocational development* (see Figure 4.4).

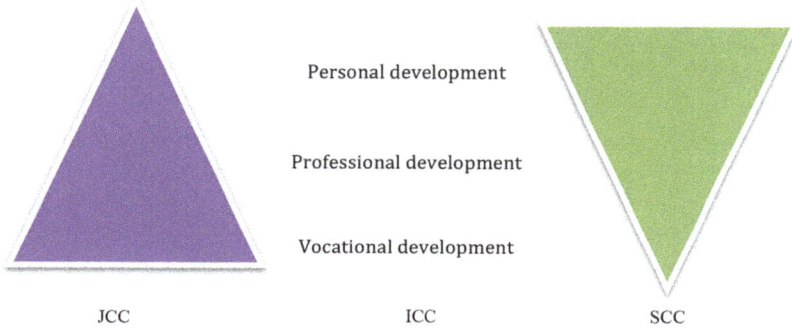

Personal development

Professional development

Vocational development

JCC   ICC   SCC

Figure 4.4: The degree of emphasis between personal, professional and vocational development in each command course
Source: Created by the authors.

Personal development refers to the extent of a person's self-awareness. Learners (or participants) are made aware of the fact that command courses are developmental in nature, with the objective of enhancing the leadership performance of junior and middle managers in the HKPF. In alignment with the theories of action learning and action research, self-awareness requires learners to be aware of their own behaviour and style so they know whether they are following best practice in modern management. They are assisted in this self-discovery process by psychometric testing. Two of these instruments are used in the SCC and ICC: the Myers-Briggs Type Indicator (MBTI) and the Harrison Assessment. Only the MBTI is used in the JCC. Psychometric profiling aside, learners are exposed to self-analysis through on-camera experiences including media training, knowledge sharing, presentations and classroom-based exercises. Arrangements are made for learners to meet with outsiders to enhance their social sensitivity and awareness of the outside world. Courses selected for this developmental area also cover the core competency requirements for 'personal effectiveness' and 'communication'. At the SCC and ICC levels, the theory and craft of leadership are included and delivered mainly through a project and an experiential learning-based approach. Small project teams work on topics covering areas such as leadership theory, motivation, policing models, a change environment and different methods of strategic policy formulation. At the SCC level, emphasis is given to 'strategic leadership'.

Professional development refers to those modules designed to enhance learners' understanding of their relationship with the organisation and the various principles under which the organisation operates. It includes field trips to both internal police formations and other police forces in greater China. Modules selected for this developmental area cover the core competency requirements for professionalism.

Vocational development covers policies, practices and procedures affecting everyday life. In general, the SCC does not focus on this area, while the JCC puts the greatest emphasis on vocational development. Figure 4.4 shows that the amount of time spent on vocational learning in the SCC is inversely proportional to that spent in the JCC. The objectives of all courses are aligned with the above schema (Hong Kong Police College 2008a).

Frequency of command courses, 2011–12

All command courses ran for three weeks with a one-day visit to the Mainland, except for the SCC, for which a two-day visit was scheduled. The HKPF organised six JCCs between April 2011 and March 2012, five ICCs between May 2011 and June 2012 and three SCCs between May 2011 and March 2012. Between 15 and 18 participants took part in each command course. The JCC included participants from the Guangdong Public Security Bureau. Both the JCC and the ICC included participants from other Hong Kong Government Disciplined Services. External participants from other jurisdictions have been availing themselves of reciprocal opportunities in the SCC. For example, in SSCs held in November 2007, there were five such officers, one each from China, the United Kingdom, Australia, the Netherlands and Singapore.[9]

---

9   Information gathered from interviews on 3 October 2011.

The HKPF does not have any plans to align command courses with one another or with any other course provided in-house—for example, the Course on Basic Training or the Inspectors' Continuation Course. The chief reason is the long time lapse between an officer's participation in each of these courses, which means any alignment would not necessarily lead to consistency in the learning experiences of participants. For example, by the time a JCC participant attends the ICC, an average of eight years has passed, by which time the original JCC will have changed in content and emphasis; the ICC cannot be aligned with both the original course and the new course. The second aspect of alignment is to decide whether officers at all levels should be taught using the same principle. Given the nature of work, scope of responsibility and degree of authority and discretion given to police officers of different levels, variations within the three command courses are expected.

Training loading and resources support in training and development

How does the HKPF invest in training and executive development, particularly the three command courses identified as the key elements? Where are the funding streams? How does the level of funding affect the staff and faculty conducting training and the quality of training delivered? What are the training costs? The following discussion uses the database and report provided by the HKPF and the authors' interview findings to address some of these questions.

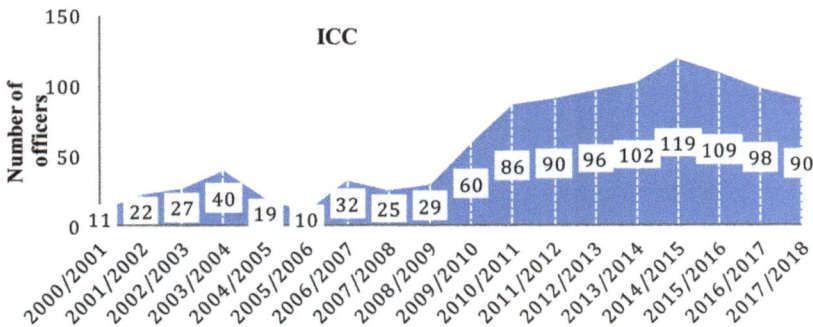

Figure 4.5: Number of officers to be trained in the Intermediate Command Course (ICC), 2000–01 to 2017–18

Source: Created by the authors (see footnote 3 above and the list of reports provided indicated in the reference list).

Figure 4.5 shows the number of officers and the percentage of each rank to be trained in the next four years of the ICC. Table 4.2 summarises the training targets of the three command courses for the years 2011–12 to 2013–14.

Table 4.2: Training targets of the three command courses, 2011–12 to 2013–14

	2011–12	2012–13	2013–14
JCC	108	186	212
ICC	90	96	119
SCC	54	56	66

Source: Hong Kong Police College (2011b).

Figure 4.6 indicates the budget (the money available to cover training contractors, presenters, training materials and the like) for the three command courses between 2006–07 and 2011–12. Figure 4.7 presents the average budget per officer trained for the three command courses over the same period, calculated by dividing the total budget by the number of participants. Note that the budget does not increase in line with the growing number of officers trained.

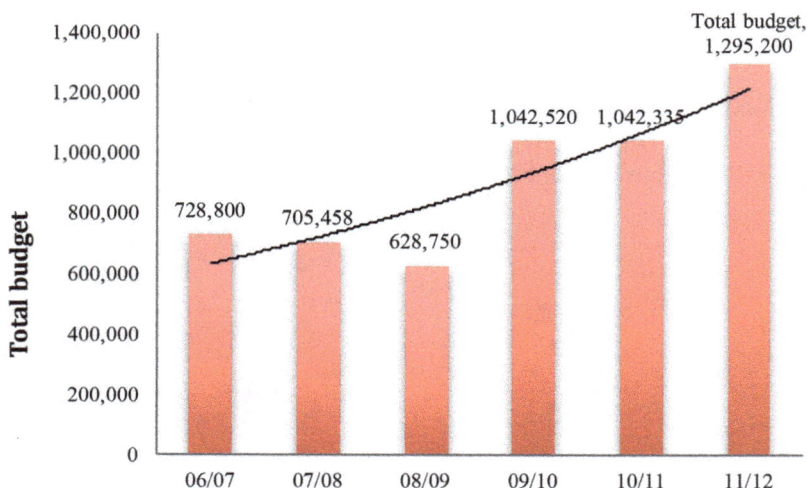

Figure 4.6: Total budget for running the three command courses, 2006–07 to 2011–12
Source: Created by the authors.

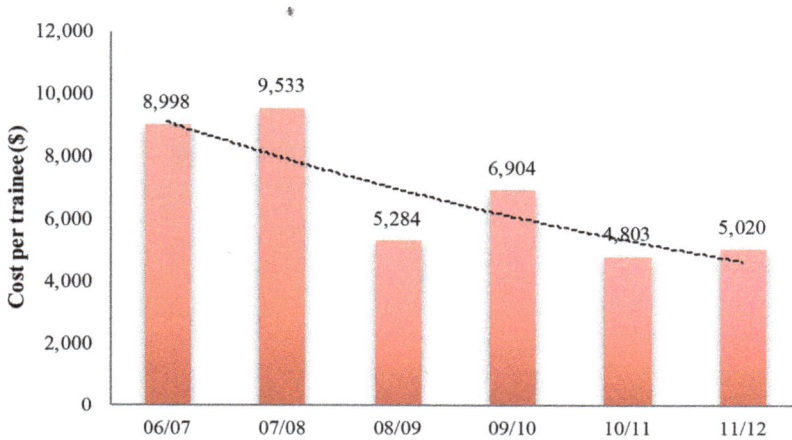

Figure 4.7: Budget for running the three command courses per officer trained, 2006–07 to 2011–12
Source: Created by the authors.

The investment in each command course cannot be measured simply by looking at the budget. Instead, the time-cost for participants should also be incorporated. The time-cost (as of October 2011, based on 18 officers per three-week command course) is as follows:

- SCC: HK$1,037,796 (A$173,544)
- ICC: HK$864,145 (A$144,505)
- JCC: HK$625,911 (A$104,667).

Based on a two-week course, the time-cost is as follows:

- SCC: HK$691,864 (A$115,696)
- ICC: HK$576,094 (A$96,336)
- JCC HK$417,274 (A$69,778).[10]

The HKPF has also organised the Overseas and Mainland Development Training (OMDT) and Overseas Vocational Training (OVT) programs. Before the start of each financial year, the HKPF sources appropriate courses for officers. The Financial Comptroller will allocate a lump sum to cover OMDT expenses. The OMDT is open to all ranks while the OVT is designed for specific purposes, usually to meet the formation

---

10   Information provided by the HKPF on 3 October 2011.

commanders' needs. The personnel wing of the HKPF is given responsibility for nominating suitable officers to attend the OMDT. The Deputy Commissioner (Management) endorses the proposed nomination and the allocation of OMDT. The Director of the HKPF endorses the proposed nomination and the allocation of OVT.

Included in the list of institutions for the overseas development programs are seven from the United Kingdom, six each from the United States and Australia, four from Canada and one each from Austria, Germany, Indonesia, Malaysia and the Netherlands. Examples of courses offered by these institutions are the Executive Leadership Program, Police Officers' Command Course, Law and Enforcement Management Program and International Fellow Exchange Program. Seventeen institutions in China are listed in the Mainland Development Training, including the National School of Administration of China, Chinese People's Public Security University and local police colleges and universities such as Sun Yat-sen University, China Foreign Affairs University, Peking University and Tsinghua University. These institutions offer courses in their (Advanced) National Studies Program, National Strategies Program, Police College Study Program, and so on.[11]

For the year 2011–12, 77 police officers were to be nominated to take part in the OVT program. At the time of writing, eight officers at or above the rank of superintendent, 50 inspectorate officers, 15 junior police officers and two technical staff had been nominated, with two further nominations pending.[12] Officers will be sent to Thailand (21 places), Singapore (20 places), the United States (12 places), the United Kingdom (11 places), Canada (four places), Mainland China (three places), Australia (two places) and Germany, Switzerland, New Zealand and Indonesia (one place each).

The HKPF has sent police officers to attend courses organised by the CSTDI. In 2010–11, 24 seminars (10 of which focus mainly on current issues in Hong Kong and China and 14 on vocational topics) and 49 job-related (to civil service) programs were organised. The CSTDI does not charge the HKPF for running all these courses because they are not police-specific.[13]

---

11 Information provided by the HKPF on 11 October 2011.
12 Information provided by the HKPF on 3 October 2011.
13 Information provided by the Hong Kong Police College on 12 October 2011.

Funding streams for training and development programs

The key service provider in the HKPF is the Hong Kong Police College. The Superintendent Management Learning Division (SMLD) is responsible for organising and running the ICC and SCC. A chief inspector and a non–civil service contract officer (with a grade of senior training manager, STM) assist the SMLD. The chief inspector and STM are responsible for organising and running the JCC. The HKPF uses external facilitators to help meet the heavy demand for the three command courses. In general, there are five types of facilitators:

1.   internal (HKPF) facilitators

2.   government speakers (mainly policy-level administrative officer grade)

3.   guest speakers (prominent personalities in society)

4.   consultants (paid on a commercial rate)

5.   academics (paid an honorarium).

Table 4.3 presents the Hong Kong Police College's 2010–11 expenditure and projected expenditure for 2011–12.

Table 4.3: Expenditure of Hong Kong Police College (HK$)

Items	Year	
	2010–11	2011–12 (projection)
Salary	297,913,000	249,372,930 (–16%)
Local training	16,204,000	15,215,400 (–6%)
Overseas training	8,426,060	6,766,000 (–20%)
Mainland Exchange Program	976,000	700,000 (–28%)
Administration and other	41,453,669	38,488,849 (–7%))
Total	364,972,729	310,543,179 (–15%)

Source: Created by the authors.

The HKPF has a special account to meet the costs of OMDT and OVT. Tables 4.4 and 4.5 present training statistics and expenditure for both programs.[14]

---

14   Information provided by the HKPF on 3 October 2011.

Table 4.4: Overseas and Mainland Development Training (OMDT) program

	2006–07	2007–08	2008–09	2009–10	2010–11
Number of courses	61	68	69	62	75
Number of participants	256	289	327	306	339
Actual expenditure (HK$)	5,615,662	5,370,101	6,048,505	5,110,746	7,319,577

Source: Created by the authors.

Table 4.5: Overseas Vocational Training (OVT) program

	2006–07	2007–08	2008–09	2009–10	2010–11
Number of courses	42	52	43	63	75
Number of participants	50	74	57	87	135
Actual expenditure (HK$)	983,780	1,606,906	1,333,088	1,962,665	3,328,739

Source: Created by the authors.

It is clear that the HKPF has allocated funding based on organisational priorities. All strategies are fully costed, including taking into account the indirect time cost to participants. Key training responsibilities are clearly articulated. Nonetheless, if the current training format for the three command courses remains unchanged, the HKPF will need to create 11 courses for the JCC, seven for the ICC and four for the SCC to meet its 2012 training targets. This would require a JCC almost every month of the year and either an ICC or an SCC every month. This kind of overlap raises the management issue of who will act in a rank if two ranks are attending courses at the same time.[15] Moreover, the data show that if the HKPF wants to maintain its momentum in training more middle-ranking and junior police officers, resources will be a problem. A 15 per cent cut to the budget was expected for the financial year 2012–13, and the HKPF will need to find a way to deal with reduced funding.

---

15   Interviews conducted on 3 October 2011.

Training content

The training curriculum of the HKPF covers all aspects of modern training and executive development theories and strategies. A very clear methodology underlines the three command courses, covering three modules: leadership and self, context of policing and organisational effectiveness. Varying degrees of emphasis on personal, professional and vocational development are built into the course design.

The seminars and programs organised by the CSTDI are designed to brush up officers' language, communication, management and other job-based skills. Additional topics offered by the CSTDI include:

- understanding China and Hong Kong
- civil service reform in China
- performance measurement and management in China
- socialist, command and basic law
- administrative law and judicial review
- enhancing gender awareness
- understanding of the *Equal Opportunities Ordinance*
- alternative dispute resolution (mediation and arbitration) and its application
- emotional intelligence in action
- executive health and stress management
- managing conflict
- capital work expenditure
- HRM
- supervisor management skills
- financial management
- managing public complaints.[16]

OMDT program-approved institutions offer courses to improve participants' understanding of strategic thinking, transnational policing management, global city management, advanced national

---

16   Information provided by the HKPF on 11 October 2011.

studies and strategies, sustainable leadership training, Chinese foreign affairs and national plans. The OVT program offers specialised courses that cannot otherwise be organised in Hong Kong. Examples include Protecting Infrastructure against Terrorism, International Disaster Management, Concealed Human Narcotic Detection, Comprehensive Security Response to Terrorism, Marine Electronics Installer, NMEA 2000 Training and Advanced Management, Dignitary Protective Seminar, Using the Internet as an Intelligence Tool, Terrorism Investigation and Behaviour-Based Safety and Safety Management. The content of the training curriculum reflects the different skills and intellectual capacities the HKPF requires to develop a comprehensive workforce plan.[17]

Two measures taken by the HKPF characterise the distinct nature of training strategies adopted by the Hong Kong civil service sector: the Living-the-Values Workshops and training days. In March 2011, the Force Quality Management Strategy was launched with the aim of achieving continuous improvement.

Living-the-Values Workshops

In 1997, the Living-the-Values Workshops were rolled out to provide a discussion forum for staff, aimed at:

- promoting awareness and acceptance of HKPF values
- expressing views on areas of concern
- providing feedback to senior management
- providing two-way 'buy-in', both from the top down and from the bottom up.

There have been seven 'waves' of workshops. Wave VII (commencing September 2010) focuses on overcoming barriers to professionalism in a changing world by:

- enhancing officers' awareness of and sensitivity to the need to meet the public's increasing expectations in a rapidly changing society
- enhancing officers' understanding of effective communication with all stakeholders by listening to their needs and explaining their reasoning

---

17   ibid.

- strengthening officers' belief and efforts in striving for quality service and continuous improvement in their everyday work.

The workshops are organised biannually. This is a HKPF-wide activity involving every member of uniformed staff. Training methods include role-playing, case studies, discussions and presentations. Facilitators are drawn from within the force: an assistant commissioner-level member will be invited to run training sessions for superintendents, a superintendent-level member for inspectors and inspector-level staff for junior police officers.[18]

Training days

Smaller in scale than the Living-the-Values Workshops are the training days that are scheduled annually and targeted at inspectors and junior police officers. The objectives of training days are to:

- enhance the effectiveness of participating personnel by providing them with job-related training
- facilitate personnel management and good communication
- generate and maintain a culture of living police values, a healthy lifestyle and team spirit
- teach awareness of the local situation as it affects individual job descriptions
- obtain feedback on professional issues of HKPF-wide concern.

Training days normally last a full working day and are held every six to eight weeks at the discretion of formation commanders. A minimum of five training days should be held each year in each formation. There should be no more than 50 officers participating. Training day packages are developed according to the laws, police orders and procedures in place at the time of scheduling. A training and staff relations officer (chief inspectorate rank) leads the activities. Topics covered in 2011 included Integrity Management, Handling Civil Disputes and Emotional Regulation and Working with the Media.

---

18   ibid.

The 2008 review of the workshops indicated that they should continue as one of the key instruments by which to align personal values with HKPF values, but the workshops should be continuously refined to encourage more bottom-up discussion and self-reflection.[19] Interviews with a handful of middle-level and junior police officers show they are all highly supportive of the Living-the-Values Workshops and the training days.[20] These two measures are highly regarded as tools to improve all stakeholder relationships, to reinforce a learning culture within the HKPF, to empower middle-ranking and junior police officers and, most importantly, to create a strong sense of pride, identity, loyalty and commitment to the HKPF.

In summary: Present problems and future challenges

The determination and dedication of successive HKPF commissioners since the 1970s have transformed the force into Asia's—and probably the world's—finest police force in terms of fighting crime, maintaining law and order and serving the community. The government has spared no effort in supporting the training and development of the police. Among all uniformed services, and indeed all departments, the HKPF has always been provided with generous resources to carry out its work, including the operation of the police college. With the exception of the very top positions in the force, the commissioner and his senior management make decisions on promotion and succession to senior ranks. The senior management identifies high performers at superintendent level and plans possible successions to commissioner level 10–15 years in advance. Every year, the Secretary for the Civil Service reviews the succession plan with the Commissioner of Police. Although the post of Commissioner of Police is a civil service one, it is classed as a principal office (similar to the posts of secretaries) under the Basic Law, so the officer is subject to official appointment by the Central Government of China following nomination by the Chief Executive of the HKSARG.

---

19   ibid.
20   Interviews conducted in October 2011.

One legacy of the colonial era is the relatively early retirement age for senior directorate officers of the uniformed services: 57, compared with the normal retirement age of 60 for other civil servants. The normal retirement age of police officers has remained at 55. With the expansion of university places in recent years, most new recruits now join the HKPF in their early 20s after obtaining their bachelor degree. If they enter at the rank of constable, they have to pass 10 rank promotions to reach the position of chief superintendent; if they join as an inspector, the number of promotions can be reduced to six. The most talented chief superintendent will then have to pass four promotions to reach the top post of commissioner. It is no surprise, then, that the average term of commissioners in the past two decades has been five years or less.

Nowadays, people not only live longer, they also stay healthy for longer. There is a strong case to extend the normal retirement age of Hong Kong civil servants from 60 to perhaps 63 or 65, and there is certainly an urgent case to extend the retirement age of the uniformed services, including the police, from 55 or 57 to at least 60.

In addition, while the numerous promotion ranks in the HKPF may be conducive to maintaining morale (so that one is promoted more often), it may not contribute to enhancing efficiency or a more sustainable executive development program. A review of the ranking structure in the HKPF would help to improve efficiency and eliminate unnecessary levels. We should bear in mind that the present strength of the force is about 400 police officers per 100,000 people, which is the highest per capita rate among developed cities (Singapore's police per capita ratio is about half of Hong Kong's).

As a paramilitary force in colonial times, the HKPF carried out its orders without any regard for Chinese nationalistic considerations, as it did during the 1967 riots. After Hong Kong became a Special Administrative Region of China, the Basic Law, created under the Chinese Constitution, conferred a high degree of autonomy to the HKSARG. Hong Kong civil servants do not need to declare their allegiance to the Central Chinese Government; under Article 99 of the Basic Law, they are responsible to the HKSARG only. When the HKSARG introduced the accountability system (which is a politically appointed ministerial system) for the most senior government officials one of its declared objectives was to better preserve the political neutrality of the civil service, including the police.

Until a few years ago, the impartiality of the police in handling political demonstrations was not questioned. For example, in 2003, when half a million people marched in the streets to protest against the government's proposal to enact legislation to prohibit treason and subversion against China, the police handled the demonstrations fairly and efficiently and not a single accident occurred. More recently, with the present government of Chief Executive, Donald Tsang, implementing some unpopular policies and anti-government demonstrations becoming more confrontational, the police have been accused of impeding some protest actions, particularly when the targets are the Chinese Government or their representative offices in Hong Kong.

The alleged politicisation of the police came to a head when the HKPF was accused of overdoing security arrangements for the visit of then Chinese Vice-Premier Li Keqiang to Hong Kong in August 2011. As a result, the Hong Kong press staged a protest against the severe restrictions put on their reporting and photography work. Several students were allegedly detained by the police in a building within the campus of the University of Hong Kong so they could not join the protest. A person wearing a 'June 4' slogan t-shirt was taken away to the police station as he stepped out from his residence.[21] These heavy-handed police actions resulted in strong public criticism. The police commissioner was summoned to a meeting of the Legislative Council, the University of Hong Kong conducted an inquiry and the detained students took civil action against the police. The commissioner insisted that he was not under any political pressure nor did he have any political considerations in making the security arrangements.

In the aftermath of this incident, police popularity suffered its worst rating since 1997. According to the University of Hong Kong Public Opinion Program (HKUPOP) survey conducted in September 2011, the proportion of respondents who were satisfied with the performance of the police dropped to a record low of 56.7 per cent, while the figure for those who were unsatisfied rose to a record high of 19.7 per cent. These figures may still be very respectable when compared with those in other jurisdictions but they certainly represent a warning signal to

---

21   This was in reference to the Tiananmen Square incident on 4 June 1989, when the Chinese Government sent in the military to forcibly quell student demonstrators in Tiananmen Square in Beijing.

the HKPF. How to stay politically neutral, and be seen as such, will be among the greatest challenges to the incumbent Commissioner of Police and the HKSARG.

In 2010–11, total expenditure on training in the Hong Kong civil service was about HK$950 million (A$162 million)—equivalent to 1.7 per cent of the total payroll. Of this training expenditure, departments spent 80 per cent, with the HKPF accounting for close to half of departmental spending. Although the HKPF is the largest department, with about 28,000 police officers, it still represents less than 20 per cent of the total civil service establishment and yet it accounts for 40 per cent of total government spending on training. The case of police training may offer a good model for other departments to follow provided the HKSARG is prepared to make greater efforts in training its civil servants and doubles its present expenditure on training.

References

Hong Kong Police College 2006. *Training Development Plan 2006–08*. Hong Kong: Hong Kong Police College.

Hong Kong Police College 2008a. *Common Course Review 2008*. EKW V1.3, March. Hong Kong: Hong Kong Police College.

Hong Kong Police College 2008b. *Police Training Series 7: Professionalization of police training and development*. May. Hong Kong: Hong Kong Police College.

Hong Kong Police College 2009. *Training and Development Plan 2009–2011*. Hong Kong: Hong Kong Police College.

Hong Kong Police College 2011a. *A Conceptual Framework for Command Courses*. Hong Kong: Hong Kong Police College.

Hong Kong Police College 2011b. *Challenge in Police Leadership Development*. July. Hong Kong: Hong Kong Police College.

Hong Kong Police Force (HKPF) 2010. *Hong Kong Police Review 2010*. Hong Kong: HKPF.

5

Building executive capacity in the Japanese Civil Service

Hiroko Kudo

The Japanese Civil Service faces many confronting issues as it grapples with the challenges of transforming a traditional Weberian-style civil service into a modern, responsive and pro-active service. Traditionally, the Japanese Civil Service was characterised by its rigid career structures, elite hierarchies, aged cohorts of intakes, and a culture imbued with the importance of seniority. More recently it has been challenged with demands to modernise the service by placing greater emphasis on management, executive leadership, innovative thinking and problem-solving, promotion by merit, gender equity, and more open-minded 'participant centred' training. Although many influences on Japanese governance go back centuries, Japan in the postwar period has faced many social, demographic, economic and political challenges. Its population is declining and rapidly ageing, and after a postwar boom its economy has largely stagnated. Political change and uncertainty marked by a succession of very short-term government administrations have now become the norm, despite conservative governments led by the Liberal Democratic Party largely holding a hegemonic grip on power. Amidst the malaise of political volatility, Japan has made a number of attempts in recent decades to undertake administrative reforms along with some out-sourcing and down-sizing initiatives—often to become frustrated by the lack of implementation or political will to drive them. In recent years more extensive plans for fundamental cultural change in the civil service and changes to the recruitment and selection of staff have been announced which have more potential to modernise government administration and provide the necessary leadership and delivery capabilities for the future.

This chapter is in three parts. The first part outlines the current structure of the Japanese Civil Service, briefly describing its history, its main features and its present size. The second part describes the development of the current human resource development policies of the civil service, focusing on the training undertaken by the National Personnel Authority (NPA) and by other institutions. The third part explains the recent civil service reforms and focuses on two proposals by the NPA: one on recruitment and the selection system and the other on the civil service training system. The chapter concludes by addressing the most challenging question: how to sustain capacity while coping with the imperatives of changing competencies.

Antecedents of the Japanese Civil Service

The modern system of public administration in Japan was largely established in the late nineteenth century, after the Meiji Restoration in 1868. During this period, Japan's political, governmental and related public institutions were established based on models drawn from European counterparts. At the same time, Japan evolved its administrative systems and procedures to support such institutions. Daily practice in these organisations tended to preserve traditional Japanese values, with a formal set of procedures operating in tandem with powerful informal ones. Over this period, the Japanese public service enjoyed a good reputation and, indeed, contributed enormously to the nation's remarkable progress, combining traditional organisational values with the application of modern theories and techniques.

This situation changed drastically after World War II. Despite its strong reputation for efficiency, effectiveness, productivity and prestige, the Japanese bureaucracy was forced to change. Campaigns to reduce the size of government—in terms of both costs and staff—resulted in the Japanese Government becoming the smallest among the industrialised democracies and having the fewest administrators relative to population size of any country in the Organisation for Economic Co-operation and Development (OECD).

After World War II, Japan started its dazzling climb as the world's 'economic miracle' (Clesse et al. 1997). One of the most popular explanations for this development is that power in Japan was centralised in the hands of 'Japan Inc.'—a ruling triad consisting of the elite of the bureaucracy, the ruling political party (the Liberal Democratic Party, LDP) and big business (Hayao 1993; Mishima 1998).[1] According to this view, the bureaucracy was the key of the three actors, helped by its long traditions, prestige and expertise. The importance of the Japan Inc. view in creating this 'iron triangle' of administrative, political and economic elites has been used both to explain the 'economic miracle' of the 1960s and 1970s and to account for the present difficulties Japan faces in conducting systemic reform (Kerbo and McKinstry 1995; McVeigh 1998; Price 1997).

A cogent example of this view is provided by Curtis (1999), who focuses particularly on the '1955 regime'[2] (see Stockwin 1997a, 1997b). Curtis suggests that the system was maintained by four mutually supporting pillars: 1) a broad public consensus to make Japan a leading global economic force; 2) the presence of large interest groups with close links to political parties; 3) total one-party dominance; and 4) a prestigious and powerful bureaucracy.

As the country moved from an industrial to a post-industrial economy, the interests of business, farmers and labour became more diverse and the Japan Inc. alliance weakened (Curtis 1999).[3] Political representatives called *zoku*, which literally means 'tribe', represented special interests. *Zoku* were members of the Japanese Parliament— usually from the dominant LDP—who specialised in a particular policy area and had close personal contacts with public servants in their corresponding ministries or bureaus. Hence, the 'iron triangle'

---

1   In this view, the ruling triad is united in promoting high economic growth above all else while at the same time subordinating Japan's defence and foreign policy more generally to that of the United States.
2   Also called the '1955 system'.
3   Curtis (1999: 44) describes it as 'a shift from interest group politics to the politics of special interests'.

relations underpinning the Japan Inc. development model were reinforced at the level of these policy communities or sub-governments (Hayao 1993; Callon 1995).

Despite being a major player in these 'iron triangles', the bureaucracy was still perceived as a beacon of competency and integrity, safeguarding the national public interest against the short-sighted behaviour of politicians (Koh 1989; Curtis 1999).[4] This reputation, however, was significantly eroded, particularly in the 1990s, by a number of widely criticised policy failures and high-profile scandals involving public servants.

Scandals and concerns about political corruption are certainly not new to Japan, with many such instances of varying degrees of seriousness (Curtis 1999). The important differences between Japan's most recent scandals and those in previous decades are that they now appear far more frequently and have more visibly involved bureaucrats (Stockwin 1997a, 1997b). One of the most prominent scandals in postwar Japan was the 1988 'recruit scandal', which involved 'insider stock' deals. The scandal claimed many top politicians; however, what was even more shocking to the public was the revelation that senior public servants were also involved.

The powerful Ministry of Finance was one of the institutions most affected by the scandals of the 1990s. For instance, in 1995 it was discovered that a high-ranking official in the ministry had failed to report to the tax authorities money he had received from donors (Hartcher 1998). In 1998, a former director-general of the ministry was arrested for leaking information in return for bribes. Then two of the ministry's bank inspectors were arrested for revealing information to several banks regarding the timing of upcoming inspections in return for expensive hospitality at restaurants, nightclubs and golf clubs. The decision of then prime minister, Ryutaro Hashimoto, to set up a committee that would eventually prepare the Ethics Law was a direct consequence of these scandals. However, the much publicised

---

4   Curtis (1999: 55) summarises the bureaucrats' position as follows: 'Recruited by competitive examination from among the best and the brightest graduates of Japan's most prestigious universities, especially from the Faculty of Law of the University of Tokyo, Japan's bureaucratic elite possessed high morale, a sense of mission, and a reputation for competence and integrity ... the image of the Japanese bureaucrat was one of a man of ability and dedication who had forgone opportunities for material gain to serve the nation.'

scandals proved to be only the tip of the iceberg, as it emerged that many more Ministry of Finance officials had allegedly accepted illicit 'entertainment' provided by private financial institutions (Brown 1999; Kaneko 1999).

Another scandal was the '*jusen* bailout' during 1995 and 1996, in which the Ministry of Finance made the highly contentious decision to use taxpayers' money to bail out many *jusen* (loan companies) that had become bankrupt through ill-advised decisions during the bubble years (Inoguchi 1997). This was an example of both policy failure and serious misconduct. Inoguchi (1997) suggests that this preferential decision can be explained in part by the fact that these *jusen* were popular destinations for *amakudari* (literally 'descending from heaven')—career civil servants who move to the private sector after retirement. Not only were the prestige and reputation of the bureaucracy diminished following the *jusen* scandal, but also there were indications that their actual power decreased.

Another practice that regularly caused public outrage was that of *kankansettai*: the wining and dining of officials from the central bureaucracy by their counterparts in local government. The latter have always claimed that if they did not entertain central bureaucrats, they would not receive the necessary information and appropriate funding from the Central Government (Inoguchi 1997).

In short, all these scandals have their roots in the traditional values and practices of the public service. Although the Japanese public service continued to value its prestige as well as its competence—and, on occasions, even claimed a 'high morality'—some of its practices were no longer acceptable in the light of modern global standards. The private sector would naturally engage in wining and dining to help foster better relationships, but many public servants were not aware that such practices could be seen as a bribe. Similarly, gift-giving is a traditional cultural practice showing respect and gratitude and is not necessarily connected to a specific interest. Nevertheless, many still have difficulty understanding that gift-giving can cause problems not only for the givers but also for the recipients. Traditional practices thus clash with the adoption of new ethical standards designed precisely to prohibit many of these traditions, but which may leave officials feeling that by not doing these things their counterparts will consider them to be lacking politeness and respect.

The introduction of modern ethical management into the bureaucracy was triggered by three notable events. First, after the 'recruit scandal' surfaced, the Cabinet made a decision—'Regarding the Enforcement of Official Discipline' (December 1988)—stating that government officials should refrain from acts that could invite public suspicion. Second, following the wave of scandals in the mid-1990s, the Council of Vice-Ministers reached an agreement in 1996 requiring each ministry to establish its own code of conduct for contact with people or entities from the private sector or from other public organisations whose interests are affected by the decisions of public servants. Those who violated the code could be reprimanded under the National Public Service Law (Kaneko 1999). The council also provided a model code for ministries. Despite these efforts, the scandals continued, leading Hashimoto to establish a committee to draft guidelines for service-wide ethical behaviour in 1998. The Ethics Law was finally promulgated on 13 August 1999 (Japanese Government 1999). It prescribed a system-wide code to replace the individual codes of the ministries (Goda 2001; Japanese Government 2000).

Political and administrative reform, 1990s–2000s

In the 1990s, faced with growing economic problems and the gradual unravelling of the 1955 Japan Inc. regime, there emerged a vibrant discourse among the elite in favour of political reform. In 1993, the government of Morihiro Hosokawa was formed from an alliance of eight separate political parties. This government was the first not to include the LDP since the establishment of the '1955 system'. Hosokawa had an ambitious reform plan that included restrictions on donations to political parties, increased public subsidies for parties, harsher penalties for corruption and proposals for electoral reform.[5] However, the government lasted only until April 1994, having achieved only part of its electoral reform agenda. Under the reformed electoral system, 200 members of the lower house would be elected in 11 regional districts under proportional representation and 300 in single-member districts, in place of the traditional multimember districts that had been blamed for pork-barrelling behaviour (Stockwin 1997a).

---

5   A law was introduced only in November 2000, prescribing penal sanctions for Diet members and members of local assemblies if they received financial gain in return for efforts to influence the awarding of contracts or administrative positions.

One of the preoccupations of administrative reform from the 1990s has been to reduce the size of government in terms of both cost and staff. This history of downsizing has today produced a country with both a government and a public administration system that are the smallest among industrialised democracies. In the 1960s and again in the 1980s the Provisional Commission for Administrative Reform (PCAR) made significant cutbacks and devolved power to local governments. Furthermore, it delegated power to public corporations in the 1960s and undertook a program of privatisation in the 1980s (Furukawa 1999; Masujima and O'uchi 1995).[6]

The main administrative reform of the 1990s was initiated by prime minister Hashimoto, who ranked this goal as his government's top priority. As a result, administrative reform was driven by two developments mentioned above: increasing scepticism over the integrity of the bureaucracy because of its policy failures and misconduct, and widespread calls for drastic economic reform that would also involve administrative reform (Mishima 1998: 969–70). Hashimoto also promised to reduce the number of government personnel by at least 10 per cent over 10 years.

The reform package initiated by the Hashimoto government and implemented under prime minister Keizō Obuchi after 1998 went further than simple cutbacks. First, in line with the new public management movement, the Japanese legislature, the Diet, approved the *Policy Evaluation Act* in 2001, which introduced a performance management system (Kudo 2002, 2003). The Act was inspired by the US Government's *Government Performance and Results Act* of 1993; however, it is more decentralised than the US version and gives more freedom to ministries and agencies to organise their own systems of evaluation (Yamamoto 2003). Second, the government reorganised and consolidated the national bureaucracy. One office (the Office of the Prime Minister) and 22 ministries and agencies became one office (the Cabinet Office) and 12 ministries and agencies. This reorganisation

---

6   The first significant administrative reform initiated by prime minister Yasuhiro Nakasone in the mid-1980s was characterised by Thatcherism and Reaganomics; Japanese reform was not an exception to these trends. The main strategy included privatisation and deregulation. In fact, Nakasone successfully privatised the national railway, the public telecommunications company and various public monopolies. This reform was remarkable not only for its success, but also for the fact that it fully introduced the global trend of public sector reform to traditional Japanese public administration.

was enacted in 1998 and came into effect in 2001. These changes forced wideranging institutional and managerial transitions in the bureaucracy.

Political and administrative reform, 2000 – present

The brief overview provided above shows how Japan's stable and economically successful postwar political system began unravelling in the last quarter of the twentieth century (Jain and Inoguchi 1997). The historical model suggests that the elite bureaucracy provided concrete policy ideas to the ruling LDP, which delivered the plans and laws, enabling industry to grow consistently (until the end of the boom). This, in turn, gave financial resources back to the party. Industry continued to lobby ministries and agencies. Many bureaucrats-turned-politicians provided the necessary knowledge and expertise to move into politics; bureaucrats-turned-executives provided necessary links and information to industry. Business helped deliver votes to politicians; meanwhile, the bureaucracy and politicians provided incentives, subsidies and protection to business. This cosy arrangement prevailed throughout the postwar boom.

Then, in more recent decades, the economy stagnated and the 'iron triangle' model began to dissipate. The key features of the decline were: the reduction of the bureaucracy's power and prestige; an increasingly unpredictable and concerned electorate that became less tolerant of corruption; and the failure of governments to capitalise on the initially strong desire for reform (Campbell 1999). This decline influenced the policy agenda, which consisted of newly proposed reforms aiming to introduce 'global standards'. Eventually, a number of scandals acted as catalysts for moving reform proposals up the government's policy agenda (but see Black 2004).

The LDP government managed to survive until 2009, but only towards the end of its term did it announce plans for civil service reform. The Japanese Government began to realise there was an urgent need for structural reform, especially in its public administration, because of the nation's existing fiscal problems and rapidly changing demographics. It was conscious that Japan had a shrinking population and an ageing society, and yet had amassed a large public debt. Hence, the government announced its intention to reduce the total number of civil servants gradually over the course of a decade. In particular, the administration of Junichirō Koizumi (2001–06) and the succeeding LDP administrations drew up plans for civil service reform, declaring the total number of civil servants would be halved in 10 years. The reform, however, was implemented only slowly.

The demise of the LDP and the election of the Democratic Party of Japan (DPJ) as Japan's government in 2009 changed the traditional relationship between politics and bureaucracy, perhaps forever. Suddenly, the number of political appointments made by the government increased; accordingly, the political leadership of the DPJ was able to rule with greater authority. The DPJ government then made radical changes to many aspects of the civil service, including its selection processes, training requirements, leadership development and management practices. A major public service reform plan was submitted to the Diet on 3 June 2011, but was long left undiscussed in the Diet, due to other priorities, including the reconstruction plan following the Great East Japan Earthquake of the same year. There was a consensus among the main political parties on the future direction of the civil service, including the need for salary reductions, improvement of working conditions, establishment of a new management organisation for the civil service and the development of new talent to manage a range of new problems. Due to the dissolution of the House of Representatives on 16 November 2012, however, the proposal was scrapped.

After winning the 16 December 2012 election, the LDP restarted discussions of the reform plan and submitted a renewed version, which included the establishment of the Cabinet Bureau of Personnel Affairs, to the Diet on 5 November 2013. The amendment was enacted on 11 April 2014 after a long and difficult debate (Japanese Government 2014).

Meanwhile, relations between national and local government bureaucracies changed markedly. Many public services once delivered by local governments were now being delivered by private providers and non-governmental organisations. This meant that the functions of both national and local public servants changed: the role of public servants in local government shifted away from that of a direct provider to one of service coordinator, and the competencies required of national public servants changed from legally oriented to economic and technology oriented. At the national level, what are now required include stronger leadership, greater innovation and creativity in managerial skills, language knowledge and facilitation and coordination abilities. These changes require more adequate recruitment systems to select suitable candidates and to innovate training content and style.

Current structure and composition of the Japanese Civil Service

Although Japanese governments have always accused the civil service of being too big, it remains the smallest among OECD countries. In fact, when comparing the number of public employees with the population, Japan has 36.4 public servants per 1,000 citizens when the defence forces are included and only 34.3 if the figure is limited to administrative personnel. In comparison, the United Kingdom has 74.8 public servants per 1,000 citizens (71 for administrative personnel only), France has 88.7 per 1,000 citizens (84.2 for administrative personnel only) and the United States has a ratio of 65.5 per 1,000 citizens (58.6 for administrative personnel only).[7]

The total number of *national* public employees in Japan is 641,000, which constitutes around 18.9 per cent of the total of 3,384,000; *local* public employees make up 81.1 per cent (about 2,744,000). Of national public employees, about 342,000 (or 53.4 per cent) are classified as 'regular service' and about 298,000 (or 46.6 per cent) as 'special service'; the latter include ministers, vice-ministers, ambassadors and so on (approximately 500), as well as judges and court staff (about 26,000), Members of Parliament and their staff (about 4,000) and the defence forces (about 268,000).

The majority of the first category of 'regular service' civil servants operates under a system of pay and conditions imposed by the National Personnel Authority (NPA). Those under the NPA scheme are subject to the Remuneration Law and constitute 275,000 in total (42.9 per cent of all national public employees), which include: general office workers (approximately 152,000); diplomats (about 5,400); tax office workers (about 52,600); imperial, prison and coast guards (about 46,900); air traffic controllers, patent office examiners, and so on (about 7,700); doctors, nurses, pharmacists and other health workers (about 3,000); and researchers (about 1,500). There is a small portion of regular service public employees who are not subject to

---

7   Based on 2013 data for Japan and 2012 data the United Kingdom, France and the United States (NPA 2015a).

the Remuneration Law, including prosecutors (approximately 2,600), national forest employees (about 4,700) and employees of Specified Incorporated Administrative Agencies (about 64,900).[8]

The NPA is also in charge of recruitment, human resource management (HRM), career design, skills and training, and capacity building of civil servants who belong to its pay scheme. Other institutions have their own HRM systems, training and capacity-building systems. For example, the Ministry of Defence has established its own HRM scheme, which is different to that of the NPA, and has its own National Defence Academy and other educational and training institutions. Since its establishment on 30 May 2014, the Cabinet Bureau of Personnel Affairs has been in charge of the HRM of top managers, the government's general HRM policy and its management and revision (Japanese Government 2014).

Among national public employees, there are three levels of career path, and each commences with its own recruitment examinations. Table 5.1 shows the recruitment examination results for these three categories in the 2014 financial year. Numbers within parentheses indicate female recruits. As can be seen from the table, the pass rate for each level is very low, implying high standards are expected.

Table 5.1: Recruitment numbers for the national civil service, 2014

Type of examination	Number of applicants	Number of successful candidates	Number of applicants employed
Career-track position	23,947 (7,105)	2,080 (441)	651 (231)
Staff position (bachelor level)	35,508 (11,178)	6.183 (1,741)	2,734 (824)
Staff position (high school diploma level)	12,482 (3,777)	1,902 (602)	846 (309)
Others (bachelor level)	35,693 (10,855)	4,339 (1,455)	1,753 (550)
Others (high school diploma level)	32,343 (6,393)	4,190 (1,027)	1,738 (417)

Source: NPA (2015b).

---

8   These numbers were published by the Cabinet Bureau of Personnel Affairs on 1 July 2015, with the exception of that for the Specified Incorporated Administrative Agencies, which was published on 1 January 2014. The latter was renamed the Agencies Engaged in Administrative Execution in April 2015.

The figures show there are comparatively few so-called career civil servants, or 'fast streamers' as they are known. However, these recruits are more likely than those of other levels to go on to become senior managers. The number of female employed applicants has increased dramatically in the past two decades, from 6.1 per cent in 1990 to 38.8 per cent in 2015. Nonetheless, a glass ceiling is still evident for women, with few reaching senior or even middle-management levels. Women form only 3.3 per cent of senior management (director level at headquarters and head level at regional offices) and 6.4 per cent of middle management (deputy director level at headquarters and division director level at regional offices). Of the unit chiefs (the first managerial position), female managers constitute 18.9 per cent, which is still much lower than the percentage of female staff at entry level.[9] Considering the need to ultimately achieve gender equality, the government has developed a policy to increase female management to up to 5 per cent at director level and 10 per cent at deputy level by 2016. The government has been promoting events to attract female university students to the civil service, and the NPA has been placed in charge of proposing concrete measures to create the necessary conditions.

The rigid civil service career system has long been criticised in Japan. In response, the NPA changed the recruitment and career system in 2012. Instead of the previous three categories (Level I, Level II and Level III), new categories are divided into a career-track position and two staff positions (bachelor level and high school diploma level) with much more flexible career paths. There has also been longstanding criticism of the retirement age for civil servants. The current reform plan includes proposals to change the retirement age—and with it the typical career path—as well as the contracts of civil servants. Since the traditional practice of *amakudari* (whereby career civil servants move to the private sector after their early retirement—a practice that is in fact forced on them by the career structure) has come under scrutiny in recent times, the reform plan outlines a rise in the retirement age from 60, at present, to 65 by 2025.[10] A newly introduced 'reappointment

---

9   As of 2013.

10   These former top administrators often receive a significantly higher wage, which is some compensation for their relatively low wage as public servants compared with top positions in the private sector. At the same time, this practice allows the ministry to provide opportunities at the top for younger promising public servants. Through personal ties, this practice also allows for a smooth and better relationship between bureaucracy and business.

system' has allowed retired personnel to stay in the public service on renewable contracts of up to one year. The number of reappointed staff between the ages of 60 and 65 is increasing drastically. In the 2014 financial year, 3,072 retirement-age staff were transferred to these temporary, renewable contracts. In accordance with these changes, life planning after retirement has become increasingly important and must complement career design during employees' time in the civil service.

Human resource development in the Japanese Civil Service

On-the-job training (OJT) has been the most important training style in Japan for both the public and the private sectors. As well as OJT, the NPA provides and coordinates various types of training for civil servants, including administrative training, training by position level and training for employees of local organisations. Furthermore, there are:

- long-term overseas fellowship programs that enable civil servants to attend foreign graduate schools
- short-term overseas fellowship programs that provide opportunities to work in foreign government agencies and/or international organisations
- domestic fellowship programs for study at Japanese graduate schools.

These systems of dispatching personnel for training also include a private sector training program. In this section, the nature of Japanese civil services training will be illustrated.

During the 2013 financial year, various ministries offered 32,491 training courses and seminars for 888,399 participants. The NPA offered 211 courses that were open to all ministries, in which 8,507 national civil servants participated. More than 90 per cent of the training courses are closed courses run within each ministry for their own staff and about 7 per cent are open to national civil servants from all ministries. About 70 per cent of the courses focus on specific content, about 60 per cent last between 20 and 40 hours (three days to one week) and approximately 20 per cent last between 41 and 80 hours (one to two weeks). About 20 per cent of courses are directed towards senior and middle management and one-quarter of all participants were managers, although the low participation of senior managers is an issue.

Courses differ in their style of operation: half are day courses and another half use retreats, at least in part. The number of e-learning or correspondence courses has increased in recent years, although they still make up only a small percentage of all courses. Almost all courses conduct participant evaluation or feedback to check the effectiveness of the training and improve the content. The total cost for national civil service training in 2009 was ¥9.07 billion (A$122 million), which is ¥12,000 (A$148) per participant. These figures have been declining since 2004.

National Personnel Authority training

The major components of training courses are provided by the NPA. The institute's training spectrum ranges from recruitment to HRM. It also deals with ethical issues as well as complaints from staff. The NPA provides joint training for senior personnel of all government sectors and ministries. As described in the NPA's *Guide to Public Administration Training* (2015c), the purpose of this training is, through training courses and the exchange of ideas between trainees:

> [T]o enhance qualities and skills of personnel necessary for implementing relevant government measures and policies—from a broad perspective, with a flexible mind-set, great sensitivity and high ethical standards, and with well-developed international awareness, maintaining a national scope ... through discussion and experience working together, to deepen mutual understanding and reliance between participants ... [and] through all training courses, to strengthen a sense of mission as a servant for the whole nation, transcending the frames of government sectors and ministries. (NPA 2015c: 2)

In the 2010 financial year, the training courses offered by the NPA changed drastically, and it began to offer a greater number of shorter courses and established new leadership empowerment courses. The last started as a pilot project in the 2010 financial year, and was developed and incorporated into the civil service training program in the 2011 financial year. These changes are part of proposals recommended to the NPA by the Committee for Public Officers' Training and Capacity Building,[11] which met regularly between June 2008 and March 2009 (coincidentally at the same time as the Expert Meeting for Reconsidering Recruitment and Examination). Based on these experiences, this section aims to explain the changing conditions of the Japanese Civil Service and corresponding efforts to provide capable personnel to cope with the new challenges facing Japanese society.

In 2012 the recruitment and selection procedures for national civil servants changed drastically—also as a result of the Expert Meeting's recommendations[12]—and the new training programs were designed to accommodate these changes. Three principles guide the new training:

1. mutual enlightenment, which centres on a 'participation-oriented curriculum' that places emphasis on group discussion and exchange of opinions relating to policy issues and specific measures of each government sector and ministry

2. a wide variety of exchange between different areas, encouraging broader points of view through 'knowledgeable lecturers capable of discussing up-to-date topics, and demonstrating an awareness of problems' (NPA 2015c: 2)

3. participant-oriented training, conducted through 'retreat training at a facility distant from the workplace to facilitate multifaceted exchange and mutual understanding … discussions with fresh and flexible ideas, and with an open mind' and a 'relationship of mutual trust developed through the free exchange of opinions and communication in and out of training courses' (NPA 2015c: 2).

The annual courses given by the NPA vary in their duration, objectives and content.[13] Of these 14 courses, numbers 13 and 14 are designed for senior managers, courses 4–9 are for middle management and courses 1–3 for future managers. Courses 10–12 are for middle managers appointed through the Staff Position Examination (former Level II and III), and open up their chances of reaching a senior

11   See the section 'Civil service reforms' in this chapter.
12   Ibid.
13   These courses are the result of modifications started in the 2010 financial year and completed in the 2011 financial year. Further adjustments were conducted in 2013 after the recruitment and examination system was changed in 2012.

management level. The courses were strengthened in 2014 when Law No. 22 of 2014 (18 April) amended the law covering national public servants and introduced a system of training for executive candidates. Courses for senior and middle management tend to feature longer discussions than the other courses and stress the importance of studying the classics. In fact, many of them have workshops on classical literature and problem solving, rather than lectures on specific topics and methods. There are also workshops on facilitation, negotiation and team building.

1. **Joint Initial Training:** This three-day course is for new employees who are likely to engage in operations such as policy planning at headquarters in the future (employees newly appointed to government positions in the second grade of the Salary Schedule for Administrative Service I, including its equivalent) in conjunction with the Ministry of Internal Affairs and Communications. It is held once a year and trained 721 participants over three days in a retreat setting in 2014.

2. **Initial Administrative Training:** This course is for employees who participated in the Joint Initial Training. It is held four times a year and lasts for five weeks in a combination of retreat and day-long formats. In 2014, 608 employees were trained in five courses, as there was an increase in appointments for that year.

3. **Third Year Follow-up Training:** This is for employees who, in principle, participated in the Initial Administrative Training, are in their third year of administrative service and are likely to engage in operations such as policy planning at headquarters. It is held four times a year over four days, in a retreat setting, and trains about 120 participants per course, totalling 477 in 2014.

4. **Administrative Training (Deputy Director Level):** The NPA offers seven courses of three-day or four-day training targeting personnel at assistant director level at headquarters in charge of operations such as policy planning and who have been promoted to this level in the past year. Since 2010, this training has been reduced from eight days (three-day in-office and five-day retreat) to three days (five courses for retreat and two courses for commuting) so that all employees recently appointed as assistant directors can participate. As it is not easy to engage participants in deep group-based discussion, policy proposal and analysis in a three-day program, two four-day courses, which are more effective

for deepening the participants' analytical skills, were launched in 2013. This course trains about 50 participants per session (386 in 2014).

5. **Administrative Training (Deputy Director Level)—International Course:** After a trial in 2012, this course was fully implemented in 2013. The course aims to help participants enhance their communication and persuasive skills in English through presentation and discussions in English with the aim of developing human resources who can respond to the globalisation of public administration in each field. A combination of commuting and retreat, the course trained 42 people in 2014.

6. **Administrative Training (Deputy Director Level)—Female Manager Training Course:** This course was launched on a trial basis to exchange ideas with female leaders in the public and private sectors and to consider their leadership, management of subordinates and working style, targeting female employees who are likely to be responsible for administrative management at headquarters in the near future and will become role models for future female personnel. In 2014, 19 women attended this course.

7. **Administrative Training (Deputy Director Level)—Dispatch Training to the Republic of Korea Central Official Training Institute and Dispatch Training Course to Republic of the Philippines:** The NPA has conducted dispatch training courses to the Republic of Korea since 2006, targeting personnel at the deputy director level at the headquarters of the Cabinet Office and ministries. This course organises visits to Korea's Central Officials Training Institute for national public employees with the aim of exchanging opinions between Japanese administrative officials and their Korean counterparts and studying the administrative situation in Korea. In addition, a visit to Philippine Government agencies was organised in 2014 and, in 2013, the course visited Singapore. There were 24 participants in 2014.

8. **Administrative Training (Deputy Director Level)—Leadership Training:** This course was launched in 2010 as a pilot project and then formally introduced in 2011. It is held once a year for 14 days (a combination of retreat and non-residential sessions), targeting officials at deputy director level at headquarters who are expected to play a central role as executive officials. There were 24 participants in 2014.

9. **Administrative Training (Director Level):** This four-day course targets officials at director level at headquarters and is organised three times a year, one day of which includes a site visit. In 2014, 96 people participated in three courses.

10. **Administrative Training (Special Course for Officer Level):** This is two weeks of training for personnel who have been appointed through the Staff Position Examinations (former Level II and III) and will shortly be promoted to unit chief positions, and whom the Cabinet Office and each ministry are planning to foster as future executive officials or whose work performance is excellent enough for them to be considered as candidates for selection for a high-level position. Three courses in 2014 trained 105 participants.

11. **Administrative Training (Special Course for Unit Chief Level):** This two-week training course is for personnel at unit chief level at headquarters who have been appointed through the Staff Position Examinations (former Level II and III) and whom the Cabinet Office and each ministry are planning to foster as future executive officials. In 2014, one of the three courses was a commuting-style course to promote the participation of personnel who are busy with their work. Three courses trained 111 participants.

12. **Administrative Training (Special Course for Deputy Director Level):** These two two-week courses are for personnel at deputy director level at headquarters who have been appointed through the Staff Position Examinations (former Level II and III) and whom the Cabinet Office and each ministry are planning to foster as future executive officials. There were 64 participants in 2014.

13. **Administrative Forum (Director Level and Executives at Headquarters):** These are two-hour forums held in the evening at the NPA conference room to provide training opportunities for personnel at director level and above at headquarters so they can exchange opinions with intellectuals in various fields. Ten forums are conducted annually and there were 660 participants in 2014.

14. **Administrative Seminar for Executives (Aspen Method):** This four-day and three-night retreat seminar is designed for personnel at deputy director-general and lead director level at headquarters. It is thinking-based training that uses various classical works aimed at training for high-level leadership through mutual conversations among participants. This course also includes participants from private enterprise and foreign governments.

During the 2014 financial year, 147 young civil servants attended foreign graduate schools, 26 were dispatched to foreign governments or international organisations, 17 entered domestic master's courses and five entered doctoral programs.

Furthermore, there are courses for specific topics, including courses: to improve participants' evaluation abilities; for newly recruited but experienced personnel; for mentoring; for female employees exclusively; and for learning personal management. There are additional training courses and seminars for basic skills and knowledge, including a course on civil service ethics and a course on manners. Courses have become shorter over the years to better complement the working lives of staff. In particular, the length of retreat courses is reducing and they are increasingly being replaced with non-residential courses.

Training by other institutions

There are also various specialised training courses offered by other institutions that are open to all national civil servants. For example, the Ministry of Internal Affairs and Communications conducts information security courses for various levels, as well as statistics courses, since it is responsible for the Japanese Bureau of Statistics. The Ministry of Foreign Affairs has its own training centre offering language and other specific courses, and outsources part of these courses to the Foundation for Advanced Studies on International Development (FASID), which organises courses related to project cycle management, development and aid, and evaluation of aid projects. The Ministry of Finance organises various open training courses for all national civil servants, while the Ministry of Education, Culture, Sports, Science and Technology offers specialised topical courses ranging from space development to nuclear energy.

There are also schools and training centres for specific categories of civil servant: the National Police Academy, the National Tax College, the Japan Coast Guard Academy and the Meteorological College, among others. These cover all levels of employee in their respective ministries.

For senior management, beyond courses at the NPA, there are opportunities to study abroad and to be seconded to international organisations or foreign governments. The number of senior managers with a master's degree and/or a doctorate from foreign institutions is increasing. Graduate schools and universities collaborate with the NPA to accept a small number of civil servants into their degree courses. Not many graduate schools and universities are directly involved in the civil service training; however, students from the law faculties and schools of traditional universities appear to form the best pool of candidates to succeed in the civil service entry examination. Students from public policy and public management schools are not as successful as students from traditional universities as their institutions have less than a decade of history and are still refining their teaching approach. The introduction of an examination category reserved for graduate school and law school graduates in 2012 was an attempt to change this situation. In 2014, law school graduates made up 45 per cent of the appointed graduate school candidates (administrative staff) and those from public policy schools 33.3 per cent. To diversify the skills of candidates and their ability to cope with global challenges, the political science and international politics examination will be drastically revised from 2016.

Civil service reforms

Reform proposal for the recruitment and selection system

The recruitment and selection procedure for national civil servants has changed since 2012 as a result of the recommendations made to the NPA by the Expert Meeting for Reconsidering Recruitment and Examination, which met between June 2008 and March 2009 and in which the author participated.

There are various factors that forced the government to reconsider the existing recruitment system. Five changes were made:

1. a full introduction of HRM based on ability and performance
2. a new examination system to guarantee diverse channels of recruitment
3. a new examination system to evaluate the planning skills of candidates

4. new examination methods to evaluate candidates' logical thinking, application skills and planning and presentation abilities

5. fair and neutral examination.

The examination system that started in 2012 has many new aspects. There are four categories of examination:

1. to evaluate high policy planning ability among candidates with a master's degree

2. to evaluate the overall skills (similar to the existing examination) of candidates with bachelor degrees, high school diplomas or work experience

3. for specific jobs and functions

4. for experienced personnel recruited from the private sector (the National Public Employee Mid-Career Recruitment Examination).

To cope with social, economic and demographic changes, the civil service has to transform itself. A new recruitment system is required to guarantee that civil servants are sufficiently competent. The recruitment system has to deal with labour market as well as systemic changes, such as the introduction and establishment of law schools (graduate level) and Master of Public Management (MPM), Master of Public Policy (MPP) and Master of Public Administration (MPA) courses. This is why the NPA decided to introduce a new examination reserved specially for these graduate students, beginning in 2012. So far, the number of employees choosing this examination is not significant, but it has been increasing and, more importantly, the success rate is much higher for this category compared with others, confirming the importance of these schools.

The existing mid-career recruitment examination guarantees mobility from the private to the public sector, as well as the recruitment of experts in a wide range of fields. The most important changes in this new system are the modification of examination content and evaluation methods. The new evaluation methods are targeted at recruiting creative and innovative personnel who are capable of logical thinking, policymaking, negotiating with others and building consensus. Thus, there will be evaluated discussion sessions in which the candidates are asked to solve problems or make policy proposals.

Particular qualities, such as excellence in languages and expertise in strategic fields (including economics, finance and engineering), will be evaluated through various new channels. One of them is the mid-career recruitment examination.

Introducing more flexible career paths is also one of the objectives of this reform. Those who enter the civil service via Level II and Level III examinations will have more opportunities than before to rise through the ranks.

Discussion and reform proposal for the civil service training system

In the 2010 financial year, the training courses offered by the NPA were modified significantly to include more short courses and to introduce leadership empowerment courses. The latter started as a pilot project in 2010, and were fully introduced in 2011. Additional modifications were made in 2013 in line with the changes to recruitment and examination introduced in 2012. These changes are among the recommendations made to the NPA by the Committee for Public Officers' Training and Capacity Building, held between June 2008 and March 2009—coincidentally, at the same time as the above-mentioned expert meeting. The author also took part in this committee.

The main issues identified in the committee's report were:

- the growing role and responsibilities of government
- the increasing frequency of scandals and policy failures
- the lack of general training to develop capable civil servants
- the growing need to provide public services efficiently and effectively
- the changing relationship between politics and the civil service.

The recommendations were as follows:

1. empower leadership, especially among senior managers
2. strengthen general capacity building
3. improve the ethical attitudes of tax managers and experts in other professional fields

4. build the capacity of managers and public servants with a market-oriented mindset

5. serve the government faithfully

6. develop broad world views, problem-solving capacities and analytical skills in public servants.

The recommendations for new training methods submitted to the NPA were:

- to develop among employees an appreciation of the value of public service
- to instil in them a sense of mission and pride
- to maintain an adequate distance from politics
- to improve employees' problem-solving capacity through case analyses
- to build integrity and ethical thinking through the study of the classics.

The recommendations also refer to the establishment of a close relationship between recruitment, training and promotion through performance-based evaluation and performance-based HRM.

Conclusion: How to cope with changing competencies through capacity building

Economic recession, fiscal crisis, globalisation, an ageing and technology-driven society, an increasingly complex social structure, a changing relationship between politics and civil services and the establishment of public policy, public management and law graduate schools are all major factors that have forced the Japanese Civil Service to change its culture. The civil service has begun the process of reform by introducing a new recruiting system and changing its training program.

New civil servants are required to have competencies in policymaking, presentation, facilitation, negotiation, consensus building, innovative and creative thinking, logical thinking and leadership. To some extent, candidates are expected to possess these competencies before joining the civil service; however, such competencies are developed and extended through executive training. The type of training is also changing: traditionally highly regarded OJT has been replaced with specific training courses and capacity-building seminars.

Social and economic changes and civil service scandals accelerated the pace of the reform of the recruitment and training systems. The latter has been modified through pilot projects, enabling experimentation with various capacity-building theories.

It is too early to make any judgements about the success of the reform process; however, there is great optimism both within and outside the civil service. The first signs from the changing recruitment system have been positive: a more diverse set of candidates sat for the examinations, including more graduate students, and human resource personnel are utilising a greater range of selection processes. The attractiveness of the new recruitment, selection and training systems will draw a higher standard of candidates to the Japanese public service, despite the recent drawback of the civil service salary cut proposed by the current government.

References

Black, W. K. 2004. The *Dango* tango: Why corruption blocks real reform in Japan. *Business Ethics Quarterly* 14(5): 603–23.

Brown, J. R. 1999. *The Ministry of Finance: Bureaucratic practices and the transformation of the Japanese economy*. Westport, Conn.: Quorum Books.

Callon, S. 1995. *Divided Sun: MITI and the breakdown of Japanese high-tech industrial policy, 1975–1993*. Redwood City, Calif.: Stanford University Press.

Campbell, J. C. 1999. Administrative reform as policy change and policy non-change. *Social Science Japan Journal* 2(2): 157–76.

Clesse, A., Inoguchi, T., Keehn, E. B. and Stockwin, J. A. A. 1997. *The Vitality of Japan: Sources of national strength and weakness*. Basingstoke, UK: Palgrave Macmillan.

Curtis, G. L. 1999. *The Logic of Japanese Politics*. New York: Columbia University Press.

Furukawa, S. 1999. Political authority and bureaucratic resilience: Administrative reform in Japan. *Public Management* 1(3): 439–48.

Goda, H. 2001. Preparation and implementation of Japan's National Public Service Law. In OECD and ADB, *Progress in the Fight against Corruption in Asia and the Pacific*, 175–9. Seoul: OECD and ADB.

Hartcher, P. 1998. *The ministry. How Japan's most powerful institution endangers world markets.* Cambridge, Mass.: Harvard Business School Press.

Hayao, K. 1993. *The Japanese Prime Minister and Public Policy.* Pittsburgh: University of Pittsburgh Press.

Inoguchi, T. 1997. Japanese bureaucracy: Coping with new challenges. In P. Jain and T. Inoguchi (eds), *Japanese Politics Today: Beyond karaoke democracy?*, 92–107. Basingstoke: Palgrave Macmillan.

Inoguchi, T. (ed.) 2008. *Human Beliefs and Values in Incredible Asia: South and Central Asia in focus—Country profiles and thematic analyses based on the Asia Barometer Survey of 2005.* Tokyo: Akashi Shoten.

Inoguchi, T. 2009. *Human Beliefs and Values in East and Southeast Asia in Transition: 13 country profiles on the basis of the Asia Barometer Survey of 2006 and 2007.* Tokyo: Akashi Shoten.

Jain, P. and Inoguchi, T. (eds) 1997. *Japanese Politics Today.* Basingstoke, UK: Palgrave Macmillan.

Japanese Government 1999. *National Public Service Ethics Law.* Law No. 129 of 1999, 13 August. Japanese Government, Tokyo. Available from: japaneselawtranslation.go.jp/law/detail/?ft =1&re=01&dn=1&co=01&x=0&y=0&ky=%E5%9B%BD%E5% AE%B6%E5%85%AC%E5%8B%99%E5%93%A1%E5%80% AB%E7%90%86%E6%B3%95&page=1 (accessed 2011).

Japanese Government 2000. *National Public Service Officials Ethics Code.* Cabinet Order No. 101 of 2000: 28 March. Tokyo: Japanese Government.

Japanese Government 2014. *Law to Amend Part of the National Public Service Act.* Law No. 22 of 2014: 11 April. Tokyo: Japanese Government.

Kaneko, Y. 1999. History of unethical conduct and recent measures to raise ethical standards in the Government of Japan. *Global Virtue Ethics Review* 1(4): 266–82.

Kerbo, H. R. and McKinstry, J. A. 1995. *Who Rules Japan? The inner circles of economic and political power*. Westport, Conn.: Praeger.

Koh, B. C. 1989. *Japan's Administrative Elite*. Berkeley: University of California Press.

Kudo, H. 2002. Performance measurement for governance: From TQM to strategic management and programme budgeting. In D. Bräuning and P. Eichhorn (eds), *Evaluation and Accounting Standards in Public Management*, 94–103. Baden-Baden, Germany: Nomos Verlagsgesellschaft.

Kudo, H. 2003. Between the 'governance' model and the *Policy Evaluation Act*: New public management in Japan. *International Review of Administrative Sciences* 69(4): 483–504.

Kudo, H. 2009. Client-orientation for good governance vs. clientelism. *The NISPAcee Journal of Public Administration and Policy* 2(2): 89–96.

Kudo, H. 2010. E-government as strategy of public sector reform. *Financial Accountability and Management* 26(1): 65–84.

McVeigh, B. J. 1998. *The Nature of the Japanese State: Rationality and rituality*. Abingdon, UK: Routledge.

Masujima, T. and O'uchi, M. 1995. *The Management and Reform of Japanese Governemnt*. 2nd edn. London: Institute of Administrative Management.

Mishima, K. 1998. The changing relationship between Japan's LDP and the bureaucracy. *Asian Survey* 38(10): 968–85.

National Personnel Authority (NPA) 2000. *Annual Report 1999*. Tokyo: National Personnel Authority.

National Personnel Authority (NPA) 2001. *Annual Report 2000*. Tokyo: National Personnel Authority.

National Personnel Authority (NPA) 2010. *Annual Report FY 2009*. Tokyo: National Personnel Authority.

National Personnel Authority (NPA) 2011. *Annual Report FY 2010*. Tokyo: National Personnel Authority.

National Personnel Authority (NPA) 2012. *Annual Report FY 2011*. Tokyo: National Personnel Authority.

National Personnel Authority (NPA) 2013. *Annual Report FY 2012*. Tokyo: National Personnel Authority.

National Personnel Authority (NPA) 2014. *Annual Report FY 2013*. Tokyo: National Personnel Authority.

National Personnel Authority (NPA) 2015a. *2015 Profile of National Public Employees in Japan*. Tokyo: National Personnel Authority.

National Personnel Authority (NPA) 2015b. *Annual Report FY 2014*. Tokyo: National Personnel Authority.

National Personnel Authority (NPA) 2015c. *Guide to Public Administration Training*. Tokyo: National Personnel Authority.

Organisation for Economic Co-operation and Development (OECD) 2000. *Trust in Government: Ethics measures in OECD countries*. Paris: OECD.

Price, J. 1997. *Japan Works: Power and paradox in postwar industrial relations*. Ithaca, NY: ILR Press.

Richter, F. J. (ed.) 1996. *The Dynamics of Japanese Organizations*. Abingdon, UK: Routledge.

Stockwin, J. A. A. 1997a. Reforming Japanese politics: Highway of change or road to nowhere? In P. Jain and T. Inoguchi (eds), *Japanese Politics Today*, 75–91. Basingstoke, UK: Palgrave Macmillan.

Stockwin, J. A. A. 1997b. The need for reform in Japanese politics. In A. Clesse, T. Inoguchi, E. B. Keehn and J. A. A. Stockwin (eds), *The Vitality of Japan: Sources of national strength and weakness*, 91–111. Basingstoke, UK: Palgrave Macmillan.

Yamamoto, H. 2003. *New Public Management: Japan's practice*. Tokyo: Institute for International Policy Studies.

6

Innovating training and development in government: The case of South Korea

Pan Suk Kim

Innovating training in government is an important topic for human resource development, and is an especially timely subject in this era of globalisation and the information society. This chapter is a personal reflection on civil service training in Korea, what makes it unique, and how it can be strengthened. The author draws upon broad experience, as both an academic and practitioner, in the field of public policy. The chapter outline is as follows. A general overview of performance management, human resource management (HRM), human resource development (HRD), training development and learning will first be provided. This will be followed by an introduction to the training system in the Korean Government, and a discussion of the Korean Government's experience of training innovation. Before concluding, lessons learned in overcoming resistance to training and in searching for the future direction of training innovation will be addressed.

In an era of globalisation, regional and global competition have increased, while budgetary cuts affected by current global economic stagnation are an unavoidable reality around the world. In such challenging circumstances, performance management is becoming a popular term and a new organisational ideology across the world.

Performance management starts with establishing performance standards, identifying relevant standards and selecting an indicator index. Performance measures then need to be decided, indicators refined and measures defined. There must be improvements to the process, the use of data for decisions to improve policies, programs and outcomes and then, of course, to progress reporting.

In certain countries, performance may not be well understood or institutionalised. To institutionalise performance management, it is necessary to provide performance awareness (to allow roles and responsibilities to be understood and performance expectations to be set and reviewed) from the outset. Performance awareness is critical for promoting an organisational culture that will adopt a performance system. When people are increasingly aware of performance, they can keep track of and identify what they should do and focus on their goals. Subsequently, a performance-focused attitude along with strategic alignment can be developed. Organisational goals should be translated into individual and team goals and the performance management process should be linked to the execution of other organisational strategies.

In performance management, because human resources and human capacity are critical, it is necessary to review HRM in a broader sense. In the human resource cycle, there are two elements: HRM and HRD. To summarise, HRM is made up of many functions, including obtaining and maintaining HR and developing employees, HR planning, performance management systems, selection and staffing, compensation and benefits, employee assistance, union labour relations, HR resources and information systems. In addition to these are HRD functions, such as training and career development and organisational job design. While HRD comprises several elements, this chapter will focus on training and development (Kang et al. 2011).

Areas and stages of training and development

Training and development (T&D) include several relevant areas: 1) training; 2) education; 3) development; and 4) learning. *Training* refers to acquisition of 'knowledge, skills, ability, values and attitude'

(KSAVA) by workers to perform their jobs better. It is more or less formal, organisation-based and somewhat technical, and is related to a person's present job. On the other hand, *education* focuses on the jobs that the individual may potentially hold in the future. *Development* refers to the activities of an organisation employing an individual or that the individual is part of, or may partake of in the future. In addition, *learning* has become a commonly used term, referring to the process of acquiring new, or modifying existing, knowledge, behaviours, skills, values or preferences, and may involve synthesising different types of information. It is individual and/or organisation based; learning occurs as part of personal development, education, training, work or exercise. Overall, *learning* is a much broader term than *training*. *Learning* could be defined as a function of observation or experience, plus practice or experimentation, and supported by reinforcement. Reinforcement here means that something is reinforced through positive and negative incentives or disciplines.

There are several prevailing theories on *learning*. Social Learning Theory (SLT) approaches the explanation of human behaviour in terms of a continuous reciprocal interaction between cognitive behaviour and environmental determinants. Determinants of human behaviour include cognitive factors (knowledge, expectations and attitude), behavioural factors (skills, practice and self-efficacy) and environmental factors (social norms, access in a community, influence on others), and all these factors determine human behaviour. Other learning theories include behaviourism, constructivism, cognitivism and connectivism. These theories lead to a number of questions: how does learning occur? What factors influence learning? How does transfer occur? Comparing all these theories is not an easy task, but a simple summary of the factors influencing learning is as follows.

- *Behaviourism* argues that the factors facilitating learning are natural stimuli, reward and punishment.
- *Cognitivism* believes that learning hinges on existing schema and previous experience.
- *Constructivism* premises learning on engagement and participation.
- *Connectivism* argues that the key to learning lies in the diversity of workers.

While various terms are used in the field, as discussed in the previous section, the most commonly used term in government is still *training*. Training has a number of phases, each of which includes additional processes.

- **Analysis:** Skill gaps need to be identified, such as gaps between needs and the current situation, which then requires a needs analysis.
- **Design:** HRD strategy as well as strategy in design must be evaluated. Blended solutions—combining a number of solutions—should be considered. Design should be structural, including blending and learning management.
- **Development:** Here, material development, performance support and training the trainer are important.
- **Deployment:** Training delivery, an exclusive training portal site (a simple web-based system that automates many of the processes involved in training management and administration), program management and flexible resourcing are needed in this phase.
- **Evaluation:** There is a need to evaluate reaction, evaluate learning, evaluate behaviour and performance or business benefit or return on investment (ROI).
- **Feedback:** Feedback follows evaluation, and includes lessons learned, revising strategies and continuous improvement.

To innovate training, there should be a review of each phase, looking to improve any weaknesses or reduce limitations. Explaining all these phases in detail is beyond the scope of this chapter.

The Korean Government training system

Legal foundations

The Korean Government has a strong legal foundation for training, which is evident in several training laws and decrees. For example, Article 50 of the *Civil Service Act* of 1949 deals with training. In 1961, the government promulgated a separate *Training Act* for civil servants. Such distinct and dedicated legislation for training civil servants is unique to Korea since, while many countries have their own civil service laws, most do not have a separate law relating specifically to training (Kim and Kim 1997; Kim 2009, 2010, 2011). As we will see, this legislative approach, coupled with a strong emphasis on adopting international best training practice—from the public but also private sectors—is unique to the Korean training experience.

Table 6.1: Korean Government legislation relating to training

1949:	Promulgated the *Civil Service Act* (Article 50)
1961:	Promulgated the *Training Act for Civil Servants*
1961:	Promulgated the *Training Decree for Civil Servants*
1961:	Promulgated the *Act for the Establishment of the Central Officials Training Institute*
1963:	Promulgated the *Local Civil Service Act*
1973:	Promulgated the *Education and Training Act for Civil Servants*
1973:	Promulgated the *Education and Training Decree for Civil Servants* (after the re-establishment of full-scale local autonomy)
1995:	Promulgated the *Education and Training Act for Local Civil Servants*
1995:	Promulgated the *Education and Training Decree for Local Civil Servants*
2015:	Revised the *Education and Training Act for Civil Servants* and renamed it the *Talent Development Act for Civil Servants*
2016:	Revised the *Education and Training Decree for Civil Servants* and renamed it the *Talent Development Decree for Civil Servants*

On the basis of the *Training Act*, the Korean Government promulgated related decrees, including the *1961 Training Decree for Civil Servants*. Particularly noteworthy is the *Act for the Establishment of the Central Officials Training Institute (COTI)* of 1961, which expanded the National Officials Training Institute (NOTI) set up in 1949 with technical support from the US International Cooperation Agency. In 1973, the Korean Government renamed the *Training Act* to the *Education and Training Act for Civil Servants*. By adding the term 'education' to the title, the government underscored its intention to enhance the capacity of civil servants. Moreover, when Korea re-established full-scale local autonomy in the 1990s, the government promulgated the *Education and Training Act for Local Government Civil Servants* as well as the corresponding decree. Thus, the Korean Government has a number of rules and regulations related to the training of government employees.

Training institutes

In terms of the organisational foundation for training, training policy is handled by the Division of Education and Training in the HRD Bureau of the Ministry of Public Administration and Security (MOPAS).[1] While there are many training institutes in the government, one of the most important is the COTI.[2] As the main training institute under MOPAS, COTI's mission is to develop high-performing government officials by providing general and specialised training, and to serve as a support centre for other public service training institutes across Korea. It also seeks to widen Korea's global network through international training and exchange activities with recognised overseas institutions. The head of COTI is a vice-minister overseeing several departments such as Planning, and Education and Training. The Planning Department in turn has many divisions, as does the Education and Training Department. In addition, COTI has a consulting and advisory group, as well as a recently launched research and development centre. Altogether, COTI employs approximately 150 full-time staff.

There are various public service training institutes in other central government agencies. Many provincial-level governments also have their own training institutes. In 1965, the Local Administration Training Institute (LATI) was established to provide learning and development for senior local government officials. This institute is now known as the Local Government Officials Development Institute (LOGODI),[3] and provides training programs for about 40,000 participants every year.

The Korean Government requires all civil servants to undertake grade-based basic (foundation) training before they can be considered for promotion or appointment. In addition, all public officials are encouraged to undertake specialised training programs to increase their knowledge and skills, to carry out their functions effectively in their respective fields. Training should also meet the needs of individuals and be aligned with relevant organisational goals and objectives. Training should be a vigorous aspect of innovative performance management. In addition, the recently added Article 11

---

1   training.go.kr.
2   coti.go.kr.
3   logodi.go.kr.

of the *Education and Training Decree for Civil Servants* emphasised that training is the joint responsibility of the officer and their supervisor. This seeks to rectify some supervisors' reluctance to release staff for training amid the focus on attending to their core work.

Training programs

The key training program in the Korean bureaucracy is the Senior Executive Program for senior civil servants (SCS), the highest level in the Korean Civil Service. The Korean Civil Service comprises nine grades, with Grade 9 the lowest and Grade 1 the highest in the hierarchy. SCS candidate development programs exist for Grades 3–4, divisional candidate development programs for Grade 4, which is a senior official's entry course, and newly promoted or appointed managers' courses are for Grade 5. At lower levels, there are training programs for Grades 7 or 9 recruited through open competitive examination. Middle to low-level government employees can access a learning program called 'Learning at All Times'.

Officers from Grades 4 to 9 are responsible for taking 100 hours or more of training annually, with 40 per cent of the learning hours devoted to work-related development and 60 per cent to personal development. The 40 hours of work-related development should correspond directly with job function and responsibilities, and officers can choose to meet this requirement through training at public or private institutions. The 60 hours of personal development could support job performance but need not be directly related to job functions—for example, a language course in French or Spanish, which might not be directly related to the job function, but satisfies the personal development function.

A criticism of this policy is that the amount of training time does not guarantee the quality or effectiveness of the training. It should be noted that governments often forget to research the outcomes needed, and so train people in unnecessary areas. This results in people with skills and knowledge that are not useful to them in job seeking, in making their job easier, in making them more useful to the organisation or in gaining promotion; it is thus a waste of resources that should have been better used.

In summary, there are three types of training programs for civil servants. Basic foundation-grade courses are delivered by public service HRD centres. Specialised courses, such as task-related, language or information communication technology (ICT) courses, are delivered by public HRD centres as well as domestic or overseas institutions commissioned by government agencies. Other courses, such as civil service ethics, integrity, training on government policy, public values (de Vries and Kim 2011) and individual learning research activity, can be delivered by public or private HRD centres. Thus, the training market has been opened up, with many private vendors delivering training for government employees.

Recommendations for innovation in the Korean Government training system

The general assumption is that there is no one 'best' strategy or method in training; to promote HR capacity, training systems and training programs should be continually improved. The public perception of government training has not been good and continuous improvement in training needs to be promoted. An immediate step towards this is to organise a reform team comprising a combination of internal and external experts, with strong support from the head of state— in Korea's case, the President.

A recent Korean experience of training innovation is outlined, based on the author's firsthand involvement in the process. In 2004, the author was invited to assume the position of secretary to the President for personal policy in the Office of the President (the so-called Blue House). In this capacity, he organised an innovation taskforce for training. This taskforce comprised directors-general (DGs) or senior officials of the Civil Service Commission (CSC) and the Ministry of Government Administration and Home Affairs (MOGAHA), DGs from major training institutes, including COTI and LOGODI, and experts from outside government, such as professors and research institute experts. Over numerous meetings, this taskforce conducted a joint comparative study and visits to domestic private companies, HRD centres and foreign government training institutes. Overseas visits included trips to the Federal Executive Institute (FEI) in Virginia, USA, and General Electric (GE) Company's training and development institute. A particular standout was GE's John F. Welch Leadership Development Centre established in 1956 in Crotonville, New York.[4] For more than 50 years, the centre has been at the forefront of real-world application for cutting-edge thinking in organisational development, leadership, innovation and change. Every year, thousands of GE employees, from entry-level workers to the highest-performing executives, journey to Crotonville for a transformative learning experience that, for many, becomes a career-defining event. GE's Corporate Entry-Level Leadership Programs offer recent college graduates prized development opportunities that combine real-world experience with formal classroom study. Experienced professionals who wish to accelerate their careers can participate in the Experienced Leadership Programs. Today, the Welch Leadership Centre serves as a powerful organisational force reminding each GE employee to never stop learning.

From this experience, a report was finalised and presented to the Korean President, key ministers and senior advisors. After the presentation, the President directed the then chairman of the CSC to implement the necessary training reform measures. At the same time, the President asked the finance minister to allocate an additional budget for training innovation. Consequently, many more training manuals, case studies and new methodologies were developed. For several months, biweekly team meetings sought to develop and implement reform measures. Moreover, each training agency had its own dedicated meeting for its own innovation.

COTI in particular had numerous meetings for low-level workers such as security guards at government buildings and cooks in the cafeterias. In order to innovate reform at the training institute, everyone was expected to do something new or better. While it is typically presumed that training reform is initiated by senior officials looking to improve training methodology and the development of trainers, in COTI's case, almost everyone was involved. For example, after reform, security guards who used to remain at their posts began instead to greet visitors to the building. Likewise, through the reforms, cooks were able to raise the quality of their food to compare with that of restaurants. Drivers who pick up staff and trainees received external

---

4   ge.com.

lecturers from Seoul and the suburbs. Administration staff started to come out of their offices to engage with external lecturers and trainees, and to survey the quality of training methodology. Researchers were able to develop better case studies, training modules and manuals, to provide stronger teaching support and administration staff. And of course, trainers were delivering better methods and improving the quality of their materials. Hence, everyone from trainers, planners and cooks to security officers, drivers and administrative staff—indeed, every member of the training institute—was encouraged to come up with new ideas to improve the quality of their preparation, planning, training and methodology, right down to the general quality of service. In sum, the training innovation in COTI started with everyone and not just a few reform agents.

In addition, the Korean Government initiated a special program to learn how to manage failures in public administration. Traditionally, the government paid little attention to learning from failures, yet there are a lot of cases of failure that offer lessons so that future mistakes can be avoided or better managed. A case in point is how lessons in public communication and conflict management can be drawn from several environmental projects where residents, in a manifestation of the 'not-in-my-backyard' attitude, refused to accommodate the establishment of a dumping ground in their vicinity.

An enabling social environment needs to be created for innovation and an accelerated learning culture, whereby various learning methods and programs will be adopted. Efforts to develop a learning and development culture should be pursued seriously in government. Those involved should progress through various learning programs and methods, such as workshops, physical exercises, and on-site and action learning. Learning and training are not just for middle or low-level employees, but are also necessary for higher-level executives, such as ministers and vice ministers. We particularly emphasise that training is needed for government executives: ministers and deputy ministers. Needless to say, training for government executives would not be the traditional classroom kind of training, but ministers and deputy ministers can have flexible learning programs such as dialogues, seminars or workshops.

It is also necessary to promote government employees' active and voluntary participation in learning communities. The Korean Government supports *dong-a-ri*, which refers to a group of people learning or a study group in government. *Dong-a-ri* guides formal as well as informal groups in solving problems. Also, various learning systems need to be established, such as action learning and mentoring. There needs to be a cultural change to utilise training programs to promote an innovative culture. In other words, HRD or training could become a part of government reform strategies. Learning organisation also needs to be built up and perhaps high-impact organisation can be chosen. Not many governments have a workshop involving the President, but Korea has the National Agenda Workshop, which was introduced during the Roh Moo-Hyun administration (2003–08). The President presides over this workshop, which often takes place at COTI and includes ministers and high-level officials. It is a dialogue between participants, to build team spirit and to understand each other. Sometimes the National Agenda Workshop becomes the basis for setting national priorities and building consensus. This is a unique kind of program for government executives. The training of top civil servants is underdeveloped in many countries, and this is a program that should be better developed in the future. However, there is relatively little public discussion on the nature of training for top civil servants (Pollitt and Op de Beeck 2010).

Additional recommendations for innovation

There are a number of different training methodologies, but a lecture is considered less effective, while the most effective method is teaching others (a person has to know the content in order to teach it). Other effective methods include practise by doing, discussion groups, demonstration, audiovisual presentations and reading to a lecture. According to the *Annual Survey Report* of the UK Chartered Institute of Personnel and Development (CIPD 2007), the most frequently used learning methods were: on-the-job training, in-house development programs, instructor-led training delivered off the job, external conferences or workshops, formal education courses, coaching by line managers, internal knowledge-sharing events, e-learning, audiotapes and videos, mentoring and buddying schemes, coaching by external practitioners, job rotation and secondments, and action learning settings.

We also need to increase training budgets. Governments must allocate substantial funds for training. The Korean National Government's training budget was approximately A$194.4 million in 2006. By comparison, one of Korea's multinational companies had a training budget of A$252.5 million—a far higher investment in training than the government's. A comparison with GE indicates even greater disparity: GE invests about A$1.3 billion each year in training and education programs for its employees.[5] The Korean Government's training budget is relatively small compared with those of multinational companies, and should be increased. Government executives and senior managers should have more responsibility for allocating funds for training. However, this issue could be dependent on the organisational structure and status of the training and development institute (Pollitt and Op de Beeck 2010); in some countries, funds come mainly from universities or independent institutes (that may operate on market principles), while in others, there are public agencies at arm's length from the central ministries and departments, or a national school with close ties to the Central Government (they may be partly or largely subsidised by funding from the relevant public agencies or have guaranteed financial allocations). Nonetheless, current economic conditions could affect funding for training and learning. Since many people are not optimistic about a quick economic recovery, the government should prepare for such challenges.

The cost of tuition for public service training in many Asian countries is too low; in some countries, trainers are paid almost nothing. In comparison, the cost of tuition in North American and European countries is substantially higher. Training elites is not cheap; in the United States, for example, two-week programs for government employees at the FEI cost almost A$7,900.[6] In the United Kingdom's National School of Government, the Modern Leaders Program costs A$8,600 for just one day. Thus, it is necessary to price tuition costs appropriately; a cheap program cannot produce high-quality results.

Moreover, poor compensation for trainers and lecturers must be changed. The Trainers and Development Institute (TDI) should not be a HR 'dumping ground' for low performers. TDI should have highly competent trainers and motivated administrative staff. Although a

5   ge.com/company/culture/leadership_learning.html.
6   leadership.opm.gov.

highly priced course is no guarantee of quality content and delivery, it is necessary to pay at least a reasonable level of compensation to trainers and lecturers. If we want to attract the best staff, we must pay attractive wages. As a general principle, better-paid, quality lecturers and trainers should deliver better training.

It would also be useful to develop and utilise a competency framework, which many organisations in the world now have in place. The Korean Government has a competency framework with three dimensions: *thinking, working* and *building relationships*. In the *thinking* dimension, the emphasis is on problem awareness and strategic thinking; the *working* dimension focuses on results and change management; and the *building relationships* dimension looks at customer satisfaction and coordination of integration. Commonly needed skills might include communication, people management, team and customer-service skills, problem-solving and technical skills. In order to assess a person's competency, various methodologies (group discussion, role-play, presentation and interview) are used. Competency assessment usually takes most of a day and evaluators carefully observe all participants before finalising competence assessment. This provides an opportunity to improve skill deficiencies in those who fail to pass the assessment procedure. This is not a symbolic exercise; the Korean Government had a failure rate of 14.5 per cent in 2009. Such a striking result caused many government officials to pay more attention to their education and development. Increasing numbers of government officials in Korea are now returning to a tertiary institution to upgrade their education.

Overcoming resistance to training

People know that training is good for one's development, but not everybody welcomes training. There is a substantial degree of cynicism and distrust from employees as well as managers. Employee cynicism may stem from their distrust of the training's effectiveness or of the training institution, and their awareness that training may lead to them losing an opportunity for promotion. Additionally, they may worry about the potential loss of opportunity or human connections that comes from spending time away at a training institute. Negative views from managers include distrust of the effectiveness of training at a given institute, concern about staffing shortages while employees are away and a potential delay in the completion of work tasks. Other reasons include: competing business pressures; lack of understanding about the value and impact of training; perceptions of learning as optional or peripheral rather than essential; lack of senior management commitment and positive role-modelling; and lack of training for managers. Also, the pressure of time is by far the most common barrier to training and learning in organisations (CIPD 2007).

It is necessary to overcome these kinds of resistance to training. What solutions exist to reduce resistance? First, it is necessary to advocate training to employees and managers. It is also necessary to enhance the awareness of benefits among employees and managers and promote the importance of training. Clear messages about the importance of training and learning should be delivered to managers. Managers should be rewarded for developing the skills of their team members; senior managers should be encouraged to act as role models; and staff development should be included in line managers' annual performance objectives. It would also be good to reflect on training results in relation to job placement, promotion and new appointments. Moreover, it is necessary to reflect on training needs and expectations through voluntary participation (self-selection) or e-HRM along with ICT applications. Finally, it is necessary to improve the quality of training and provide a pool of HR substitutes.

Conclusion: Future directions for the development of training

It is time for a paradigm shift in training and education—from provider-centred programs to customised or tailored programs that are trainee-centred; and from theory-centred programs to those that are participatory or involve training by experience. We need innovation for better training development, so it is necessary to transform knowledge delivery into a curriculum centred on problem-solving. We need to change from simple evaluation of instruction to evaluating the outcomes of training. We also need to have continuous evaluation starting from the identification of needs through to application. A typical evaluation method is to survey the satisfaction levels and collect comments from the trainees, but a better method would be to assess the longer-term impacts of training (how, and how far, it affected the behaviour of the trainees once they had returned to their agencies).

So what are some future directions for the development of training? First of all, we need to recognise that training should be perceived as an investment, rather than a cost. It is an employee's right to have training or development opportunities. We need to secure the right to choose appropriate and necessary training courses and to utilise various training methodologies—not only lectures, but also participatory and experiential training methodologies.

We need to improve training conditions. We need better trainers, better facilities and better equipment. We need to have training evaluation and feedback for trainers and trainees. Training results should be utilised for employees' placement or promotion. There must be innovation in the operation of training institutes. For example, the head of each training institute should be recruited in an open, competitive way, and he or she must be reform-minded and reform-orientated. It is therefore necessary to develop an open recruitment system to hire key officials and staff of training institutes; we need to turn those institutes into organisations that promote organisational learning to meet future challenges in government.

Finally, it is necessary to recognise that the nature of current public administration is becoming more complex, diverse, fragmented, interdependent, time-consuming, boundary-blurring and decentralised, with more stakeholders and an increasing number of dilemmas. In dealing with public affairs, many stakeholders are participating and conflicts are often developing, giving rise to an increasing number of 'wicked' problems. Capacity is fixed like a cup, but the challenges are growing and daunting, so we cannot hold them all. In other words, a small cup cannot hold all the things that overflow from a bigger bucket; a significant 'capacity deficit' can certainly be seen in the wide gap between growing demand and existing public capacity. In fact, public capacity has declined due to the shrinking role of the state, the more complex nature of problems, a lack of financial and human resources, the increasing cost of cooperative and communicative governance, the increasing number of critical citizens and a culture of resistance, as well as increasing public expectation. There is an urgent need for capacity building, but capacity building has three different levels: individual, organisational and systemic. At the individual level, the need is to improve the level of training and education. At the organisational level, the need is to improve the capacity of the organisation in its structure and management. At the systemic level, there is the need to improve the capacity of the system in modernising or innovating—for example, financial and legal systems. In an era of globalisation, and in a rapidly changing information society, we clearly need to innovate training and development in government. After all, government competitiveness is highly dependent on human capacity.

References

Chartered Institute of Personnel and Development (CIPD) 2007. *Annual Survey Report on Learning and Development*. London: UK Chartered Institute of Personnel and Development.

de Vries, M. and Kim, P. S. 2011. *Value and Virtue in Public Administration: A comparative perspective*. London: Palgrave.

Kang, S. C., Kim, P. S., Lee, J. S., Jin, J. G. and Choi, G. Y. 2011. *New Public Personnel Management*. [In Korean]. Seoul: Daeyoung Moonhwasa.

Kim, B. W. and Kim, P. S. 1997. *Korean Public Administration: Managing uneven development*. Seoul: Hollym.

Kim, P. S. (ed.) 2009. *Public Administration and Public Governance in ASEAN Member Countries and Korea*. Seoul: Daeyoung Moonhwasa.

Kim, P. S. (ed.) 2010. *Civil Service System and Civil Service Reform in ASEAN Member Countries and Korea*. Seoul: Daeyoung Moonhwasa.

Kim, P. S. (ed.) 2011. *Public Sector Reform in ASEAN Member Countries and Korea*. Seoul: Daeyoung Moonhwasa.

Pollitt, C. and Op de Beeck, L. 2010. *Training Top Civil Servants: A comparative analysis*. Leuven, Belgium: Public Management Institute of Katholieke Universiteit Leuven.

7

Civil service training in the Macau Government

Pauline Lai Pou San

The civil service of Macau faces unique challenges as it continues to transfer from a colonial bureaucracy administered by Portugal to the post 1999 system of 'special autonomy' within China, whereby the territory will administer much of its own affairs until 2049. Traditionally, Macau's civil service was characterised by a rigid ethno-linguistic hierarchy, with Portuguese nationals occupying its executive positions and middle management reserved for the Portuguese-speaking mestizo community to the exclusion of the ethnic Chinese who were and remain Macau's most populous demographic. More recently, leading up to and following the transfer of Macau from Portuguese to Chinese rule, Macau's civil service has undertaken a threefold process of 'localisation', which aims to slowly reorientate its personnel, language and law to better reflect the territory's contemporary cultural and political reality. Significantly, Portuguese-speaking civil servants have undertaken Chinese-language instruction, with Chinese-speaking civil servants being taught Portuguese. This chapter first gives a historical background to these changes, before outlining the various instruments of the Macau civil service, and how they have developed since the handover. It finally explores the process of civil service training within the territory, which has undertaken significant institutional and cultural change both before and after Macau's return to Chinese rule. The chapter concludes by emphasising the current trend of heavy investment in civil service training—increasingly conducted in mainland China—something which further underlines Macau's unique position.

Macau is a tiny peninsular enclave on the southern coast of China with a total land area of just 30.3 sq km. According to the Macau Statistics and Census Bureau, in 2013 Macau had an aggregate population of 607,500, and its government had 29,598 civil servants, including both permanent and contract staff—a high ratio of one civil servant for every 20 citizens.

From the mid-sixteenth century until 19 December 1999, Macau was a Chinese territory under Portuguese administration. During this time, it developed a Portuguese-oriented judicial and administrative system with a strong emphasis on legal-administrative roles and rules consistent with the *Rechtsstaat* tradition of government. After 1999, Macau became one of the two Special Administrative Regions of China alongside Hong Kong. Once Macau was back under the sovereignty of China, the Central People's Government appointed Macau's administrative leader, known as the Chief Executive, after an election. The *Sino–Portuguese Joint Declaration* signed in March 1987 guaranteed that Macau would operate with a high degree of autonomy until at least 2049—that is, 50 years after the transfer. The policy of 'one country, two systems' divided government responsibilities between China and Macau: the Chinese Central Government assumed responsibility for the territory's defence and foreign affairs, while Macau controlled its own legal system, police force, monetary system, and customs and immigration policies.

Civil service structure

Since Macau's handover, the Chinese Central Government has exercised the authority to appoint the Chief Executive of Macau. The Chief Executive is elected by a committee whose 400 members are nominated by corporate and community bodies. The Chief Executive is assisted by five policy secretaries (portfolio holders), who assist the Chief Executive in formulating and implementing policies and in administrative affairs, among other duties. The five policy secretaries look after the portfolios of Administration and Justice, Economy and Finance, Security, Social Affairs and Culture, and Transport and Public

Works. Under the management of these secretaries, each portfolio consists of government directorates of services, departments and divisions. The most senior officials within a portfolio are the directors of the directorates, with middle-level officials heading departments and divisions.

Macau's civil servants before the 1980s were mainly of Portuguese and Macanese, rather than Chinese, origin;[1] the former occupied all the most important political and senior civil service positions, while the latter occupied the middle-level civil service positions. The Governor of the colony (a post similar to that of Chief Executive) was appointed by the President of Portugal and the appointee was always of Portuguese extraction. Thus, these Portuguese administrators came with almost no understanding of the local culture or the traditions of the people of Macau, so many of the government policies they promulgated were not adapted to the preferences or needs of the citizens. During this time, the ethnic Macanese occupied the crucial middle-level civil service positions because they served as the language bridge between the governing Portuguese and local residents, who were mainly Chinese. Chinese residents were rarely appointed to senior civil service or even middle-level positions. Usually, ethnic Chinese were assigned to work in the security forces in positions such as police or fire officers, or alternatively they served as low-level clerks or office servants. Paradoxically, although Chinese residents in Macau generally had higher educational qualifications than the Macanese or Portuguese, their inability to speak Portuguese usually prohibited them from reaching higher civil service positions.

Civil service reform from 1999

Much was to change, however, after the transfer of sovereignty back to China in 1999. In fact, many changes in the reorientation of Macau's government and to the composition of its administration can be traced back earlier, to the signing of the *1987 Sino–Portuguese Joint Declaration*. The new government committed to developing an improved relationship with the citizenry, and it implemented many policy measures designed to suit their needs. In contrast to the situation

---

1   The term 'Macanese' refers only to mestizos of Portuguese and Chinese descent, not to those whose parents are both ethnically Chinese.

in the 1980s, now all Chinese residents were able to gain government employment and it was not uncommon for them to rise to the higher ranks. At first, many Chinese residents with university degrees were recruited into the government as senior technicians but were later promoted to managerial positions. The majority of these Chinese civil servants were recruited through a special program initially organised by the Macau Portuguese Government, in which they were sent to Portugal for one or two years to study Portuguese.

In the negotiations over the *Joint Declaration* and to ensure the smooth transfer of Macau to China, the Chinese Government requested that the Macau Portuguese Government start a process of 'localisation' in Macau. Before the handover, the localisation process was called the 'Three Localisations'—that is, the Localisation of Law, the Localisation of Civil Servants and the Localisation of Chinese as the official language. As a result, many training courses were conducted for existing civil servants to prepare for the future, and new recruitment strategies were adopted.

One of the major training exercises in which the majority of civil servants participated was language instruction in their non-native tongue. The Macau Government sent Portuguese-speaking civil servants to Beijing to learn Mandarin while Chinese-speaking civil servants were sent to Portugal to learn Portuguese.

Due to the desire of the Portuguese administrators to maintain control of most positions within the judicial system until the handover to China, the Portuguese Government of Macau did not invest in much Chinese-language training for the judiciary. And yet, one non-governmental, not-for-profit organisation, the Associaçao Promotora da Instrução Pós-Secundária de Macau (Macau Association for the Promotion of Post-Secondary Studies), carefully selected high-performing students from Chinese and English-language high schools to receive training in Portugal as bilingual legal professionals. Thus, when the handover occurred, the new government had a sufficient number of local judges and prosecutors to fill the void left by the departing Portuguese judiciary. This was the reason some of the judges and prosecutors were initially younger and less experienced than their counterparts in comparable countries. In 2003, to improve training and as a way of increasing the number of legal professionals, the Macau Government established the Legal and Judicial Training Centre (CFJ).

The Public Administration and Civil Service Bureau

Responsibilities and training programs

Before the establishment of the Public Administration and Civil Service Bureau (Serviços de Administração e Função Publica, SAFP) in 1983, each public agency carried out its own training. After the establishment of the SAFP, the training was organised centrally through the Recruitment and Training Department (RRF) of the SAFP. This department was responsible for all aspects of human resources in the civil service, including recruitment and training.

The responsibilities of the SAFP were to:

- study and propose policies for administrative reform
- establish appropriate guidelines to facilitate and monitor the implementation of policies
- develop and coordinate the government's central management of its human resources policies, especially regarding recruitment, training and retirement
- investigate and develop better procedures for performance evaluation
- establish forms of e-government and promote information technologies.

Training courses organised by the SAFP mainly targeted the routine functions of the civil service, such as administrative procedures and the implementation of the law in different contexts. Hence the content of the training courses was drawn largely from the administration of Macau's Basic Law, together with some judicial and administrative practices developed by Portugal. The training provided by RRF has focused on practical knowledge for frontline civil servants, including citizen-oriented delivery, appropriate behaviour in dealing with clients and how to administer efficiently and effectively.

Some courses were organised in accordance with an agreement signed between Portugal and Macau to provide short- and long-term training in Portugal as a means of enhancing the professional knowledge of civil servants as well as allowing them to learn new techniques.

Macau also began organising training courses with the European Union to broaden the perspectives of civil servants and enhance their international vision and understanding.

The teachers and presenters of the courses conducted in Macau were primarily high-ranking civil servants such as department or division heads of a relevant bureau. However, university academics as well as judges and prosecutors were also enlisted to teach and make presentations. The presenters of the courses held in Portugal (and some other European countries such as Belgium) were a mixture of experienced civil servants and private consultants.

In 1987, the Macau Portuguese Government issued another statute to regulate and enhance the functions of the SAFP. The new law enlarged the organisational structure of the SAFP and changed the name of the RRF to the Centre of Training for Public Administration (CFAP). CFAP's functions included organising an annual program of civil service training courses to meet the changing needs of Macau, and establishing and developing cooperative relationships between government departments and private organisations as well as between departments and Portuguese and other foreign actors, with the aim of arranging high-quality professional training activities.

Reforms to the SAFP

In 1994 the Macau Government again rearranged the organisational structure of the SAFP, mainly due to the promotion of localisation as a result of the pending transfer of sovereignty to China and to meet the needs of modernisation and the management of its human resources. The CFAP was replaced with a specialist Division of Training, which operated under the management of the Department of Human Resources.

Language training continued to remain a priority and received much government investment. After Macau was returned to China, the new Macau Government came to realise that Macau could play an important international role as a platform between China and Portuguese-speaking countries. To improve its capacity in this role, in 2010 the SAFP started a program to train translators and interpreters in second languages. Trainees first had classes in Macau, and then were sent to Portugal and Belgium to undertake linguistic and cultural immersion.

In 2009, a decade after reunification, the Macau Government promulgated another new law, to regulate the recruitment and career development of civil servants. All civil servants, including permanent and contractual staff, were brought under the same service-wide human resource management procedures. In addition, some occupational categories such as senior technician and assistant technician were to be recruited only through a central recruitment process organised by SAFP instead of under the authorisation of each bureau. This important and complex task became the exclusive responsibility of the SAFP. To fulfil the task smoothly, in 2011 the government further enlarged the purview and organisational structure of the SAFP, making it a significantly larger training agency. There were substantial increases in the number of important positions at all levels: the number of sub-directors was increased from two to three; a further three department heads were added, taking their total to nine; the cohort of division heads was more than doubled, from eight to 17; the number of senior technicians was almost tripled, from 40 to 110; similarly, the pool of technicians went from nine to 39; and the number of assistant technicians increased from 24 to 40. The main reason for such a substantial increase in the size of the agency was its increased responsibility for the delivery of civil service training and for central recruitment of senior technicians and assistant technicians.

The SAFP still operates within the portfolio and under the management of the Secretary for Administration and Justice and reports to that secretary. The current departments within the SAFP are:

- Department of Organisational Performance and Operations
- Department of Civil Service Training
- Department of Legal Affairs
- Public Information Centre
- Department of Language Affairs
- Electoral Affairs Division
- Language and Documentation Division
- Administration and Finance Division
- Public Service Welfare Division
- Personnel Recruitment and Selection Division
- Training Coordination Division

- e-Government Planning and Infrastructure Division
- e-Government IT Development Division.

In contrast to the previous system, according to the new law, civil servants who are promoted to a higher grade must have completed 80 hours of training courses, which may consist of either courses run by the relevant SAFP department in Macau or courses taken at overseas institutes. After two or three years, civil servants are expected to have undertaken another 30 hours of compulsory service-wide courses organised by the SAFP to be promoted to another higher grade; in fact, the SAFP recently expanded its organisational structure to deliver these training services. The Department of Human Resources was also renamed the Department of Civil Service Training, while the Division of Training is now known as the Division of Training Coordination. Today in Macau, any civil servant can register to attend any training course. Priority for course places is usually given to those civil servants who are recommended by their bureau to study the specific course or to those whose tasks are particularly related to the course.

In addition to these training courses and workshops, the Macau Government has adopted a policy of rotation for top-level officials. Since 2000 the government has followed a strategic policy of transferring top-level officials horizontally between bureaus to give them management and leadership experience in different fields, as well as encouraging communication between leaders and bureaus. This has become one of the main ways by which top-level officials receive practical experience in dealing with real problems, adding to what they have learned theoretically through training courses.

In 2000 the Macau Government signed an agreement with the Singapore Civil Service College (CSC) to collaborate in providing specialist training for Macau's top- and middle-level officials. These training courses have focused on policymaking and management skills, management development, the training of civil service tutors and other administrative topics. It is estimated that 3,000 officials and 70 local tutors have already participated in this training program.

In January 2011, the SAFP signed another agreement with the CSC, under which the college will assist the Macau Government in developing a strategic plan, and will also collaborate in the new

SAFP Training Centre, constructed in late 2011. This agreement also extended the 2000 agreement that assigned the CSC the task of assisting the Macau Government in training executive-level civil servants.

Conclusion

As economic and social development accelerates in Macau, demands from the citizenry for better and more responsive public services have increased. The new government has responded by being more activist in the provision of public services and in improving their quality, and as a consequence has expanded both the scale and the scope of its civil service training program. Clearly, the new Macau Government considers civil service training to be important in enhancing its capacity to deliver responsive, timely and courteous services. In the post-handover period, the government has taken on increased responsibility for funding training programs across all levels of the civil service. The government has accepted the full burden of covering the costs of all training centrally to ensure that Macau's civil servants pay nothing. This contrasts with the situation in some comparable Asian countries.

Increasingly since the handover in 1999, the Macau Government has prioritised the training of civil servants in Mainland China—and not only for language education and cultural immersion. Civil servants have also been sent to China to undertake courses such as diplomatic protocols, city and infrastructure planning in regional contexts, water management issues and financial and taxation matters. This training is already providing benefits for Macau's growth and development. As a result, despite being somewhat late in recognising the need for extensive civil service training (mainly due to Portuguese influence in its earlier forms of government), Macau has in recent years greatly expanded its commitment to training as a long-term investment in the future. It has recognised that such investment is necessary for the development of future capabilities and the management of public policies as well as for strengthening its international relationships.

8

Building executive capacity in the public service for better governance: The Philippine Civil Service[1]

Alex B. Brillantes Jr and Maricel T. Fernandez-Carag

> Leadership is the prime mover in bringing about alignment between capacity-building efforts of the public administration system and national development goals. Without effective and determined leadership, it is difficult to revitalise public administration in any country. While the importance of developing sound policy and institutional frameworks for revitalising public administration cannot be overemphasised, it is leadership that primarily drives the change process. (UN 2004: 2)

Investing in career executives in the civil service to develop and strengthen the leadership of the bureaucracy is critical. This is what Hooton (1997: xiii) calls 'executive governance', where the executives are at the 'heart of "permanent" government'. Politicians may come and go but the executive service officers remain at the helm of the bureaucracy. Hence, according to Stanton (2001: xvii), it is necessary

---

1   This chapter is adapted from a paper presented at the Taipei Conference on Building Executive Capacity in the Public Service for Better Governance, 31 October – 1 November 2011. We are grateful to Professor Tsai-Tsu Su, Professor John Wanna and James Low for the invitation to be part of this international conference.

to make government manageable, which means that 'responsible government departments and agencies are expected to carry out their missions effectively and the public shall judge the results'.

Capacity development for career executive officers is necessary for responding to the demands of the public. Building the capacity of the public administration system is both a process and a goal (UN 2004). How the public sector is structured, how it operates and the role it performs within a country play an important part in economic and social progress. In particular, the quality of government leadership has a great impact on the quality of governance, which in turn affects a region's level of development. Reforming the public sector in both developed and developing countries is not an easy task and there are many difficulties to overcome. In the past 20 years, a number of national and international forces have contributed to significantly changing the role of the state, which has resulted in the need for new skills, attitudes and behaviours among public officials at all levels. In fact, the core competencies for the public sector of the twenty-first century differ in many ways from those of the past, especially as the demands placed on public servants in terms of skills, knowledge and competency are rapidly increasing and becoming more complex. Top government leaders in developing countries are still facing old challenges while at the same time having to address new ones resulting from the many social, economic and political changes sweeping through the world (Bertucci, as cited in UNDESA 2005).

This chapter provides some historical context to the evolution of the Philippine Civil Service before focusing specifically on the Career Executive Service (CES) and the role of the Career Executive Service Board (CESB). It discusses the training and capacity development programs for career executive service officers (CESOs) and then identifies contemporary issues and concerns confronting the civil service in general, and building executive capacity in particular.

The Philippine Civil Service[2]

The evolution and development of the civil service system of the Philippines must always be appreciated within its particular historical context. The Philippines has a long history of colonisation under Spain and the United States; as a result, its political and administrative systems were designed according to the style of its colonisers. The formal introduction of the civil service system occurred under US colonisation with the establishment of the Philippine Civil Service in 1900, as reflected in *Act No. 5 (Civil Service Act)*, which also led to the establishment of the Bureau of Civil Service (BCS), with a mandate that the 'greatest care should be taken in the selection of officials for civil administration'. Since the Philippines attained political independence from the United States in 1946, various administrations have continued to reform the civil service—mostly through reorganisation interventions—with the general objective of achieving the classic three 'Es' of economy, efficiency and effectiveness. Over time, a fourth 'E'—that of equity—has been added.

There have been several highly significant pieces of legislation regarding the civil service in the Philippines, including former president Ferdinand Marcos's *Presidential Decree Number 1 of 1972*, declaring martial law, which reorganised the entire bureaucracy. The Administrative Code of 1987, issued by president Corazon Aquino through Executive Order 292, essentially reiterated existing principles and policies in the administration of the bureaucracy and for the first time recognised the right of government employees to self-organisation and to conduct collective negotiations under the framework of the 1987 Constitution. Today, efforts continue to further reform and strengthen the civil service, through the proposal of bills such as the omnibus Civil Service Code.

An interesting pattern in the politico-administrative system of the Philippines is that all administrations since 1946 have placed the reorganisation of the bureaucracy high on their agenda on their assumption of office. Among the more dramatic and visible reorganisations implemented were those by president Elpidio Quirino

---

2   For a detailed discussion of the Philippine Civil Service, please see Brillantes and Fernandez (2009).

in the 1950s (through the Government Survey and Reorganisation Commission); by Marcos on the proclamation of martial law (*Presidential Decree Number 1* establishing the Presidential Commission on Reorganisation and the implementation of the Integrated Reorganisation Plan); by Aquino in 1986 (the Reorganisation Plan of the Presidential Commission on Government Reorganisation); by president Fidel Ramos, who re-engineered and reinvented the bureaucracy in the late 1990s; by president Joseph Estrada, who established the Presidential Commission for Effective Governance; and finally, by president Gloria Macapagal-Arroyo, who introduced the rationalisation program.

The Philippine bureaucracy has essentially been shaped and influenced by its colonial heritage and legacies inherited from different political periods, each with its own administration and innovations. Now with more than 100 years of history, the civil service system continues to respond to the challenges and demands of nation-building and development, yet remains adversely affected by the political system of the country. Among the major contemporary initiatives of the civil service system is the formulation of a Civil Service Code that attempts to define a Philippine system resulting from and operating within the context of the Philippines' unique political, administrative and cultural history.

Building executive capacity: The Career Executive Service[3]

The CES constitutes the executive class in the Philippine Civil Service, which was formally introduced through Marcos's Integrated Reorganisation of 1972. This also led to the creation of the CESB in 1973, and it was during this time that the Career Executive Service Development Program (CESDP) was introduced to produce a corps of development executives who would carry out the development tasks of the 'new society' and create public understanding and acceptance of the CES as a new profession. The objective of continuously improving the quality of the civil service executive was promoted through

---

3   This section about the CES and CESB draws on the CESB website: www.cesboard.gov.ph. It also draws on Lodevico (n.d.).

the implementation of a more competitive and stringent process in 1986. This was when Aquino had assumed the presidency and there was widespread reorganisation of the bureaucracy in which it was 'purged' of 1,000 civil servants including CESOs. However, the CES was reactivated in 1988. At present, there are roughly 6,260 positions within the CES—nine times more than three decades ago.

The chairperson of the CESB plays a key role in shaping the policy directions of the board. Table 8.1 reflects a list of the accomplishments of each CSB chair within the context of building executive capacity in the public service.

Table 8.1: Former chairpersons of the CESB and their accomplishments

Onofre D. Corpuz (1973–78)	Conceptualised the CES for the Philippines, drawing from systems already in place in certain bureaucracies around the world. His original concept of the CES as a service that included all executives in government, from assistant directors to undersecretaries, with ranks designated by a number and characterised by mobility in the service, continues today.
Jacobo C. Clave (1978–81)	Approved a performance evaluation system to measure CESOs' significant contributions to national development.
Armand V. Fabella (1982–86)	Focused on developing the managerial skills of CESOs through the CESDP, a 10-month training program run by the Development Academy of the Philippines. This program included a 16-week residential training course and a two-week *barrio* (village) immersion program. It was crafted to develop camaraderie among the participants to enable them to establish lasting networks cutting across the bureaucracy.
Patricia A. Sto. Tomas (1988–95)	Initiated the shift from a training-based to an examination-based system for the acquisition of CES eligibility and rank, which broadened the base from which eligible candidates and CESOs were sourced. The examination-based system ensured two features of a good recruitment system: open competition and intense selection. This shift to an examination-based system was complemented by the inclusion of shorter training courses focusing on leadership, values, interpersonal relations and administrative efficiency.
Amado Luis S. Lagdameo Jr (1995)	Short term as chairperson. Transition from the integration of CESB to CSC[1] and then nullification of the integration in 1995.

Corazon Alma G. De Leon (1995–2001)	Established the CES eligibility requirement for appointment to third-level positions in the CSC. This requirement was created to assist the CESB in coping with the growing number of government executives seeking third-level eligibility.
Karina Constantino-David (2001 – February 2008)	Unified the third-level eligibility requirements given by the CESB and the CSC. Essential to this achievement was the clarification of the concept of the third level and its adaptation to existing realities and current limitations of law. A new instrument for the Career Executive Service Performance Evaluation System was also crafted and rolled out.
Bernardo P. Abesamis (March 2008 – present)	Pursued an integrated CES human resource development framework through the implementation of the Continuing Professional Development Program based on the CES Competency Grid developed in 2008.

[1] CSC = Civil Service Commission

Source: CESB website (www.cesboard.gov.ph).

In keeping with its mandate to form not only well-selected but also development-oriented officials, the CESB designed a shorter three-pronged core training program called the Executive Leadership Program (ELP) for its CESOs and those eligible for CES, commonly known as 'CESO eligibles'. The ELP was launched in 1993 and was shorter than earlier training programs in the CES. It was made up of three separate modules: *Salamin*, *Diwa* and *Gabay*. Since it was piloted in 1993, the ELP has produced 1,257 graduates. In a bold move in 2002, the CESB adopted a revised policy (*CESB Resolution No. 453*) on original and promotional appointments to CES ranks. This policy provides for the appointment of CES eligibles initially to Rank VI regardless of their *position*, and for the CESOs to work their way up to a higher *rank* without necessarily being promoted to a higher *position*, through demonstrated competence, sustained performance levels, completion of prescribed training programs in the CES and passing a screening process for promotion to Rank III and higher. To ensure rigorous selection, the present CESB also restored the Assessment Centre to the CESO promotion process for those who pass the Management Aptitude Test Battery (MATB). This was the case in the early 1990s.

For more than a decade to 1985, the route to CES eligibility and a CESO rank was via a training program; however, the CESB shifted from a training-based to an examination-based selection system in 1989. The new four-stage examination system based on merit and open competition enabled the institution to speed up the process of granting eligibility while ensuring that high standards for selection were met. In 1990 the CESB conducted a nationwide MATB on more than 1,000 applicants from both the government and the private sector. For the first two years, the MATB was conducted only once a year. By 1994 it was conducted twice a year and by 2000 it was conducted on a monthly basis in addition to the two annual rounds. Today the MATB is conducted in the 12 regions of the Philippines on a monthly basis, and, nationwide, bi-annually. After 1990, the CESB also adopted other methods by which officials could acquire CES eligibility and rank, including the testimonial eligibility route, accreditation of the Executive Leadership Management (ELM) Program and accepting the Master of National Security Administration (MNSA) and Master of Public Safety Administration (MPSA) courses as equivalent to passing some stages of the four-stage screening process. The testimonial eligibility route has since been suspended (Lodevico n.d.)

Designing, implementing and sustaining programs to build executive capacity

In the Philippines, the CES is the 'third level' or managerial class of career positions. Created by *Presidential Decree No. 1* to 'form a continuing pool of well-selected and development-oriented career administrators who shall provide competent and faithful service',[4] it is the highest level of career civil service as determined in the Position Classification and Compensation System. The CES is also a public personnel system separate from that of the first two levels in the Philippine Civil Service. The first level includes clerical, trades, crafts and custodial positions whether in non-supervisory or supervisory capacities; and the second level comprises professional, highly technical, scientific or other highly specialised positions in a supervisory or non-supervisory capacity requiring at least a bachelor degree or equivalent as determined by the Civil Service Commission (CSC). The CES operates on the 'rank concept'. CESOs are appointed

---

4   This was the first Presidential Decree: PD No. 1 issued by former President Ferdinand Marcos on 24 September 1972 after declaration of Martial law on 21 September 1972 for the establishment of the Career Executive Service.

to ranks and assigned to CES positions; hence, they may be reassigned or transferred from one CES position to another and from one office to another but not more than once every two years. In this respect, the CES is like the armed forces and the foreign service, in which officers are also appointed to ranks and assigned to positions. Positions in the CES are the career positions above the level of division chief staff who exercise managerial functions. Table 8.2 shows the aforementioned positions.

Table 8.2: Positions in the Career Executive Service

Undersecretary
Assistant Secretary
Bureau Director
Bureau Assistant Director
Regional Director
Assistant Regional Director
Department Service Chief
Other executive positions of equivalent rank as identified by the CESB

Source: CESB website (www.cesboard.gov.ph).

The CESB

The CESB is the governing body of the CES. It is mandated to promulgate rules, standards and procedures on the selection, classification, compensation and career development of members of the CES. The CESB comprises eight members: the chairperson of the CSC and the president of the Development Academy of the Philippines (DAP) as *ex officio* members, and six others appointed by the President of the Philippines for a term of six years. Day-to-day operations are handled by the CESB Secretariat, headed by an executive director and a deputy executive director. Five operating divisions are tasked to handle specific program areas.

To be part of the CES, the aspiring candidate must undergo the CES eligibility examination process, which has four stages: 1) written examination; 2) assessment centre; 3) performance validation; and 4) board interview.

If the candidate is conferred CES eligibility and complies with the other requirements prescribed by the CESB, his or her name is then included on the roster of CES eligible candidates. He or she may then be assigned any CES position and appointed to a CES rank by the president on the recommendation of the CESB and will then become a member of the CES. Table 8.3 indicates the six CESO ranks in the CES ranking structure, with CESO I the highest rank (with an equivalent salary grade of 30) and CESO VI the lowest (with an equivalent salary grade of 25).

Table 8.3: CES ranking structure

CESO rank	Salary grade
CESO Rank I	SG 30
CESO Rank II	SG 29
CESO Rank III	SG 28
CESO Rank IV	SG 27
CESO Rank V	SG 26
CESO Rank VI	SG 25

Source: CESB website (www.cesboard.gov.ph).

Training and career development program for CESOs

A crucial CESB program is training and career development for CESOs. The CESB, through *Board Resolution No. 812* of 17 August 2009, approved and promulgated the *Omnibus Rules, Guidelines and Standards on the Continuing Professional Development System for the Career Executive Service* (*CPDS-CES*). The *CPDS-CES* serves as the overarching framework of policies, rules and standards for the development, implementation and evaluation of all capacity-building programs to be offered for the career and professional development of CESOs and CESO eligibles in the civil service.

These capacity-building programs include training and career development programs based on the need for CESOs who are not only good managers but also effective leaders. The CESB has lined up a number of training and other career development interventions to provide a range of experiences, knowledge and skills necessary for effective job performance. Career development in the CES follows a framework that responds to the CES officials' career development needs from the time they enter the CES up to preparations for retirement from the service. Thus, it aims to complete their 'whole person development' as a CESO.

CESB training programs are designed to improve the competency not only of CESOs but also of the third-level eligible candidates, to nurture in them a deeper sense of commitment to public service and to help them understand the CES as a program of government, a culture and a way of life. However, in the case of third-level eligible candidates, only those occupying at least a division chief position or its equivalent, unless otherwise provided, may participate in the training and human resource development programs of the CESB. These programs include Executive Leadership Program courses and CESB-accredited training courses.

Executive Leadership Program

The ELP is currently the foundational training program for CESOs and CEO eligibles. It includes three courses corresponding with a three-pronged leadership and management framework of: 'knowing one's self' (*SalaminngPaglilingkod* or *Salamin*), 'relating to others' (*DiwangPaglilingkod* or *Diwa*) and 'leading the organisation' (*GabayngPaglilingkod* or *Gabay*). The program also includes the Community-Organisational Attachment Module (COAM), a learning integration course.

SalaminngPaglilingkod (Salamin)

Salamin, a course on self-examination, is anchored on the premise that the best leaders are those who have a good understanding of themselves, their values and their leadership style. Learning modules are built around, and have the objective of, enhancing the identified Competency Standards for CESOs.

The learning outcomes of *Salamin* include making participants:

- reflect on their values given their primary roles as family members, members of the community and government executives
- examine the leadership requirements of the bureaucracy and their organisations and how they fit into these

- relearn the struggles and aspirations of the common people towards increased responsiveness in government policies and programs
- from this experience, articulate and refine their values and leadership style and gain a renewed commitment to public service.

DiwangPaglilingkod (Diwa)

Diwa, a course on interpersonal relations, is based on the premise that good leaders are those who have a deep understanding and appreciation of how they and other people inside and outside the organisation influence each other in their behaviour and interpersonal relations. It emphasises participatory management and effective teamwork in achieving organisational goals and objectives. It also aims to address how to deal with the public and other stakeholders more effectively— one of the main concerns of executives—as well as how to deliver the highest service possible. Learning outcomes of Diwa are aimed at eliciting productive behaviour from subordinates and teams to achieve public service excellence and to positively influence the behaviour of superiors and peers for cooperation and support.

GabayngPaglilingkod (Gabay)

Gabay provides learning modules aimed at addressing the executive's need to remain effective on the job and to impart a deeper appreciation of government policies and programs. It seeks to provide:

- enhanced awareness and greater appreciation of the demands and challenges facing a public manager
- a wider perspective on the environment of public management around which leadership and managerial responsibilities are exercised
- familiarity with the planning and organisational processes and the information and communication technology (ICT) governance and management concepts that are essential in the development of organisations
- additional knowledge on how to optimise government administrative support systems for effective decision-making and management.

Gabay also exposes participants to a community organisation that enables the sharing of competencies, insights and managerial experiences and the ability to work on governance and development concerns with local officials, civil society and community stakeholders.

COAM (Community-Organisational Attachment Module)

COAM is the final module of the ELP. Together with the *Salamin*, *Diwa* and *Gabay* modules, it aims to:

- widen the scope of, increase and strengthen the key leadership and managerial competencies of career executives via real-life and structured immersion in a community organisation
- foster an environment and cultivate partnerships for learning where executives can share their competencies, insights and experiences in managing organisations and work on governance and development challenges and imperatives with local government officials, civil society and private sector leaders and other community stakeholders
- encourage executives to individually and collectively explore, adopt and advocate meaningful, innovative and results-focused approaches for re-examining governance and leading reforms in the public sector.

CESB-accredited training programs

The CESB is not the only agency that designs and implements executive development programs for the civil service; other agencies also have their own custom-made programs. To complement CESB learning activities and provide CES executives with a further continuing executive development program, the CESB works in partnership with reputable training institutions to offer programs that address specific leadership and managerial competencies.

Descriptions provided by the relevant training institutions appear in a modified form below.

Communicating Change through Media

This is a two-day seminar provided by Blas F. Ople Policy Centre and Training Institute with workshops designed to equip participants with the knowledge and skills needed to communicate using the media in a fast-paced and evolving environment. CESOs, as policy advocates of government programs and services, play key roles in promoting messages of positive change and good governance. They must be adept in public diplomacy and skilful in the art of public communications to build networks of support within and beyond traditional constituencies. The seminar introduces concepts and best practices regarding the online marketing of government programs and services.

Seven Habits: Applications for Managers Workshop

This is an intensive hands-on, two-day workshop run by the Centre for Leadership and Change. It helps participants build a strong cadre of leaders capable of leading with character and competence. Managers and leaders learn to define their contributions, develop greater influence, leverage hidden resources, give constructive feedback and unleash the full potential of their team against critical priorities. This workshop is designed to help CESOs enhance desired behaviours learned in *Salamin*, *Diwa* and *Gabay* sessions.

Power Principle Workshop

This workshop helps CESOs develop desired competencies for leading in a continuously changing environment and for networking for productive partnerships. It teaches participants a new paradigm of power: the 'principle-centred power'—the ability to *influence* others' behaviour rather than to control, change or manipulate it. The Centre for Leadership and Change provides this workshop.

Leadership: Great Leaders, Great Teams, Great Results

This is another training course provided by the Centre for Leadership and Change. It provides participants with the mindset and tools to execute CES core competencies and help them as leaders discover how to inspire trust and build credibility with people, define a clear and compelling purpose, create and align systems of success, unleash the talents and energy of a winning team and align the essential systems of execution, core work processes and customer feedback.

Change Leadership

This is a practical course provided by Human Resource Innovations and Solutions (HURIS) on managing and handling the constant stream of changes in today's complex world. This two-day program includes research on individual and organisational change dynamics and hands-on exposure to practical change leadership tools and practices.

Managerial Leadership

This is another training program run by HURIS, which goes beyond the basics of planning, organisation and leadership for results by highlighting, through experiential insights, the core underlying principles of these fundamental managerial practices. The program is based on real cases and covers the latest research and best practices, and the participants gain a wide and practical perspective of managerial tasks and leadership responsibilities.

Performance and Results Management

This course provides participants with the opportunity to master the skills of managing employee performance and building a results-focused work culture through coaching. It covers the skill areas of crafting behavioural goals, selecting predictive metrics of performance and motivating people to produce consistent results. Learning is stimulated through a combination of research-based lectures, role-playing, management simulations and film clips.

Strategic Thinking

This course deals with a comprehensive overview of strategic thinking skills including systems thinking, critical reasoning and creativity. Through an interactive and engaging mix of presentations, role-playing and management simulation exercises, participants acquire insights and skills on improving their grasp of strategy formulation and strategic learning.

The New Leadership Style for the Twenty-First Century

Peter Drucker predicted that the leader of the future will be one who asks while the leader of the past is one who tells. This course seeks to present the secrets to becoming a successful leader in the twenty-first century. Focused on self-mastery and emotional intelligence, participants practise coaching, conflict management and handling difficult employees.

Policy Appreciation Course

This three-day program provided by the DAP is aimed at equipping senior CESOs with the requisite concepts and skills to be effective producers and consumers of policy analysis. The course guides senior CESOs and their principals not only to make informed policy choices but also to implement these choices in the public interest. Specifically, the course enables participants to be more aware of the value of policy analysis and of the role policy plays in shaping the activities of government. Participants better understand the theoretical underpinnings and components of policy analysis, the range of policy tools and techniques as well as the process that must be followed and the conditions that must be met to ensure the quality and feasibility of policy outcomes. They also develop an understanding of how the policymaking process applies to practical situations; indicate where to find policy-related methodological resources and information; realise or situate their role as CESOs in the entire policy process; and reflect together on the role each institution can play in sound policymaking.

Creative Innovations and Reforms for Committed Leadership and Effectiveness (CIRCLE) Forum Series

This is a series of monthly, multi-sectoral forums conducted nationwide, showcasing exemplary, pioneering and influential leaders from the CES and various fields of governance and development, who interact with government executives in interactive learning experiences while dissecting important issues relating to governance and development. These leaders distil and share their insights and practical know-how in achieving strategic institutional and sectoral outcomes and in realising their personal and professional goals while confronting day-to-day executive challenges. This is a major professional development program of the CES Career Development and Life-Long Learning Strategic Framework, and an executive who attends and completes it earns credit points. It also promotes the CESB's core objective of providing meaningful, innovative and effective mechanisms for:

- the personal and professional development of members of the CES
- strengthening strategic networks and engagements with key sectors who share the same mission of improving governance, managing partnerships and promoting development and change.

CES Executive Leadership and Wellness Camps

These camps are part of the CESB's advocacy to promote total wellness, work–life balance and sustained productivity among government executives. They include:

- learning activities on maintaining relationships and a healthy lifestyle
- sessions to enhance longevity and increase productivity at work
- holistic stress management that deals not only with physical and emotional but also spiritual and social wellbeing aspects.

Follow-up sessions are also conducted to equip participants with further motivation, knowledge and practical tips.

CES Thought Leadership Congress

The CES Thought Leadership Congress (CES-TLC) is a thematic and scholarly forum showcasing pioneering and influential citizen leaders from the Philippines and other nations who have made valuable and enduring contributions in various disciplines. This program immerses government executives in hands-on, face-to-face and life-based learning encounters with these champions, exemplars and luminaries, who distil their ideas and insights; impart their wisdom and inspiration; and share their visions and stories of struggle, discovery and hope. It is planned and regularly conducted by the CESB in cooperation with its partner institutions as a whole-day symposium every semester in metropolitan Manila and in different regional capitals.

CES Leader's Enterprise Attachment Program

The CES Leader's Enterprise Attachment Program (LEAP) is a structured immersion-attachment program open to all CESOs and eligible candidates of good standing in the CES. The program exposes these public sector executives to new organisations and work environments in carefully selected private sector enterprises. In partnership with the chosen enterprise, the CESB facilitates the immersion attachment with the professional guidance of an enterprise-based volunteer mentor (or 'learning partner') within a fixed period, linking the private and public sectors in developmental synergy. The program builds a dynamic learning environment by partnering career executives and managers from both sectors in the creation and application of knowledge, skills and new technologies; in sharing insights and experiences; and in jointly addressing vital corporate governance problems and issues. As a key element in the vision of a strengthened CES, LEAP's primary goals are improved levels and quality of productivity—primarily demonstrated in high-value, efficient and sustained levels and quality of work performance achieved by developing and institutionalising vital technical competencies among CESOs and eligible candidates, resulting in optimal organisational effectiveness. Leading to these goals are the upgrading of competencies and nurturing key leadership and managerial competencies of career executives through structured immersion at (or 'attachment' with) model institutions.

CES Management Apprenticeship Program

The CES Management Apprenticeship Program (MAP) is a two-year, government-wide, on-the-job and multi-modal leadership and managerial capability development program that prepares third-level eligible candidates for entry into the CES. The program incorporates the development, implementation and monitoring of standardised in-service immersion modules by the CESB in partnership with various government agencies, clustered into sectors. These modules, which candidates are required to undergo, include:

- MAP Foundation Course Series (MAP-FCS)
- MAP Continuing Professional Education Program (MAP-CPEP)
- corporate policymaking and strategic planning activities
- international study visits, exchange programs, conferences and other overseas professional development activities
- fixed-term cross-sectoral postings in the government sector
- the formulation of the MAP *Terminal Report*.

The completion credits earned are considered partial fulfilment of prerequisites for a third-level eligible candidate to qualify for CESB endorsement for initial appointment to a CES rank.

CES Fellows Program

This is a development-oriented off-site learning program that seeks to provide opportunities for CESOs to explore new avenues and apply tools for their career development while working on leadership and governance challenges outside the agency work environment. It is designed primarily to strengthen CESO core professional competencies and improve their executive performance. It is a management intervention granted as a reward or privilege, which allows CESOs to engage in external development work (with pay) as an alternative to the performance of regular/standard office functions. CES Fellows have the option of working as volunteers, development facilitators, technical experts or consultants, educators, program/project managers or coordinators, or in other roles in various fields. CES Fellows work on a part-time or full-time basis through postings ('attachments') to:

- selected organisations and institutions, whether local or international
- other government agencies
- local governments
- non-governmental or community-based organisations either in the Philippines or in another developing country.

Fellows may also engage in self-initiated or existing institutional or academic-based development work on strategic and urgent socioeconomic or ecological development issues.

Executive Placement Program

This program is designed to promote the placement of CESOs and CESO eligibles in CES positions. It is classified under two major subprograms.

- Executive Placement Program: This aims to match the placement participants' career options with the needs of the bureaucracy as determined by the agencies and/or the Office of the President Search Committee. It requires strategic and continuing partnership with the agency and gathering and maintenance of information regarding agency-specific requirements and the expertise and career options of the placement participants to enable job matching.

- Placement Assistance and Referral Program: This aims to assist CESOs and eligible candidates requesting short-term or one-time endorsement.

Performance management

The performance of CES officials is evaluated annually through the CES Performance Evaluation System (CESPES) developed and administered by the CESB and installed in all departments and agencies as part of the performance management system focusing on third-level executives. It was developed to reflect the significance of the third level (which numerically represents only 1 per cent of the entire bureaucracy) as the determining factor of the quality and type of service that the rest of the bureaucracy offers to the public.

Like its predecessor, the CESPES measures the accomplishments of CESOs using the Performance Contract (PC), as well as their behavioural competence using the Behavioural Competency Scale. Accomplishments (referred to as milestones) are classed as either 'leading and innovating' or 'regular or routine'. *Leading and Innovating* (LI) milestones are policies, programs, projects or procedures that the CESOs create for the department or agency. They are innovations and reforms that aim to improve the quality of the department's or agency's structures, operations and resources. They are 'value-adding' measures that are developed and implemented within a given period—with a definite start and end. In contrast, *Regular or Routine* (RR) milestones are the outputs of functions or activities within the accountability of and performed by CESOs on a regular basis in the work setting. These may include outputs resulting from the performance of technical and administrative functions needed to sustain day-to-day operations in an office. The percentage of LI to RR milestones depends on the rank of the CES officials and is determined by the department or agency: the higher the position level, the higher the LI. CES officials are encouraged and expected to perform increasingly more innovative functions as their position level increases. This, to a degree, describes and justifies why they deserve the status and salary received.

A superior rates CESOs on the basis of their accomplishments using a scale of one to seven:

1. unacceptable
2. below average
3. solid performance
4. good solid performance
5. above average
6. commendable
7. exceptional.

Superiors and subordinates alike rate CESOs on the basis of their behavioural competence using the Superior and Subordinate Rating Forms of the Behavioural Competency Scale, respectively. They are given a questionnaire of 30 statements indicating the attributes of government executives. They then rate CESOs according to how often these qualities are observed—again, using a scale of one to seven, with one being 'never' and seven being 'always'.

The role of the NUCESO

The energies and potential of graduates of the CES Program are harnessed through the National Union of Career Executive Service Officers (NUCESO). CESOs are treated to a variety of interventions designed to promote effective networking and greater camaraderie, as this is seen to have a positive effect on government programs. The NUCESO was formed when two CES organisations (the National Council of CES Organizations, NCCESO, and the ELP Alumni Association) merged. It aims to:

- keep alive and dynamic the ideals and purposes of the CES
- enhance the competencies of CESOs as public managers and leaders and encourage them to advocate programs for their agencies and communities in the pursuit of CES objectives
- promote and strengthen camaraderie between and among the CESOs in government
- extend assistance to individual CESOs in the recognition and protection of their rights as career executives
- provide a forum for discussion and resolution of issues concerning the national interest

- implement projects that will contribute to the achievement of government goals
- not engage in any government unionism.

Issues, gaps and challenges in career service and executive development[5]

The Philippine bureaucracy has been beset with problems that need to be resolved to sustain a class of honest, accountable and responsible civil workers who deliver public service in the most effective and efficient way possible. Some challenges have adversely affected the bureaucracy so much that poor public service practices and negative bureaucratic behaviour have been embedded in Philippine culture and incorporated into its system of governance. Executive development intervention and the CES are responsible for their share of the challenges and problems in the bureaucracy.

Failure to implement policies

Unfortunately, some major policy reforms that would have strengthened the institution never gained ground. Policy proposals have been designed and advocated in the years since the reactivation of the CES in 1988, but most have been shelved due to a lack of political support. In 1993, the NCCESO began the arduous task of lobbying for the passage of a proposed bill strengthening the CES. The Association of ELP Alumni also consolidated its forces to push for the same bill. However, it never went further than committee-hearing level in both chambers of Parliament. A proposal to grant a significant premium to CESOs—which would have set a material difference between a CESO and non-CESO—suffered the same fate. The proposal was shot down early because of a lack of funding. The initiative to develop a mechanism for performance-based tenure started in 1989 but never

---

5   This section has been written with the assistance of 'A manifesto for the next government: A proposed Philippine Civil Service reform agenda', prepared by PA 208 Class (Philippine Administrative System) under Professor Alex Brillantes Jr UP National College of Public Administration and Governance, University of the Philippines, second semester, 2009–10.

went beyond the proposal stage because it was considered unfeasible. Ambitious plans to establish a CES training centre or a CES college never got further than the drawing board.

The pieces of legislation governing the Philippine Civil Service remain scattered across different laws, decrees, letters of instruction and executive orders. The absence of a comprehensive civil service law has sometimes caused confusion among civil servants; many laws overlap and some have become obsolete.

Politicisation of the bureaucracy

Politicisation of the bureaucracy is an issue in the Philippines because civil service appointments continue to be made according to political pressure. This destroys the principle of merit, undermines security of tenure and demoralises career civil servants. Politicisation exists despite various programs designed to maintain high standards in the civil service by attracting the best and brightest leaders. Over the years, various presidents, particularly Macapagal-Arroyo, have exercised presidential privilege and circumvented the merit and fitness stages of civil service appointment by instating 10,000 civil service personnel—mostly in executive positions (David 2005). The prevailing culture of political patronage undermines the government's efforts to professionalise the bureaucracy and improve the capabilities of government workers to serve the public effectively and efficiently.

Ethics and accountability in the Career Executive Service

The issue of ethics and accountability in the CES continues to permeate the government and the bureaucracy on a massive scale despite the profusion of laws and the existence of numerous agencies designed to curb corruption. With good governance as the prevailing dictum in effective public administration, society now demands more accountability from civil servants in the performance of their duties. Never before in the history of its administrative system has Philippine society demanded as much accountability as it does today. Survey results indicating a very high public perception of corruption in the public sector as well as the ranking of the Philippines among the world's most corrupt countries seem to indicate that now more than ever civil servants are expected to tell the people truthfully how they have been performing their tasks. For instance, according to the Social Weather Stations (2010), the annual proportion of managers seeing 'a lot' of corruption in the public sector has been steady at two-thirds since 2005. Almost all of them see it happening at the national level; progressively fewer see it at the provincial, city and barangay levels. In SWS 2015, a record-low 39 per cent say most companies in their sector of business give bribes to win public sector contracts (see Box 8.1 below). Accountability is seen as a key not only to good *government* but also to good *governance*.

Box 8.1. Highlights of the SWS Survey on Corruption

The survey found a record-low 39% saying most (11% almost all, 28% most) of the companies in their line of business give bribes to win public sector contracts, surpassing the previous record-low of 41% in 2012 and 2013

Of the 36 government institutions rated for sincerity in fighting corruption in the 2015 survey, 21 got favorable ratings, 9 neutral, and 6 unfavorable

The net ratings of sincerity (computed as % *sincere* minus % *insincere*) in fighting corruption was very good for the Securities and Exchange Commission (+63), Social Security System (+57), Philippine Stock Exchange (+55), Office of the President (+54), and Dept. of Trade and Industry (+51)

It was *good* for the Filipino business associations (+49), Supreme Court (+42), Civil Service Commission (+41), Dept. of Education (+43), Sandiganbayan (+37), Office of the Ombudsman (36), Commission on Audit (+36), and Dept. of Justice (+34)

It was *moderate* for Dept. of Health (+28), Government Service Insurance System (+27), Dept. of Social Welfare and Development (+24), their own Barangay Government (+19), Dept. of Finance (+15), Presidential Commission on Good Government (+15), Governance Commission for GOCCs (+12), and their own City Government (+12)

It was *neutral* for Dept. of Interior and Local Government (+9), the Trial Courts (+6), Dept. of Environment and Natural Resources (+6), the Armed Forces of the Philippines (+4), Dept. of Budget and Management (–7), Dept. of Transportation and Communication (–2), the Senate (–2), Bureau of Internal Revenue (–4), and Commission on Elections (–6)

It was poor for Dept. of Agriculture (–10), Philippine National Police (–16), Dept. of Public Works and Highways (–21), House of Representatives (–25), and Land Transportation Office (–26)

It was *very bad* for Bureau of Customs at –55

Source: The 2014/15 SWS Survey of Enterprises on Corruption, www.sws.org.ph.

Public image and reputation

Public service delivery continues to be a central criticism of the bureaucracy. Unfortunately, civil servants are generally viewed as incompetent, slow, rude and inefficient in rendering public service. They are viewed as influence peddlers and products of political accommodation and therefore do not possess the high degree of excellence, professionalism, intelligence and competence needed to be able to serve the public well.

Weak public service values are evident among government workers. They lack dedication and commitment in providing public service. It has been observed that the civil service has lost much of its service development orientation. Government service is no longer considered 'public service' but rather a job that public officials and employees need to support themselves and their families, forgetting that the public is the reason for the existence of the bureaucracy. That said, in spite of such a negative perception, we are aware that there are many gems in the bureaucracy—unheralded but dedicated public servants.

Inadequate remuneration for CESOs

Low compensation packages for executives (including low salaries) hinder the recruitment and retention of the best and brightest. The pay scale in the civil service does not compare with equivalent technical and supervisory positions in the private sector.

Outdated systems and procedures

Outdated systems and procedures are a problem in many agencies, resulting in inefficiency, as people in government are more concerned with adherence to rules than with the achievement of results and job productivity. The problem is exacerbated by the inability of agencies to keep up with the latest advances in information technology.

Recommendations

Mindful of the need to address these issues and concerns urgently, implementing the following recommendations would contribute towards building executive capacity and transforming the Philippine bureaucracy into a model of excellent, reliable, efficient and desirable public service.

Enact a Civil Service Code

Codifying laws and relevant directives governing the civil service into a single, comprehensive statute (as sought by Senator Aquilino Pimentel Jr with Senate Bill Number 1162) would give the Philippine Civil Service system much-needed and long-awaited legal authority. Senators Panfilo Lacson and Jinggoy Estrada have filed other bills proposing the adoption of a Civil Service Code.

Implement periodic evaluation of capacity-building programs

Enhance partnerships with non-governmental actors

Cooperation should be encouraged between providers of executive training towards building capacity.

Continue to recognise outstanding CESOs for their performance

An example of recognition of CESO performance is the Gawad Civil Service (CES)[6]—a motivational approach for CESOs to excel in the field of public service and good governance. This presidential award recognises CESOs for exemplary performance and significant contributions, particularly in the areas of innovation, information and communication technology, social services, administrative reforms and public policy. The search for worthy recipients aims to inspire members of the CES to live up to the ideals of the organization as well as recognize exceptional accomplishments to encourage consistent performance and to promote excellence among members of the

---

6   The Filipino term 'Gawad' means to give or confer or as a noun, it is an award.

CES community. Gawad CES is open to all CES Officers and Third-Level Eligibles who are presidential appointees and are appointed to CES positions. The Gawad CES winner will receive a plaque with the Presidential Seal and Php100,000 cash reward.

Finally, the framework developed previously by the authors, and illustrated in Figure 8.1, may be considered in reforming public service for good governance. Capacity-building interventions may be targeted at all four areas of reform, but should pay special attention to changing the mindsets and behaviour of those in the public service, especially leaders and those occupying executive positions, as discussed in this chapter.

Figure 8.1: Reform framework for building executive capacity in the public sector for better governance

Source: Brillantes and Fernandez (2010).

Indeed, building executive capacity is part of the overarching vision of reforming public administration for good governance. As indicated above, four elements are needed to achieve not only good governance (UNDP 1997) or 'good enough governance' (Grindle 2005), but also 'better governance':

1. reforming institutions, structures and processes
2. leadership
3. reforming behaviours and mindsets
4. citizen engagement.

Conclusion

Starting from a discussion of the historical context of the Philippine Civil Service, this chapter has discussed the various capacity-building programs available to CESOs. The primary strength of the Philippine CES is its members; the CESOs who have undergone the rigours of merit and fitness to serve in the bureaucracy. On the other hand, with identified challenges such as the politicisation of the Philippine bureaucracy, among other issues, there is a need to re-examine policy directions and standards, program values and priorities and procedures.

Capacity-building programs for the CES need to be reviewed to improve them. In this way, training programs, whether internally or externally provided, will be objectively evaluated in terms of their effectiveness, efficiency and even affordability. The CESB must continue its efforts to attract high-quality professional CESOs to work in the public service through adequate compensation packages. Aside from monetary or material rewards, the government should motivate the CES with awards for outstanding CESOs, such as the Gawad CES.

To maintain fairness and equality, the CESB should continue its informal regulatory function by defining how training providers are chosen. This will improve training programs in the future by eliminating poor training providers. The board must also continue to enhance its own regular training programs and look at how these can be improved. It is hoped that the recommendations made in this chapter will contribute to building executive capacity in the Philippines CES for public service for better governance.

Indeed, as suggested earlier, one of the challenges of training is whether or not it has made an impact on the CES. The reform framework (Figure 8.1)—particularly developing leadership and reformed mindsets, paradigms and behaviour—is the ultimate objective of any training and capacity-building program. Reformed mindsets and behaviour, including those at the executive level, are essential for capacity-building programs to be truly effective and sustainable.

References

Bekke, H. A., Perry, J. L. and Toonen, T. A. (eds) 1996. *Civil Service Systems in Comparative Perspective*. Bloomington: Indiana Press.

Brillantes, A. B. and Fernandez, M. T. 2008. Is there a Philippines public administration? Or better still, for whom is Philippine public administration? *Philippine Journal of Public Administration* 52(2–4) (April–October): 55–80.

Brillantes, A. B. and Fernandez, M. T. 2009. Philippines. In P. S. Kim (ed.), *Public Administration and Public Governance in ASEAN Member Countries and Korea*. Seoul: Deayoung Moonhwasa Publishing Company, pp. 207–20.

Brillantes, A. B. and Fernandez, M. T. 2010. Toward a reform framework for good governance: Focus on anti-corruption. *Philippine Journal of Public Administration* 54(1–2): 87–127.

Career Executive Service Board (CESB) n.d. *Career Executive Service Board*. Available from: cesb.gov.ph (accessed 2015).

Career Executive Service Board (CESB) 2007. *2007 Annual Report*. Quezon City: Career Executive Service Board.

Career Executive Service Board (CESB) 2009. *2009 Annual Report*. Quezon City: Career Executive Service Board.

Career Executive Service Board (CESB) 2010. *Dynamism Amidst Change: 2010 annual report*. Quezon City: Career Executive Service Board.

Career Executive Service Board (CESB) 2011a. *The Public Manager* 23(1) (January–March).

Career Executive Service Board (CESB) 2011b. *The Public Manager* 3(4) (April).

Civil Service Commission (CSC) n.d. *Civil Service Commission*. Available from: csc.gov.ph (accessed 2015).

Condrey, S. E. and Maranto, R. 2001. *Radical Reform of the Civil Service*. Lanham, Md: Lexington Books.

David, K. 2005. Combating Corruption in the Philippines: Are we Plundering Our Chances or Doing it Better? Diliman Governance Forum Working Paper Series No. 2.

Grindle, M. S. 2005. *Good enough governance revisited*. A Report for DFID with reference to the Governance Target Strategy Paper, 2001. Cambridge, Mass.: Harvard University.

Hays, S. W. and Kearney, R. C. 2003. *Public Personnel Administration: Problems and prospects*. 4th edn. Upper Saddle River, NJ: Prentice Hall.

Hooton, C. G. 1997. *Executive Governance: Presidential administrations and policy change in the federal bureaucracy*. New York: M. E. Sharpe.

Lodevico, B. V. n.d. Thirty years: The story of the career executive service. Available from: oocities.org/vynkeziah/frontpage1.html (accessed 3 June 2014).

National Economic Development Authority (NEDA) 2011. *Philippine Development Plan 2011–2016*. Pasig City, Philippines: National Economic Development Authority.

Rhodes, R. and Weller, P. 2001. *The Changing World of Top Officials: Mandarins or valets?* Philadelphia: Open University Press.

Senate Bill No. 1162 2007. *Civil Service Code*. Proposed by Senator Aquilino Pimentel. 14th Session.

Smith, M. J. 1999. *The Core Executive in Britain*. London and New York: Macmillan & St Martin's Press.

Social Weather Station 2015. The 2014/15 SWS Survey of Enterprises on Corruption: Record-low 32% of executives have personal knowledge of corrupt transaction with government in the last 3 months. SWS: Quezon City. Available from: www.sws.org.ph.

Social Weather Station 2010. The 2010 SWS Survey of Enterprises on Corruption. SWS: Quezon City. Available from: www.sws.org.ph.

Stanton, T. 2001. Government Loans in L. Salamon, (ed.) *Handbook of Policy Instruments*. New York, Oxford University Press.

Stanton, T. H. and Ginsberg, B. 2004. *Making Government Manageable: Executive organisation and management in the twenty-first century.* Baltimore: Johns Hopkins University Press.

Theakston, K. 2000. *Bureacracts and Leadership.* London and New York: Macmillan & St Martin's Press.

United Nations (UN) 2004. *Role of Human Resources in Revitalising Public Administration: Report of the secretariat.* New York: United Nations. Available from: unpan1.un.org/intradoc/groups/public/documents/un/unpan014910.pdf.

United Nations Department of Economic and Social Affairs (UNDESA) 2005. *Human Resources for Effective Public Administration in a Globalised World.* New York: United Nations.

United Nations Development Programme 1997. Reconceptualizing Governance. Discussion Paper Series No. 2. New York. United Nations.

9

Milestone programs for the administrative service in the Singapore Public Service

James Low[1]

Scope and approach

This chapter examines executive training in the Singapore Public Service: who are the people behind the executive leadership of the Singapore bureaucracy? What is their training? Who conducts the training? How does this training build capacity in the Singaporean bureaucracy? By addressing these questions, this chapter seeks to enlarge the existing body of knowledge, especially in light of the current dearth of literature on the subject of training in the Singapore Public Service and the country's public administration.

For meaningful discussion, this chapter focuses on the role of centralised training. In Singapore, bureaucracy training is undertaken centrally and at the various agencies of the public service. Agency-based training includes content catering to specific portfolio needs such as the use of specialised equipment (for example, firearms in the

---

1   Thanks to Professor John Wanna, Professor Hon S. Chan, Professor Andrew Podger and other colleagues for their guidance in writing this chapter. While all their suggestions were instrumental in shaping the arguments herein, I bear responsibility for the chapter, including all errors that may arise.

military and police) or inducting officers into peculiar organisational culture (for example, regimentation in uniformed services). Some agencies also have informal mentorship or coaching programs as part of leadership development efforts. Individual officers may also be sent for postgraduate courses in universities. Making an inventory of all such non-centralised training, from executive programs and coaching for individual officers to agency-based courses, will undoubtedly be a complex exercise. More importantly, such non-centralised training is not reflective of developments across the bureaucracy and cannot be meaningful for cross-bureaucratic analysis. Rather, this chapter will focus on centralised training to explore the role of executive training in the context of the Singapore Public Service.

While official government records on the Singapore bureaucracy are not readily available, a mine of official information can be found in the public domain. The challenge lies in accessing official documents recording decision-making—commonly available in the archives of countries such as Australia, the United Kingdom and the United States under freedom of information legislation. Such is the nature of the Singapore Administrative Service that detailed official information is scant. Nevertheless, the approach in this inquiry is to trawl for data in the open domain for primary sources. Records such as annual reports, curriculum material and information brochures found at the National Archives of Singapore, the National University of Singapore Library and Singapore's National Library provide useful primary materials. News reports can cross-reference other primary records. Data from previous research such as interviews of officials by undergraduates for their academic tasks, found at the National University of Singapore, will also be drawn on.

The discussion that follows will begin with a historical and political background of the Singapore Public Service before introducing the Administrative Service—the executive leadership of the bureaucracy. It will then address the key subject of the chapter: the training of Administrative Service Officers (AOs). The topic will be elaborated on by identifying the Civil Service College (CSC) and its Institute of Policy Development (IPD) as the centres through which AOs are trained. The focus is then on Milestone Programs—the system of continuous training throughout the careers of AOs. By attuning AOs to the policy milieu, Milestone Programs build up AOs' capacity to formulate and implement policies. In other words, the training is responsive to the context of the work of AOs. More importantly, this chapter shows that by helping to attract the best and brightest to provide leadership for the bureaucracy, Milestone Programs contribute to developing Singapore's capacity for effective governance.

The Singapore Public Service: Background

Singapore today, with its high standard of living and economic vibrancy, has come a long way since gaining self-government in 1959 after 140 years of British colonial rule. A small island (710 sq km) without natural resources, relying on imports for all essentials, it generates an impressive gross domestic product (GDP) of S$304 billion (A$297.3 billion). This is a more than 145 per cent increase from the figure at decolonisation; per capita GDP has also grown 45 per cent since 1959 to S$57,603 (A$56,300). Unemployment is a low 2.1 per cent; infant mortality is only two per 1,000 live births; and the literacy rate is 97 per cent. Singapore's multiracial population—an ethnic Chinese majority and substantial Indian and Malay communities—lives in general harmony and the crime rate is low. This stability and modern amenities make Singapore one of the most liveable cities in the world.

The Singapore Public Service is often given little credit for the leading role it played in the country's modernisation. Singapore's transformation is typically attributed to the strategic foresight and political will of founding prime minister, Lee Kuan Yew, and his colleagues in the People's Action Party (PAP) (see, for example, Turnbull 1989; Drysdale 1984; Chew and Lee 1991; Lam and Tan 1999; Tan 2007; Latif 2009; Ng 2010; Ho 2000: 149). There were scholars who argued that the public service was made up of civil servants wielding 'power and privilege without accountability to the public and who may eventually become the real rulers of the country' (Chan 1975: 68; see also Seah 1999: 253). Proponents of this 'administrative state' model were really pointing to the bureaucracy as a source from which the ruling party coopted talent. The credit for Singapore's development continued to be accorded to the political elite.

Political visions, however, had to be translated into policies—and this depended on the bureaucracy. Singapore's early strategy to attract foreign investment needed civil servants to market the fledgling state across the world to draw in overseas capital. Engineers were responsible for erecting factories to make industrialisation a reality. Improving living standards required architects to plan new public housing zones, doctors and nurses to administer primary health care and teachers to provide education. Even as the maturing state sought infrastructural expansion and more sophisticated economic strategies, converting these broad strategic ideas into actionable policies, and then carrying them out, rested on the shoulders of the country's civil servants, from senior bureaucrats to rank-and-file frontline officers. Significant credit for Singapore's modernisation is due to the public service, which turned the strategic foresight of the political elite into reality.

The Singapore Public Service today is regarded as 'one of the most efficient and least corrupt in the world' by the UN Public Administration Network (UNPAN 2005) and other international indicators.[2] Unlike counterparts in some post-colonial states, Singapore's bureaucracy and its leadership have not interfered in the political arena. Unique even to civil services of developed countries, the Singapore Public Service has gone beyond efficiency and integrity to position its officers to 'anticipate, welcome and execute change' (PSD 2011). From harnessing technology to delivering government services, it has gone on to adopt concepts and tools such as scenario planning and horizon scanning to prepare for unforeseen crises that may arise in the future—a sign of its growing sophistication. Efficient, incorrupt and faceless behind its political masters, the Singapore Public Service is quintessentially 'professional' by Westminster standards.

A large body of literature covers various aspects of this professionalism. Quah has written extensively on the bureaucracy's management of personnel, particularly through the Public Service Commission, and the fight against corruption.[3] Quah (1987) also studied the bureaucracy's ability to implement policies formulated by the political leadership and his 1985 work covered statutory boards, a subject also addressed by Lee (1975). Recent works by other scholars analyse administrative reforms, such as those by Koh (1997) and Jones (2002) (see also Quah

---

2   Under 'Institutions', Singapore ranked first of 133 countries from 1999 to 2011 (World Economic Forum 2011: 4, 14).
3   On the Public Service Commission, see Quah (1971; 1972; 1996a: 492–506). On corruption, see Quah (1978; 1989: 841–53; 2003: 180–97).

1994, 1996b). In 2010, Quah published *Public Administration Singapore Style*, compiling themes of his work thus far: statutory boards, the Public Service Commission, compensation, bureaucratic reforms and anti-corruption efforts.

Yet the role of training in this professionalism is virtually ignored in the public administration literature. As Simon (1976) points out, training—by preparing staff to reach satisfactory decisions on their own—frees the organisation from the constant exercise of authority. Giving officers the knowledge and loyalty to act in the organisation's interests but using their own discretion is especially critical for large organisations dispersed across different locations. Training thus allows a bureaucracy to carry out daily functions effectively. Yet the importance of the subject is not matched by the significance accorded it in Singaporean public administration literature. Training has largely been discussed as part of broader topics such as personnel management. There are two rather comprehensive perspectives on training within larger discussions—namely, Seah (1971) and Lee (1977)—and several undergraduate theses (Sim 1985; Lai 1995; Siow 1998), but these are outdated.

From colonial bureaucracy to the Singapore Public Service

The genesis of the Singapore Public Service is in a colonial bureaucracy that was discriminatory and disconnected from the populace. The administration set up after the island's 1819 colonisation restricted executive positions to 'natural-born British subjects of pure European descent on both sides' (Seah 1971: 12). Locals could only fill rank-and-file positions, working as policemen, peons, clerks and the like. Even when tertiary education qualified locals for higher positions, their service conditions never matched those of their European colleagues. European officers, despite effectively governing the colony, did not receive any training preparing them to govern. Courses in administration before their overseas deployment equipped them for general service across the British Empire rather than in specific colonies. British bureaucrats thus arrived in Singapore without an understanding of the local population and culture.

Discriminatory staffing only ended towards the end of the colonial period. In 1957, after years of agitation for localisation of the bureaucracy, barriers against local officers being promoted into the elite Administrative Service were at last removed.[4] A century after the Northcote–Trevelyan reforms required the British Civil Service to make appointments based on an individual's qualifications, deserving local officers in Singapore were finally able to access the apex of the bureaucracy. Besides the consolidation of wide-ranging schemes of service into four divisions (see Seah 1971: 30), the introduction of meritocracy represents the most enduring bureaucratic reform of the colonial era. Meritocracy continues to be the guiding principle for recruitment and promotion in the present-day Singapore Public Service.

The bureaucracy's aloofness from the populace did not improve even late in the colonial period. As a colonial institution, the bureaucracy had long regarded itself as a sovereign's agent ruling over imperial subjects. Even local rank-and-file civil servants were generally overbearing and rude towards the local people; street-level bureaucrats such as police and postmen were notorious for petty corruption. Senior civil servants, on the other hand, were typically sequestered in offices away from the 'man on the street'. Postwar reforms might have allowed more local officers into the executive echelons of the bureaucracy, but with a population that was overwhelmingly non-English speaking, even illiterate, the introduction of a merit-based system into a bureaucracy in which English was the lingua franca only perpetuated existing disconnectedness.

After the British grant of self-government in 1959, the newly elected PAP government initiated a series of measures that had far-reaching effects on the bureaucracy. To begin with, the Singapore Public Service, emerging from the colonial bureaucracy, was apprehensive about the seemingly pro-Chinese PAP.[5] Cuts to their pay and

---

4   Chief Secretary to Permanent Secretaries and Heads of Departments, CSO, CO215/53, Vol. III, 22 November 1956, MF862/1087.

5   A civil servant at that time recalled that 'when the PAP came in, the first fear was really the image which they had of being extreme, of being pro-communist and of being anti-civil service … With such a strong political party coming in, with a certain amount of antagonism to the old Civil Service which has stood for the colonial masters and implemented the will of the colonial masters, to put it in the language of the extreme left, the running dogs of the British, what future was there for these civil servants?' (Goh Sin Tub, Oral interview transcript, NAS, Accession No. 001422, Reel 4: 39).

a tightening of disciplinary regulations by the PAP soon after taking power led civil servants to protest and some even resigned (Singapore Government 1960). Senior officers were then sent to the newly set up Political Study Centre for courses on the context of policymaking since 'because of past training and background of the civil service in the traditions of the British system, particularly the colonial system … they have not been made aware of the importance of keeping in touch with the masses'.[6]

While the PAP's immediate measures might be an assertion of its authority over a hostile colonial-era bureaucracy, tightening of discipline—particularly anti-graft efforts—set in motion the eventual professionalisation of the bureaucracy. Socialisation of officers away from colonial apathy led to a public service consciousness of the importance of the context in which policies have to be formulated and implemented. Its 50 years of uninterrupted rule over the country also means that the PAP's initial claim of authority over the bureaucracy has over time cemented the centrality of its political control over the public service.

The Administrative Service

The Administrative Service is another colonial legacy, continuing to provide leadership for the Singapore bureaucracy. Its exact origin is not clear, but Seah (1971: 11a; see also Sim 1985; Lai 1995) believes it began with the 1882 introduction of the Eastern Cadetship, evolving into the Malayan Civil Service in 1934. The Singapore Administrative Service probably emerged as part of a distinct Singapore Civil Service after the island was separated from Malaya after World War II. Today, the officers of the Singapore Administrative Service continue to provide the senior leadership of the Singapore Public Service. Most permanent secretaries and chief executives heading the 15 ministries and 50 statutory boards are AOs. As of 2010, there were 277 AOs, constituting 0.2 per cent of the 127,000-strong public service (Ong 2011).

---

6   Singapore Government press statement, 'Civil service political study centre', 28 July 1959, JK/INFS.JL.119/59.

In line with meritocratic principles, entrance into the apex of the Administrative Service is based on qualifications and is highly stringent. AOs are typically scouted from among the best and brightest of 18-year-old high school leavers. Those who excel academically and exhibit leadership abilities are offered Singaporean Government scholarships sponsoring their tertiary studies in prestigious overseas universities. On graduation, these 'scholars' are required to serve in the public service, typically in the Management Associates Program, in stints of three to four years at one or two government agencies (SAS n.d.(b)). If performance at these junior policy positions is deemed 'outstanding', they are then absorbed into the Administrative Service. AOs who do not perform to expectation during their probation of one to two years can choose other schemes of service in the public service. Entrance into the Administrative Service, in other words, is not direct and involves a highly rigorous process.

On confirmation of their appointment by the Public Service Commission, AOs are held to demanding standards as these generalists are rotated across the public service. Each posting spans two to three years to expose them 'to a broad spectrum of policy work and acquire knowledge, experience and expertise in government administration, economic, security and social fields' (Teo 2001). Regular postings are also meant to evaluate them in different job contexts for their suitability for promotion to senior positions. These postings and promotions are decided by the Special Personnel Board of senior permanent secretaries, whose standards are exacting. AOs who meet the standards after two to three postings are promoted to the SR9 grade as directors heading departments, typically at age 32 (Teo 2007; PSD 2010). The SR9 grade's S$365,000 (A$357,000) annual remuneration illustrates the policy of high pay to attract and retain talent. In comparison, the MX9 grade director in the general public service receives no more than S$264,000 (A$258,000).[7] AOs with potential for higher leadership positions after two to three directorships are promoted into Public Sector Leadership—that is, chief executives of statutory boards and deputy and permanent secretaries of ministries.

---

7   While there are no official data on MX9 salaries, the monthly salary at the midpoint of MX9 grade was revealed as S$13,750 (A$13,400). Assuming the typical 13-month payment and three months' performance bonus, the annual salary of the mid-scale MX9 officer is S$220,000 (A$215,000) (Teo 2012). Internet discussions listed the MX9 monthly salary range from $10,580 to $16,540 (A$10,300 to A$16,200) and typical bonuses as four months (Salary Singapore 2011).

However, if 'an officer's potential is assessed to be below that of at least deputy secretary when he reaches his mid-30s, he will be counselled to leave the Administrative Service' (Teo 2001: 5). The tenures of public sector leaders are capped at 10 years to allow leadership renewal but also to accommodate rapid mobility up the ranks.

Critics argue that AOs 'should work their way up' (Koh 2006; see also The Straits Times 2006; Loh 2007; Lim 2008). Rapid promotion and postings may have shielded AOs from experience implementing policies on the ground and working with everyday citizens. While they may excel at writing papers and table-top planning, some AOs—detractors allege—may lack 'soft skills' such as working with people: from members of the public to their staff and peers. The Public Service Division (PSD) clarified that AOs 'are subject to stricter requirements and higher expectations … those who do not measure up to the high standards are asked to leave or transfer to another Service' (Ong 2007). In response to criticisms of AOs' high pay, the minister in charge of the civil service pointed out:

> [T]here is no perfect method for doing this benchmarking … We do not want pay to be the main reason for people to join us. But we also do not want pay to be the reason for them not to join us, or to leave after joining us. (Teo 2007)

Training AOs

Most of the training for AOs, as for other public service officers, is conducted by the Civil Service College (CSC). The CSC is a statutory board established by legislation specifically to provide training for the Singapore Public Service. Its status as a statutory board affords it greater autonomy than government ministries in areas such as financial arrangements and human resource management. For example, the CSC has the liberty to offer greater remuneration to attract staff. As with all statutory boards, the CSC reports to a parent ministry, which, appropriately, is the public service's Personnel Management Ministry, the PSD, which, in turn, is located within the Prime Minister's Office. Providing CSC management with oversight and strategic guidance is a board of directors. Chaired by the Permanent Secretary of the PSD, this board also includes permanent secretaries of several ministries, chief executives of other government agencies and senior executives from the private sector (CSC 2014).

The CSC currently has three training departments. Apart from the international training arm, the two local training departments allow the CSC to train about 40,000 public officers each year, or one in every three officers (CSC 2008b: 9). The bulk of this training is conducted through the Institute of Public Administration and Management (IPAM). The range of courses caters to officers from Division 1 to Division 4, and includes induction skills training (human resource management, fiscal planning, information and communications technology, and so on) and pre-retirement planning—almost a cradle-to-grave offering of training in the career of a public officer (CSC 2008a).

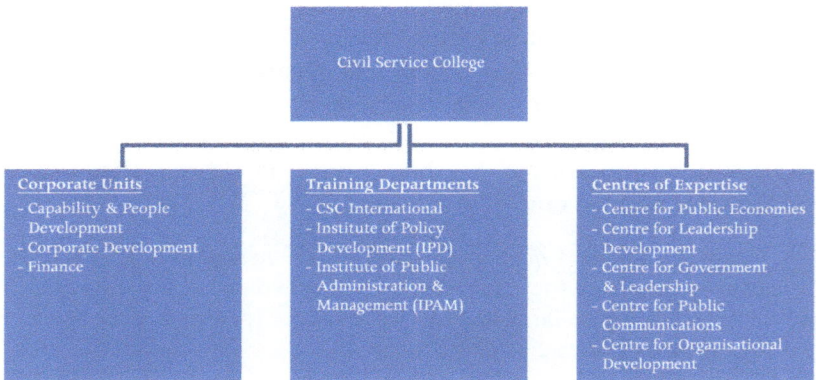

Figure 9.1: CSC organisational structure
Source: CSC (2013b).

Institute of Policy Development

The department in the CSC responsible for training AOs is the Institute of Policy Development. The IPD was established in 1993 as the original Civil Service College—a name it held until 1996, when it was renamed and merged with IPAM to form part of the current CSC (CSC 2013a).

From the start, the IPD was set up as a dedicated institute to provide leadership training for AOs (Hu 1992). Before 1993, their training had been conducted through the Civil Service Institute, IPAM's predecessor. The focus on skills training by the Civil Service Institute resulted in neglect of policymaking perspectives deemed critical for AOs as they rose through the ranks in their careers (Lai 1995: 33).

The IPD, consequently, was established to provide AOs with specialised training in management, leadership, policy and strategic planning skills and to provide them with an international outlook.

Beyond skills training, the IPD's courses aimed to foster among AOs a sense of national teamwork. Pointing to France's Ecole Nationale d'Administration (ENA; National School of Administration) and Malaysia's National Institute of Public Administration (INTAN) as examples of where strong bonds were forged among elite administrators, the then Minister for Finance lamented that Singapore did not have a focal point to preserve traditions and transmit values. By bringing AOs together from their routine posts scattered across the bureaucracy, the IPD's courses could inculcate a sense of 'national team work necessary for the survival and progress of a small country like Singapore' (Hu 1992). Older AOs could share their 'baptism by fire' experiences with younger officers who did not have policymaking exposure (interview with Tan Boon Huat, cited Lai 1995: 33). The founding head of the IPD saw the institute as 'a repository of old wisdom, and as a generator of new ideas' (Mahbubani, cited in Lai 1995: 34). Its mission was spelled out as being:

> To foster … in addition to the prevailing strengths of competence, dedication, integrity and meritocracy … a strong sense of tradition, *esprit de corps*, enhanced managerial skills, a sensitive understanding of the new evolving political and economic realities and commitment to a long term vision of a secure, stable and successful Singapore. (Mission statement, cited in Lai 1995: 34)

While it is prepared to train participants in administrative skills, the IPD was clearly intended to imbibe within the Administrative Service elite a common sense of values and outlook—a goal that continues to feature prominently in the IPD's collateral material today.

The IPD's instructional objective appears geared towards providing practitioner-based policymaking lessons, rather than an academic curriculum. The IPD's original formulators aimed to draw on varied expertise to address its courses. In its collateral material, it states that the trainers engaged to share 'insights on governance, policy and leadership' are apparently 'senior public sector leaders' (CSC 2013a)—that is, permanent secretaries and deputy secretaries of ministries and chief executives of statutory boards. Unlike trainers external to the bureaucracy, these public sector leaders are not paid for the training they conduct (Lai 1995; CSC 2013a), although time away from their offices to conduct such training constitutes a kind of cross-subsidy within the public service. Other speakers invited to engage with participants are leaders from the private sector. Throughout the IPD's website and publications, there is no reference to theoretical or academic frameworks in its programs.

The IPD offers a variety of training programs. These include policy forums that are used to keep officers abreast of 'live' policy issues so that 'officers are better prepared to think and act from a wider national perspective' (CSC 2011c). Workshops and seminars, such as the Strategic Perspectives Conference, where public sector leaders (that is, permanent secretaries, deputy secretaries and chief executives) engage with participants, 'engender shared understanding of national opportunities and challenges, and galvanise collective action' (CSC 2011d). Scenario Planning Workshops featured on the IPD's website are coorganised with the PSD's Strategic Policy Office to imbue in participants the aptitude 'to anticipate and deal with the challenges before they occur, and to harness opportunities that arise' (CSC 2011d).

Milestone Programs

The IPD's main mode of training for AOs are the Milestone Programs—a series of intensive training sessions extending for several weeks and scheduled at key points (or 'milestones') in an officer's career (CSC 2003: 26; 2005: 13, 44). A senior official in the PSD interviewed in the 1990s revealed that participants were identified and scheduled for Milestone Programs by the PSD based on their potential for higher responsibilities (interview with Tan Boon Huat, cited in Lai 1995: 54). The performance of these participants in the Milestone Programs would be used by the PSD as a reference point for their assessment.

As the medium of continuous training for AOs throughout their careers, these programs naturally focus on equipping AOs with several key competencies. In a work that probably enjoyed access to the CSC and the PSD, Saxena (2011: 107–8) compiled a list of competencies fundamental to developing management and leadership capacity among AOs: the capacity to be flexible and agile; an ability to analyse the macro/global situation and its relationship to micro/local conditions; and being able to generate a variety of solutions and possibilities in diverse situations.

The types of Milestone Programs offered appear to have diversified in recent years as IPD's participant base has expanded beyond AOs to include officers in the mainstream public service who exhibit significant leadership potential. This chapter will focus on IPD's three main Milestone Programs for training AOs:

- Foundation Course
- Senior Management Program
- Leadership in Administration Program.

The Foundation Course

IPD's entry-level Milestone Program for AOs, the Foundation Course (FC), essentially exposes new AOs to the policymaking milieu. Sim (1985: 36) traced the FC's origins to 1979 when the Training Advisory Council observed that new Administrative Service recruits hailed from different universities locally and abroad. There was a need to acquaint these officers, particularly newly returned scholars, with Singapore's political, social, economic and administrative environments and those of its neighbouring countries. At the same time, the FC was intended to foster esprit de corps among the new officers. Though the FC was transferred to the IPD in 1993, having been run through the Civil Service Institute since its introduction, its aim remains to induct new AOs in the first year of their career. In recent years, the FC has reportedly been brought forward to the pre-absorption Management Associate Program phase (CSC 2007: 10, 36). In any case, participants—newly returned graduates—would be in their mid-20s and probably in their first or second year in the public service.

During the nine-week course, new AOs and management associates are introduced to 'values, knowledge and skills' essential for leadership careers in the bureaucracy (CSC n.d.). These are drawn out through adventure learning, learning journeys, case studies, workshops, self-facilitated discussions on policy papers, role-play, presentations and dialogue with experts. The FC also includes overseas study trips to countries in the Association of Southeast Asian Nations (ASEAN). Besides equipping participants with an understanding of the

South-East Asian neighbourhood, these trips allow officers to foster good relations with the foreign officials hosting them. In a 2003 interview, Bilahari Kausikan, a permanent secretary in the Ministry of Foreign Affairs, summed up the FC experience:

> When you join there is a Foundation Course for Administrative Service Officer[s] from all ministries. They have a formal program given to all ministries and they will be taken around to a good number of ASEAN countries to visit our missions there and so on. When you go around with a bunch of fellows for three months a certain bonding occurs and it's meant to occur. (Barr and Skrbis 2008: 229)

The Senior Management Program

The Senior Management Program (SMP) is a six-week course for director-level officers focusing on policy implementation and preparing officers for future leadership positions (CSC 2006: 17). AOs would form the bulk of participants although the class would also include director-level officers from the mainstream civil service, identified by the PSD to have potential for senior appointments (interview with Zee Yong Kang, cited in Lai 1995: 39). This mixture of AOs with other emerging leaders of the civil service would serve the purpose of building team spirit and cohesion among the administrative elite, as well as bringing broader perspectives to the classroom. With the SR9 grade of AO directors pegged at age 32 and AOs reaching director grade after two to three postings of two to three years each, most participants would be in their early to mid-30s, having served about six to eight years in the Administrative Service. The syllabus concentrates on the finer details of translating policy intent at the strategic level to implementation as well as public consultation and public communications. The curriculum appears to have high-level inputs, as evidenced in a 2007 report. Themes for that year's SMP were apparently drawn up from 'Public sector leaders advance, a discussion involving senior officials [topics discussed included sustaining] good governance, forging new social compact, ensuring security and globalization, and hyper-competition' (cited in CSC 2008b: 26). Like other Milestone Programs, SMPs involve meetings and discussions with policymakers and leading personalities in the media and private sector (CSC 2006: 17). India and China are typical destinations for the SMP's overseas study trips, perhaps in view of their rising economic status and geostrategic implications for Singapore's regional environment. As revealed by an IPD official in the 1990s, while the SMP does not guarantee participants automatic promotion, it is almost a prerequisite for their progress to the next grade (interview with Zee, cited in Lai 1995: 39).

The Leadership in Administration Program

The IPD's pinnacle Milestone Program, the Leadership in Administration Program (LAP), spans five to six weeks and aims to prepare a cohort of about 25 officers at deputy secretary and chief executive level for permanent secretary positions—the highest office in the Singapore Public Service (CSC 2007: 36). Based on an AO's typical advancement through two to three rotations across the public service, participants would have spent between four and six years as directors before attending LAP and so would be in their mid-40s. As in the SMP it would not be surprising to find some LAP participants from the mainstream public service and so older in age given their slower career progression compared with that of AOs. Such a mixture of participants is in keeping with the intention to bring a diversity of experiences into the classroom and to strengthen esprit de corps among these bureaucratic elite, although there is no information in the public domain to confirm this.

The syllabus seeks to stimulate participants to think critically about the future of Singapore and how the public service should respond, and reviews fundamental principles that will project Singapore forward (CSC 2007: 36). Much attention is also given to processes and challenges in policy implementation, organisational leadership, management skills, and understanding prevailing trends in the political, economic and social sectors as well as the region around Singapore. Emphasis has in recent years been devoted to facilitating whole-of-government coordination and organisational change. During study trips to China and India, arrangements are made for participants to meet with fellow public sector leaders in the region. Permanent Secretary Bilahari recalls 'at the most senior level you have six weeks with a bunch of peers. Basically that is a far more conscious process of bonding, or elite formation if you want' (Barr and Skrbis 2008: 244).

Other types of Milestone Programs

In 2008, a new Milestone Program called the Leadership Development Program (LDP) was introduced between the FC and the SMP. The AOs targeted would probably be in their late 20s or about 30, after spending two to three years at junior policy positions following their FC stint, and before promotion to directors. The LDP, in the words of the head of the civil service, 'helps young Administrative Officers to develop an understanding of self, cultivate the ability to develop others, build teams and to drive change' (Ho 2009).

In 2009, 'BEACON' was rolled out for newly appointed management associates. It aims to raise their 'self-awareness … by giving them a better understanding of their personal strengths and areas of development' (Ho 2010). No further information could be obtained about this program, including what the abbreviation BEACON might represent. While management associates have their own dedicated Milestone Program, it is not clear whether they are then excluded from the FC, to make that course a Milestone Program focusing only on newly absorbed AOs.

Funding

While there is no publicly available information on the funding of these Milestone Programs for the AOs, IPAM's *Training Directory* offers a hint. IPAM's Strategic LEAD Program for directors from the mainstream public service is priced at S$2,782 (A$2,720) per participant (CSC 2008a: 24–5). However, the Strategic LEAD Program is a five-day course while IPD's SMP spans six weeks. Without more details of each program, simply multiplying the price of the Strategic LEAD Program with the six weeks of the SMP is speculative and not a meaningful deduction. Suffice to note that even this simplistic calculation would mean a very high price per participant. Factor in the costs involved in overseas study trips and the opportunity costs of the time given by senior public sector leaders and the investment in the training of AOs is undoubtedly high.

There is evidence to suggest that at least part of the funding for IPD's Milestone Programs is borne by the PSD. For IPAM's training programs, the participants or their agencies pay half the course fee. The remaining half is paid by the PSD through its Public Service for the 21st Century Office (PS21 Office), which is responsible for leading changes across the bureaucracy (PSD 2011). Indeed, as the parent ministry of the CSC and the personnel management arm of the public service, the PSD is certainly a source of funding for the CSC's training programs. In the 2011 Singapore Government Budget, the PSD reported allocating 'S$24.6 million [A$24.06 million] for the development of training programs, enhancement of methodologies and tools for public sector leadership development, organisational and employee development, as well as staff selection and assessment' (Ministry of Finance 2011).

This amount is clearly in addition to the regular training subsidy provided by the PS21 Office for an individual officer's development. With the IPD the primary training arm of the Administrative Service, part of this budgetary allocation—especially that relating to 'public sector leadership development'—should go towards funding the IPD's Milestone Programs for AOs.

A more significant observation that can be drawn from the review of financial data is that a steady stream of funding for training is provided regardless of national economic performance. Even during periods when Singapore suffered recession—in 2003 as a result of the Severe Acute Respiratory Syndrome (SARS) epidemic, and between 2008 and 2009 after the Global Financial Crisis—the CSC's revenue from training was healthy (see Table 9.1). In fact, the CSC's income from training in 2008 and 2009 grew substantially, to S$35 million (A$34.2 million) and S$36 million (A$35.2 million) respectively, when compared with figures in the preceding three years (CSC 2010: 12). A review of the CSC's annual reports for these periods also indicates that the IPD continued with its scheduled Milestone Programs for AOs without any sign of disruption from the economic fallout. Singapore's commitment to providing training for its AOs, and officers across the public service generally, is evidently firm regardless of the country's economic conditions.

Table 9.1: CSC revenue from training

	2002	2003	2004	2005	2006	2007	2008	2009
Revenue from training	S$38m	S$34m	S$34m	S$30m	S$27m	S$26m	S$35m	S$36m
Income from consultancy	S$3m	S$3	S$4m	S$5m	S$8m	S$9m	S$7m	S$2m
Research	n/a	n/a	n/a	S$1m	S$2m	S$2m	n.a.	n.a.
Government grant	n/a	n/a	n/a	n/a	n/a	S$5m	S$7m	S$15m
Other income	S$2m	S$2m	S$5m	S$3m	S$3m	S$2m	S$1m	S$1m
Total revenue	S$43m	S$39m	S$43m	S$39m	S$40m	S$42m	S$50m	S$54m
Training as a percentage of total	88.37%	87.18%	79.07%	76.92%	67.50%	61.90%	70.00%	66.67%

n/a not applicable

n.a. not available

Source: CSC (2003, 2004, 2005, 2006, 2007, 2008b, 2009, 2010).[8]

Evaluation, relevance and responsiveness

Given the significant cost and time involved, including attention from public sector leadership, some form of evaluation should be expected for these Milestone Programs. While official evaluation of the IPD's Milestone Programs is not publicly available, Lai (1995: 41) reported that participants typically completed evaluation forms that 'are elaborate in order to assess their satisfaction with the course and if refinements are in order'. There were no written examinations because the IPD was not an academic institution. Official data in the public domain indicate that evaluation is based on participant feedback on a five-point rating. In the 2001–03 *CSC Annual Report*, LAP participants gave a score of 4.19 for the course, while the IPD's average rating in 2004 for all its programs was reported as 4.46 (CSC 2003: 29; 2006: 18). While in-depth evaluation is not available, the continuation of these expensive programs suggests they have been found effective and relevant by the bureaucracy.

---

8   The CSC stopped publishing revenue data after this period.

The relevance of Milestone Programs appears to be a fundamental factor. Detailed documents on the design of specific sessions in these programs are once again not available. A study of references to these programs in public material reveals constant emphasis on 'practitioner perspective', 'implementation' of public policy, 'public consultation' and 'public communication'. Interestingly, such a focus on policy implementation and public engagement coincides with some of the starkest criticisms of AOs—that is, that they do not have sufficient exposure to the operational details of policy implementation due to their fast-track promotion and rapid job rotation, and that AOs lack the people skills to effectively interact and engage with members of the public. In a recent article, the director of the IPD reiterated this emphasis on the practitioner-based teaching model. By getting senior officers to recount their practical experiences with junior officers, 'sharing could legitimately encompass good practices as well as learning points from policies that did not pan out as anticipated' (Maniam 2011: 71).

More than the relevance of practical lessons learnt, these Milestone Programs are particularly useful as platforms of socialisation. As noted earlier, the process of putting groups of AOs together for several weeks, making them undergo intensive activities—whether classroom-based discussions or overseas study trips—has the effect of forging a strong sense of bonding among them. A constant reinforcement of particular messages towards policymaking, even if these are practical approaches and devoid of ideology, could condition these AOs into a uniform world view of the milieu in which they need to formulate and implement policies. Periodic reunions in the form of more senior-level Milestone Programs as each cohort rises up their career ladder would serve to deepen the socialisation process and strengthen their sense of camaraderie. While 'group think' can be a real risk, at the same time such socialisation offers advantages in policymaking: it builds up a common language that facilitates communication and deliberation and develops a strong network of contacts, if not friendship, between the policymaking elite. Even as they are dispersed across various ministries throughout the bureaucracy, such informal bonds facilitate inter-agency collaboration increasingly necessitated by emerging issues of governance. In recent times, the IPD seems to purposefully position its Milestone Programs as platforms for cultivating such whole-of-government bonding among its AO participants. Maniam (2011: 71) writes:

> The value of such interactions across agencies is both analytical, in inculcating understanding among future leaders of how government operates as a system, not just as discrete silos; as well as in the formation of social capital, through networks and bonds of trust developed over the various leadership programs.

Hence, the relevance of the Milestone Programs lies in their ability to relate the classroom curriculum to the actual policy work milieu, but also their ability—through the socialisation of the bureaucratic elite—to develop capacity for governance.

One way in which the CSC seeks to ensure the relevance of its Milestone Programs may be through actively engaging the leadership of the bureaucracy. As pointed out earlier, it was found that themes of a particular Milestone Program had been drawn up from a discussion of public sector leaders—that is, permanent secretaries, deputy secretaries and chief executives (CSC 2008b: 26). By involving them as trainers to directly engage with program participants, these senior officials would be able to impart real-life policy lessons: dilemmas of and debates about policy options, the intricacies and undocumented tacit details of policy implementation, possibly even lapses and blunders of certain policy episodes. The public sector leaders of other ministries and agencies who sit on the CSC's board of directors provide another quick channel of feedback to ensure the relevance of training. By virtue of their senior positions in the bureaucracy, these officials are naturally conscious of the key strategic issues facing the country and so would have an understanding of the needs of the public service. As 'end-users' of training coming from agencies whose officers have been dispatched and thus are able to assess the relevance and effectiveness of training, these public sector leaders would also be able to provide feedback on training and how it can be improved.

Whether by design or by coincidence, structuring the CSC as a subordinate agency of a strategic ministry such as the PSD may also have contributed to the relevance and responsiveness of its training. As a statutory board of the PSD, the CSC is exposed to direct and frequent interactions with the PSD—such as meetings and events— exposing it to the range of human resource issues and priorities facing the division. Another interesting observation is that several key members of CSC's senior management hold concurrent appointments in the PSD. For example, the dean and chief executive officer (CEO) of the CSC is concurrently deputy secretary (development) in the PSD (highlighted in Figure 9.2). The CSC's director of the Centre for Governance and Leadership was at the same time the director of the PSD's Strategic Policy Office. Such concurrent appointments at the training agency and the central ministry, and locating the training institution within the ambit of the ministry, link up the training institution with the strategic level of the bureaucracy to ensure training is relevant.

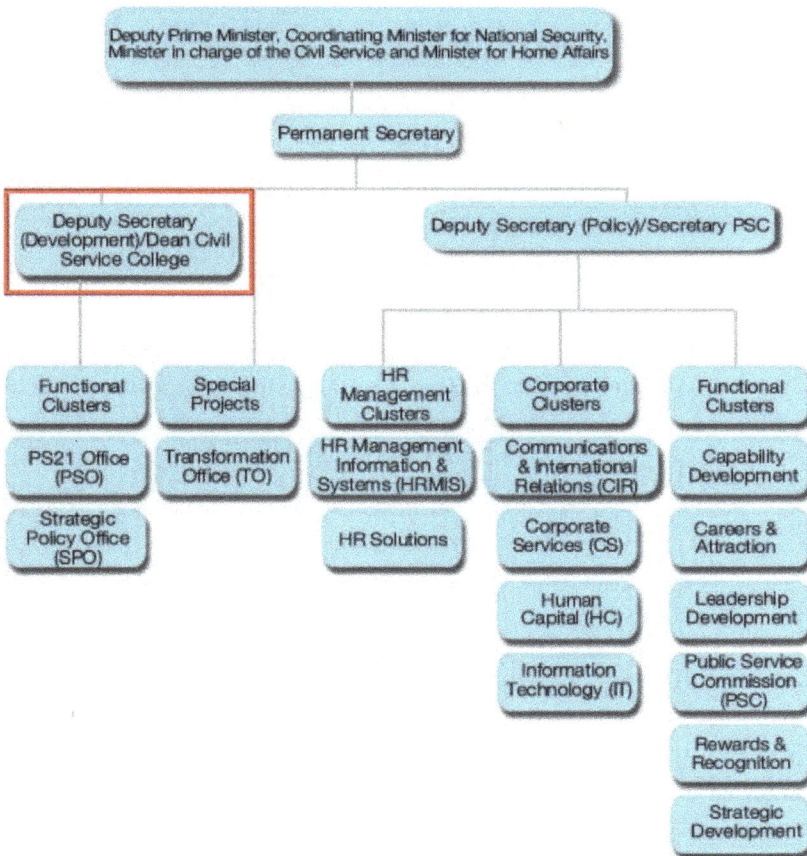

Figure 9.2: PSD organisational chart
Source: CSC (2011b).

From the PSD's perspective, these Milestone Programs serve a broader personnel management purpose beyond the development of AOs. To be sure, Milestone Programs constitute the centrepiece in the suite of continuous training and development programs for AOs.[9] When included in recruitment collateral, these programs and continuous training opportunities become a marketing tool to attract talented candidates into the Administrative Service. The PSD could effectively use Milestone Programs as an incentive—or a disincentive, by withholding an officer's nomination for a program—alongside performance appraisal and promotion as a tool for personnel management. Milestone Programs thus constitute an important part of the PSD's strategy to attract, retain, assess and develop talent through the Administrative Service.

Conclusion

Capacity building is a complex and multidimensional undertaking (UNPAN 2006: 17) and may not have been the specific and deliberate goal of the Singapore Public Service. The country's stability and high standard of living today result from a wide-ranging approach to developing the economy, improving social services and securing its international relations while strengthening public administration, rather than a single goal to develop capacity for good governance. Nevertheless, the high level of professionalism—efficient, incorruptible and non-partisan—exhibited by the Singapore Public Service suggests it has over time developed a level of capacity for effective governance.[10]

That the public service is growing its capacity for effective governance is clearly evident from the training of the Administrative Service elite, as has been discussed in this chapter. The relevance and responsiveness of the Milestone Programs to the policy milieu and

---

9 These range from Community Attachment Programs for the young officer and postgraduate degree or executive programs as the officer progresses in their career, to serving as director on the governing boards of government-linked companies and statutory boards as a senior AO (SAS n.d.(a)).

10 'Governance' is defined by the United Nations as 'the exercise of economic, political and administrative authority to manage a country's affairs at all levels. It comprises the mechanisms, processes and institutions through which citizens and groups articulate their interests, exercise their legal rights, meet their obligations and mediate their differences' (UNPAN 2006: 3).

shifting strategic directions show that the public service seeks to attune AOs to the context in which policies will have to be effectively formulated and implemented. The shunning of academic theories in favour of an emphasis on the practitioner's perspective reinforces the real-world context in which officers will have to deliberate on and deliver policies. Parallel to the curriculum, the fostering of esprit de corps between each cohort of AOs through spending long hours in class together also facilitates interagency cooperation or 'whole-of-government coordination' when addressing issues straddling multiple portfolios. At the same time, the many discussions of policy issues within the framework of 'baptism by fire' stories from senior public sector leaders at these Milestone Programs serve to orient AOs towards common values espoused by the bureaucracy such as public service and integrity. More significantly, for a small country fixated on nurturing talent amid its lack of natural resources, the Milestone Programs are part of a sophisticated strategy to attract, develop and retain the best and brightest among its citizenry to lead the bureaucracy. Thus, the training of executives in the Singapore bureaucracy is more than an end in itself; by helping to recruit and develop talent in the administrative elite, Milestone Programs for the Administrative Service are a mechanism for building capacity for good governance.

The unique aspects of the Singaporean context must be taken into account when attempting to derive any (universal) lessons from its experience in capacity building. Being such a small island with a relatively small population certainly aids administration. The Singapore Public Service involves one level of government that is not encumbered by the complications of municipal, provincial or federal systems. The Singapore bureaucracy has also benefited from the support of a consistently strong political leadership with the continuity of the ruling political party. Even in its support of training in the bureaucracy, as noted by one CSC official in the mid-1990s, 'when some senior officials were unwilling to attend some courses because of the demands of their jobs in the Ministry, the first Deputy Prime Minister was able to command their attendance' (interview with Zee, cited in Lai 1995: 36). The advantages afforded by compactness are not to dismiss or downplay the complexities of administration faced by the Singapore bureaucracy; indeed, these phenomena may create their own sets of issues, which are beyond the scope of this chapter. Suffice to note that part of the rise in professionalism is aided by Singapore's unique geographical and political context. Rather than offering lessons, perhaps this chapter can conclude with some observations.

Singapore's experience suggests that the relevance and responsiveness of training can be aided by facilitative structures. Locating training institutions under the oversight of key strategic agencies allows broad or overarching goals to be quickly communicated to training institutions, for translation into a curriculum aligned with strategic objectives. Changing priorities can be similarly cascaded and training rapidly adjusted. In Singapore's case, apart from locating CSC within the ambit of the PSD, appointing leaders in the CSC to concurrent positions within the PSD undoubtedly facilitates communication between the personnel management ministry and its training agency. Such organisational structures can help align training so that it is more relevant and responsive to the broader priorities of the bureaucracy.

Another observation of the Singapore Public Service is the heavy involvement of its public sector leadership in the training process. Permanent secretaries and deputy secretaries by virtue of their positions of office are highly attuned to the strategic issues facing the country and the bureaucracy. They are in the best position to design training programs that will prepare young leaders to deal with these issues. Indeed, public sector leaders are by far the best trainers to impart real-life policy lessons from dilemmas and debates they have themselves experienced. The price of this dedication to leadership development is naturally the opportunity cost to bureaucratic leadership doing what they are supposed to do: lead, rather than train. Singapore has somehow managed to strike a delicate balance, involving permanent secretaries and chief executives, to keep the CSC's training relevant.

All governments have competing priorities and limited resources, and training in this context is often the victim of a more compelling agenda and lack of funding. In Singapore's case, the healthy state of its economy may have allowed it to invest heavily in the training of its public sector leaders even amid economic downturns. Nevertheless, the huge amount of money invested in developing these public sector leaders points to the importance accorded by the government to the bureaucracy, its leadership and the key role they play in the economy and the country. This discussion of Singapore's experience raises some questions for reflection: how important is the leadership to an organisation? How important is it for an organisation that their leadership is developed? How much money and time is an organisation willing to invest in its leaders and their development?

References

Barr, M. and Skrbis, Z. 2008. *Constructing Singapore: Elitism, ethnicity and the nation-building project*. Denmark: NIAS Press.

Chan, H. C. 1975. Politics in an administrative state: Where had the politics gone? In C. M. Seah (ed.), *Trends in Singapore*, 51–68. Singapore: Institute of South East Asian Studies.

Chew, E. and Lee, E. (eds) 1991. *A History of Singapore*. Singapore: Oxford University Press.

Civil Service College (CSC) n.d. *Milestone Programs*. Singapore: Civil Service College. Available from: cscollege.gov.sg/page.asp?id=55&pf-=1 (accessed 6 June 2011) (site discontinued).

Civil Service College (CSC) 2003. *Sharpening Minds Beyond Public Service Excellence: Civil Service College 2001–03*. [Annual report]. Singapore: Civil Service College.

Civil Service College (CSC) 2004. *Beyond Public Service Excellence, Moving Forward: Civil Service College 2003–04*. [Annual report]. Singapore: Civil Service College.

Civil Service College (CSC) 2005. *Renewing Our Commitment: Civil Service College 2004–05*. [Annual report]. Singapore: Civil Service College.

Civil Service College (CSC) 2006. *The Future: InSight—Civil Service College 2005–06*. [Annual report] Singapore: Civil Service College.

Civil Service College (CSC) 2007. *Developing People, Connecting the World: Civil Service College 2006–07*. [Annual report] Singapore: Civil Service College.

Civil Service College (CSC) 2008a. *Institute of Public Administration and Management: Training directory 2008*. Singapore: Civil Service College.

Civil Service College (CSC) 2008b. *Transformation: Civil Service College 2007–08*. [Annual report] Singapore: Civil Service College.

Civil Service College (CSC) 2009. *Annual Report 2008–09*. Singapore: Civil Service College.

Civil Service College (CSC) 2010. *Annual Report 2009–10*. Singapore: Civil Service College.

Civil Service College (CSC) 2011a. Official website. Singapore: Civil Service College. Available from: cscollege.gov.sg (accessed 22 August 2011).

Civil Service College (CSC) 2011b. *Management Team*. Singapore: Civil Service College. Available from: cscollege.gov.sg/page.asp?id=32 (accessed 22 August 2011) (site discontinued).

Civil Service College (CSC) 2011c. *Policy Forums*. Singapore: Civil Service College. Available from: cscollege.gov.sg/page.asp?id=164 (accessed 6 June 2011) (site discontinued).

Civil Service College (CSC) 2011d. *Workshops and Seminars*. Singapore: Civil Service College. Available from: cscollege.gov.sg/page.asp?id=163 (accessed 6 June 2011) (site discontinued).

Civil Service College (CSC) 2013a. *History of CSC*. Singapore: Civil Service College. Available from: cscollege.gov.sg/About%20Us/Pages/Our-History.aspx (accessed 6 June 2011).

Civil Service College (CSC) 2013b. *Organisational Structure*. 1 April. Singapore: Civil Service College. Available from: cscollege.gov.sg/About%20Us/Organisation%20Structure/Pages/default.aspx (accessed 6 June 2011).

Civil Service College (CSC) 2014. *Board of Directors*. Singapore: Civil Service College. Available from: cscollege.gov.sg/About%20Us/Organisation%20Structure/Pages/Board-of-Directors.aspx (accessed 3 June 2014).

Department of Statistics 1983. *Economic and Social Statistics: Singapore 1960–1982*. Singapore: Department of Statistics.

Department of Statistics 2011. *Singapore in Figures 2011*. Singapore: Department of Statistics. Available from: singstat.gov.sg/pubn/ reference/sif2011.pdf (accessed August 2011).

Drysdale, J. 1984. *Singapore: Struggle for success*. Singapore: Times Books International.

Ho, K. L. 2000. *The Politics of Policy-Making in Singapore*. Singapore: Oxford University Press.

Ho, P. 2009. Opening address by Head, Civil Service, 2009 Administrative Service Dinner and Promotion Ceremony, Public Service Division, Singapore, 30 March. Available from: app. psd.gov.sg/data/ASDpercent2009percent20-percent20HCS percent20Speech.pdf (accessed November 2011) (site discontinued).

Ho, P. 2010. Opening address by Head, Civil Service, 2010 Administrative Service Dinner and Promotion Ceremony, Public Service Division, Singapore, 30 March. Available from: app.psd.gov. sg/data/Adminpercent20XServicepercent20Dinnerpercent202010p ercent20-percent20HCSpercent20Speech.pdf (accessed November 2011) (site discontinued).

Hu, R. 1992. Government setting up college for top civil servants. *The Straits Times*, 11 July.

Jones, D. S. 2002. Recent reforms in Singapore's administrative elite: Responding to the challenges of a rapidly changing economy and society. *Asian Journal of Political Science* 10(2): 70–93.

Koh, A. 2006. Scholars should work their way up. *The Straits Times*, 16 December.

Koh, G. 1997. Bureaucratic rationality in an evolving developmental state: Challenges to governance in Singapore. *Asian Journal of Political Science* 5(2): 114–41.

Lai, T. 1995. Administrative training in the Singapore civil service: An evaluation of recent changes. B.Soc.Sci.(Hons) academic exercise, National University of Singapore, Singapore.

Lam, P. E. and Tan, K. Y. L. (eds) 1999. *Lee's Lieutenants: Singapore's old guard*. Sydney: Allen & Unwin.

Latif, A. 2009. *Lim Kim San: A builder of Singapore*. Singapore: Institute of South East Asian Studies.

Lee, B. H. 1975. *Statutory Boards in Singapore*. Singapore: University of Singapore.

Lee, B. H. 1977. The Singapore Civil Service and its Perceptions of Time. Honolulu: University Microfilms International.

Lim, G. 2008. Young civil servants need course in street-cred. *The Straits Times*, 27 May.

Loh, M. (M. F.) 2007. Civil servants have the best of both worlds. *The Straits Times*, 6 March.

Maniam, A. 2011. Preparing public officers for new modes of governance. *Ethos* 10 (October): 66–71.

Mercer 2010. Quality of living worldwide city rankings 2010. Mercer. Available from: mercer.com/press-releases/quality-of-living-report-2010 (accessed August 2011) (site discontinued).

Ministry of Finance 2011. *Singapore Budget 2011: Expenditure overview, Prime Minister's Office*. Singapore: Ministry of Finance. Available from: singaporebudget.gov.sg/budget_2011/expenditure_overview/pmo.html (accessed August 2011).

Ng, I. 2010. *The Singapore Lion: A biography of S. Rajaratnam*. Singapore: Institute of South East Asian Studies.

Ong, P. 2011. Opening address, 2011 Administrative Service Dinner and Promotion Ceremony, Administrative Service, Singapore. Available from: adminservice.gov.sg/NR/rdonlyres/BDD309D6-4EDE-4EA9-B988-AA21E5A86D4C/0/OpeningAddressbyHeadCivilServiceMrPeterOngatthe23rdAdministrativeServiceDinnerandPro.pdf (accessed August 2011) (site discontinued).

Ong, T. H. 2007. Civil service is not an iron rice bowl. *The Straits Times*, 8 March.

Public Service Division (PSD) 2010. Civil servants to get 2-month year-end payment. Press Release. Website. Available from: psd. gov.sg/data/ PSD%20press%20release%2024112010.pdf (accessed August 2011) (site discontinued).

Public Service Division (PSD) 2011. Website. Available from: psd.gov. sg/ (accessed August 2011).

Quah, J. S. T. 1971. The Public Service Commission in Singapore: A comparative study of its evolution and its recruitment and selection procedures vis-a-vis the Public Service Commissions in Ceylon, India and Malaysia. M.Soc.Sci. thesis, Department of Political Science, University of Singapore.

Quah, J. S. T. 1972. *Origin of Public Service Commission in Singapore*. New Delhi: Indian Institute of Public Administration.

Quah, J. S. T. 1975. Administrative reform and development administration in Singapore: A comparative study of the Singapore Improvement Trust and the Housing and Development Board. PhD thesis, Florida State University, Tallahassee.

Quah, J. S. T. 1978. *Administrative and Legal Measures for Combating Bureaucratic Corruption in Singapore*. Singapore: Chopmen.

Quah, J. S. T. 1985. Statutory boards. In J. S. T. Quah, C. H. Chee and S. C. Meow (eds), *Government and Politics of Singapore*, 233–58. Singapore: Oxford University Press.

Quah, J. S. T. 1987. Public bureaucracy and policy implementation in Singapore. *Southeast Asian Journal of Social Science* 15(2): 77–95.

Quah, J. S. T. 1989. Singapore's experience in curbing corruption. In A. J. Heidenheimer, M. Johnston and V. LeVine (eds), *Political Corruption: A handbook*, 841–53. New Brunswick, NJ: Transaction Books.

Quah, J. S. T. 1994. Improving the efficiency and productivity of the Singapore civil service. In J. P. Burns (ed.), *Asian Civil Service Systems: Improving efficiency and productivity*, 152–85. Singapore: Times Academic Press.

Quah, J. S. T. 1996a. Decentralizing public personnel management: The case of the public sector in Singapore. In S. Kurosawa, T. Fujiwara and M. A. Reforma (eds), *New Trends in Public Administration for the Asia-Pacific Region: Decentralization*, 492–506. Tokyo: Local Autonomy College, Ministry of Home Affairs.

Quah, J. S. T. 1996b. Transforming the Singapore civil service for national development. In H. K. Asmerom and E. P. Reis (eds), *Democratization and Bureaucratic Neutrality*, 294–312. New York: St Martin's Press.

Quah, J. S. T. 2003. Singapore's anti-corruption strategy: Is this form of governance transferable to other Asian countries? In J. B. Kidd and F.-J. Richter (eds), *Corruption and Governance in Asia*, 180–97. Basingstoke, UK: Palgrave Macmillan.

Quah, J. S. T. 2010. *Public Administration Singapore Style*. Singapore: Talisman Publishing.

Salary Singapore 2011. *Civil Service Pay Scale in Singapore*. Singapore: Salary Singapore. Available from: salarysingapore.com/civil-service-pay-scale-in-singapore.html (accessed August 2011).

Saxena, N. C. 2011. *Virtuous Cycles: The Singapore public service and national development*. Singapore: United Nations Development Program.

Seah, C. M. 1971. Bureaucratic evolution and political change in an emerging nation: A case study of Singapore. PhD thesis, Victoria University of Manchester, Manchester.

Seah, C. M. 1999. The administrative state: Quo vadis? In L. Low (ed.), *Singapore: Towards a developed status*, 250–70. Singapore: Oxford University Press.

Sim, S. H. 1985. Training in the Singapore Administrative Service. B.Soc.Sci.(Hons) academic exercise, National University of Singapore, Singapore.

Simon, H. A. 1976. *Administrative Behaviour: A study of decision-making processes in administrative organisation*. New York: The Free Press.

Singapore Administrative Service (SAS) n.d.(a). *Continuous Training for the Administrative Service.* Singapore: Singapore Administrative Service. Available from: adminservice.gov.sg/AS/TrainDev/ (accessed 17 August 2011) (site discontinued).

Singapore Administrative Service (SAS) n.d.(b). Website. Available from: adminservice.gov.sg (accessed August 2011) (site discontinued).

Singapore Government 1955. *Singapore Annual Report 1954.* Singapore: Government Printing Office.

Singapore Government 1960. *Singapore Annual Report 1959.* Singapore: Government Printing Office.

Siow, V. 1998. Training in the Singapore civil service: The way forward. B.Soc.Sci.(Hons) academic exercise, National University of Singapore, Singapore.

Spann, R. N. 1973. *Public Administration in Australia.* Sydney: V. C. N. Blight.

Tan, S. S. 2007. *Goh Keng Swee: A portrait.* Singapore: Editions Didier Millet.

Teo, C. H. 2007. Ministerial Statement by Minister for Defence, Annex 1. *Parliamentary Debates Official Report,* 9 April. Singapore. Available from: nas.gov.sg/archivesonline/speeches/view-html?filename=20070409992.htm (accessed August 2011).

Teo, C. H. 2012. Closing speech by Deputy Minister, Coordinating Minister for National Security and Minister for Home Affairs, Parliamentary Debate on Political Salaries, 18 January. Available from: app.psd.gov.sg/data/DPM ClosingSpeech18 percent20Jan2012.pdf (accessed January 2012) (site discontinued).

Teo, E. 2001. The Singapore public service: A development-oriented promotion system, Presentation to Conference on Career Development of Public Servants in the 21st Century, Taipei, 19–20 December. Available from: app.psd.gov.sg/data/PSspeechTaipeiDec01SpCivilSvc.pdf (accessed August 2011) (site discontinued).

The Straits Times 2006. Don't knock us, our rice bowls are not iron. *The Straits Times*, 16 December.

Turnbull, C. M. 1989. *A History of Singapore, 1819–1988*. Singapore: Oxford University Press.

United Nations Public Administration Network (UNPAN) 2005. *Republic of Singapore: Public administration country profile*. New York: United Nations Public Administration Network. Available from: unpan1.un.org/intradoc/groups/public/documents /un/unpan023321.pdf (accessed August 2011).

United Nations Public Administration Network (UNPAN) 2006. *Definition of Basic Concepts and Terminologies in Governance and Public Administration*. New York: Committee of Experts on Public Administration. Available from: unpan1.un.org/intradoc/groups/ public/documents/un/unpan022332.pdf (accessed August 2011).

World Economic Forum 2011. *The Global Competitiveness Report 2010– 2011*. Geneva: World Economic Forum. Available from: weforum. org/docs/WEFGlobalCompetitivenessReport2009-10.pdf (accessed August 2011) (site discontinued).

10

Senior civil service training in Taiwan: Current concerns and future challenges

Su Tsai-Tsu and Liu Kun-I

Although Taiwanese Civil Service positions are still attractive to young people[1] due to their high job security and lucrative retirement pensions, the current civil service system does not enjoy as much power or receive as much respect from citizens as it did in the past.

To restore public confidence in the civil service system, the Taiwanese Government is determined to improve the calibre of the civil service, focusing particularly on top-level officials. The Examination Yuan (Branch), the highest authority responsible for the recruitment, selection and management of all civil service personnel, approved the Civil Service Reform Plan in June 2009. One major objective of the plan is to enhance the training of high-ranking officials to improve decision-making and leadership skills.

---

1   According to statistics released by the Ministry of Examination, the number of people who registered to take the Junior and Senior Civil Service Examinations reached a record high in 2010 and 2011. (wwwc.moex.gov.tw/main/content/wfrmContentLink.aspx?menu_id=268. Accessed 3 July 2012.)

The capacities of top-level civil service members are naturally held in higher regard than those of their subordinates in the bureaucratic hierarchy. People expect those serving at the top—the cadre of the civil service—to be equipped with strategic foresight and up-to-date knowledge to steer the nation through tough challenges. Hence in 2010, with the support of President, Ma Ying-jeou, and the Legislature, the Examination Yuan established the National Academy of Civil Service (NACS) under the Civil Service Protection and Training Commission (CSPTC).[2] With the training of high-level officials as one of its most important tasks, NACS has since designed and vigorously implemented a series of training programs.

Before the NACS was established, the Directorate-General of Personnel Administration (DGPA)[3] of the Executive Yuan was the main institution in charge of training high-level officials. In September 2009, not long after the Examination Yuan started its Civil Service Reform Plan, the DGPA also announced a comprehensive high-ranking training package. This package consisted essentially of two parts: 1) Top Executive Leadership seminars held domestically; and 2) Globalisation and Leadership workshops held abroad.

The establishment of the NACS and the Examination Yuan's desire to cultivate high-level officials appeared to be in competition with the DGPA. Although this unique two-track training system offers the benefits of healthy competition, such as increased budget allocation and richer curriculum design, the system may encounter problems relating to the unclear division of tasks and responsibilities, duplicated resource investments and the loss of economy of scale, given the small number of senior-ranked civil service members being trained. The result is continuing debate about the benefits and costs of duplication and overlap in administrative organisations (Landau 1969, 1991; Felsenthal 1980; Knott and Miller 1987; Lerner 1987).

---

2   The NACS was not a new institute. Its antecedent is the National Civil Service Institute (NCSI), which was founded in 1999 under the supervision of the CSPTC of the Examination Yuan. It was restructured, up-scaled and renamed NACS in 2000 and designed to focus on training high-level civil servants and to offer lifelong learning programs and international exchanges for civil servants.
3   The antecedent organisation of the DGPA, the Central Public Administration, was established in 1967 and was responsible for the overall personnel administration of all the ministries and agencies under the Executive Yuan. In February 2012, the Central Public Administration was upgraded to the Directorate-General of Personnel Administration as part of a larger governmental reorganisation.

Is it desirable to maintain this duplication in the senior service training system in Taiwan? Does it breed problems of coordination and result in redundancy and waste of resources or does it foster healthy competition and restore capacity for innovation? Under this centralised dual-track training system, what types of training curricula are provided to senior civil service members, and are they adequate to help senior civil servants cope with complex issues in our newly democratised and globalised society? So far, little effort has been made in academic circles to address these questions.

This chapter begins with an overview of Taiwan's senior civil service system. It then explains the dual-track training system and describes the core training programs developed for high-level officials by the Examination Yuan and Executive Yuan. Finally, the chapter summarises recent changes in executive civil service training and concludes with a discussion of the future challenges facing this dual-track training system.

Overview of the senior civil service

Before the twenty-first century, an effective civil service system was considered the backbone of the administrative machinery and was credited for the outstanding economic performance that led to Taiwan becoming one of the four 'Asian Dragons'[4] by the end of the 1990s (Wade 1990; Clark 2000; Cheung 2005). In the past decade, however, harsh challenges including worldwide financial crises, national disasters, food insecurity, environmental degradation and other social and economic problems related to globalisation have brought a great deal of frustration to the Taiwanese Civil Service. Evidence suggests that in the face of rising public dissatisfaction, the once competent Taiwanese Civil Service has degenerated into bureaucratic passivity and has gradually decreased its leadership and initiative in policymaking (Tan 2000; Tang 2004; Berman et al. 2012).

---

4   The four 'Asian Dragons' refers to Taiwan, Singapore, South Korea and Hong Kong. These four economies maintained exceptionally high economic growth rates between the 1960s and the 1990s.

While the sudden international economic uncertainties and a fast-changing globalised world have understandably affected the responsiveness of civil servants in their efforts to cope with such dynamic changes in Taiwan, scholars have pointed out that the island's democratisation process in the past two decades is also responsible for declining bureaucratic capacity (Tan 2000; Painter 2004). Under the one-party dominant authoritarian regime lasting from the late 1940s to the late 1980s, the working environment of Taiwan's civil servants was mostly insulated from electoral politics. Civil servants during that period enjoyed a relatively high degree of autonomy and were not under much public pressure or legislative oversight in making and implementing policies. Entering the post-democratisation era, however—particularly after two major political regime changes in the 2000 and 2008 presidential elections—civil servants found themselves losing party patrons and forced to answer to various political pressures (Tan 2000: 49). Demanding citizens, aggressive legislators, rent-seeking interest groups and a nosey mass media have had the combined effect of transforming the once insulated bureaucratic organisation into a fishbowl. Adjustment to the new politics has compromised the effectiveness of the civil service.

There are 14 grades of civil service positions across three ranks:

- elementary (G1–5)
- junior (G6–9)
- senior (G10–14).

This chapter relates to training for high-level officials or top civil servants—that is, grade 10–14 civil servants. However, as will be explained later, G9 civil servants are in some cases included in training.

The most important civil service examinations in Taiwan include the elementary, junior and senior examinations for recruiting ordinary administrative personnel.[5] On passing the elementary examination, for which there are no educational prerequisites, candidates are assigned to a G1 position. The junior examination requires at least a high school

---

5   While the elementary, junior and senior examinations are designed for recruiting ordinary administrative personnel, another important type of civil service examination is the Special Examination, which is designed to recruit manpower for government agencies requiring personnel with specialised capacities (such as diplomats, national security personnel, prosecutors and judges) or to recruit from disadvantaged groups including disabled and indigenous peoples.

education, and those who pass this examination are assigned a G3 position. The senior examination is divided into three levels, with Level 1 requiring a bachelor degree, Level 2 a master's degree and Level 3 a doctorate. Those who pass Levels 1, 2 or 3 of the senior examination are assigned to G6, G7 and G9 positions respectively. Currently, there is no civil service examination placing candidates directly into senior positions (G10 or higher).

Table 10.1 displays the ranking structure of the Taiwanese Civil Service and its composition. By the end of 2011, there were 342,643 civil servants in Taiwan.[6] Among them, 121,935 were elementary-rank personnel, 208,188 were classified as junior rank and 12,520 were in the senior ranks, representing 35.6 per cent, 60.8 per cent and 3.7 per cent, respectively, of the entire civil service. As expected, senior-rank civil servants comprise the smallest group of all three ranks and yet they are key figures in the bureaucracy who wield great power and greatly impact the effectiveness of public policies. Undoubtedly, the government takes the training of senior personnel seriously despite their relatively small number.

Table 10.1: Composition of the Taiwanese Civil Service (as at the end of 2011)

Rank	Grade	Number of people	Percentage
Elementary	G1–G5	121,935	35.6%
Junior	G6–G9	208,188	60.8%
Senior	G10–G14	12,520	3.7%
Total		342,643	100.0%

Source: Calculated from official statistics released by the Ministry of Civil Service (mocs.gov. tw/pages/detail.aspx?Node=1038&Page=3620&Index=4. Accessed 3 July 2012).

With such high expectations imposed on them, senior-rank officials are the focus of training and development. Another reason to invest more in Taiwan's top-level personnel training is the aforementioned closed employment system for senior civil servants. Generally speaking, the current civil service recruiting system in Taiwan is flexible enough to encourage outsiders from the private sector to

6   The civil servants listed in Table 10.1 include personnel working in central and local governments. This includes civil servants working in administrative offices, public enterprises, hygiene and medical services, and public schools. Political appointees, elected agency chiefs and public school teachers are excluded.

enter the public sector at elementary and junior ranks. As indicated previously, depending on the type of civil service examination passed, new public sector entrants typically enter at G1, G3, G6, G7 or G9 grade. Yet as Su (2010: 614) points out, with a few exceptions, senior-rank positions (G10–G14) are not open to individuals outside the civil service.[7] Instead, positions categorised G10 or higher can be reached only through regular promotion processes inside the bureaucracy for existing civil servants. Consequently, almost all senior civil servants must serve in the bureaucracy for years before reaching executive level. Though this lengthy process may result in the senior civil service being an experienced team, many lose their ambition and innovation after years of immersion in rigid and tedious red tape (Shih 2006). Therefore, compared with their more diversified junior colleagues in the public sector, the homogeneous senior-rank officials are in greater need of training and development.

Dual-track training system

Taiwan's unique dual-track training system for senior civil service members has much to do with its complex constitutional and political arrangements. In the spirit of the five-power constitution, which was created by founding father, Dr Sun Yat-sen, the five Central Government branches—the Executive Yuan, Legislative Yuan, Judicial Yuan, Examination Yuan and Control Yuan—are independent and form a system of checks and balances. Among them, the Examination Yuan and Executive Yuan share power and responsibility for the establishment and maintenance of a competent civil service system. Specifically, the two major institutions in charge of senior civil service training are: 1) the NACS of the CSPTC under the Examination Yuan; and 2) the Civil Service Development Institute (CSDI) of DGPA under the Executive Yuan. The bilateral relationship between the two training institutions is shown in Figure 10.1.

---

7   Before 1994, college professors and citizens holding overseas graduate degrees were eligible to compete in the Senior Special Civil Service Examination, which was held infrequently. After passing the exam, the individual would be assigned to a G10 posting and would become a senior-ranked civil servant. The qualification rate for this Senior Special Examination between 1968 and 1988 was approximately 25 per cent, with 1,946 people competing and 503 passing the examination. The examination—criticised as unfair and often tailor-made for the privileged—was abolished in 1994. For a detailed discussion, see Shiau (2006).

| Examination Yuan | Civil Service Protection and Training Commission (CSPTC) | National Academy of Civil Service (NACS) |

| Executive Yuan | Directorate-General of Personnel Administration (DGPA) | Civil Service Development Institute (CSDI) |
| | Individual ministries and agencies | Agency-based training centres |

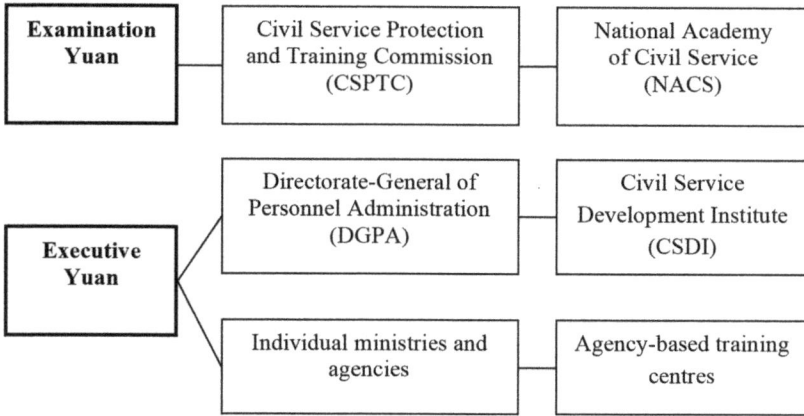

Figure 10.1: Senior-rank civil service training institutions
Source: Created by the author.

According to the 1946 Constitution, the Examination Yuan is the independent authority in charge of making and implementing public personnel policies, including civil service training. However, aiming to strengthen the dominance and influence of executive power, the then ruling party established the Central Personnel Administration (renamed the DGPA in 2012 as part of a larger governmental reorganisation) under the Executive Yuan in 1967. Later, after constitutional amendments and rounds of negotiations between the Executive and Examination yuans, a line was drawn to divide jurisdiction for personnel training between the two branches. The agreement at that time was that the Examination Yuan would focus on training new recruits, rank promotion and political neutrality, while the training of senior servants would be the responsibility of the Executive Yuan, except for those who served in non-executive branches (CSPTC 2000). Specifically, in the jurisdiction of high-ranking personnel training, the Executive Yuan assumed responsibility for public employees affiliated with the Executive Yuan, whereas the Examination Yuan was in charge of training for top officials employed by the other four branches, including the Examination Yuan, Legislative Yuan, Control Yuan and Judicial Yuan. The Executive Yuan is the largest of the five branches in terms of employee size: more than 90 per cent of civil servants work in the Executive Yuan, meaning the Examination Yuan would be implementing top-level civil service training for only

10 per cent of employees. Therefore, it is clear that, at least before the establishment of NACS of the Examination Yuan, the Executive Yuan played a much more important role in training senior civil servants.

To carry out the training assignments agreed on through negotiations and constitutional amendments, the DGPA of the Executive Yuan set up the CSDI in 1996 and the CSPTC of the Examination Yuan founded the National Civil Service Training Institute in 1999, which was restructured and upgraded to the NACS in 2010. Before 2000, each training institution had its own jurisdiction with regards to training senior civil servants. The division between the Executive and Examination yuans with regards to senior civil service training was clear and unambiguous and there was little duplication or overlap.

In late 2008, however, the new members of the Examination Yuan and its new president, John Kuan, began to change the operation of this dual yet parallel training system.[8] At that time, the Global Financial Crisis and the resulting economic recession hit the nation hard, and concerns about an incompetent civil service were widespread in society. Hence, with the support of President Ma and the Legislative Yuan, the Examination Yuan successfully modified the CSPTC Organisation Law in 2009, adding medium- and long-term development training for high-level civil servants to the list of its organisational responsibilities. Although the definition and essence of 'medium- and long-term development training' are somewhat ambiguous, the new clause in the CSPTC Organisation Law clearly expands the training jurisdiction for the CSPTC of the Examination Yuan. Previously, the Examination Yuan trained only senior-rank personnel serving in non-executive branches—representing less than 10 per cent of total senior personnel. Now, it has an enlarged jurisdiction reaching all five branches, so long as the program is considered mid- or long-term development training. Essentially, the old parallel dual-track training system—in which two training authorities had different jurisdictions for training and little duplication—has been changed to an overlapping dual-track system. The two training authorities may now target the same group of senior civil servants as potential trainees.

---

8   The Examination Yuan has a president, vice-president and 19 members, all of whom are special appointees nominated by the nation's President. These individuals are appointed to six-year terms on confirmation by the Legislative Yuan. All policies and major issues are deliberated and decided on jointly by members at Examination Yuan Council meetings.

In anticipation of the expanded jurisdiction and a higher training demand, in 2010 the Examination Yuan quickly incorporated the existing NCSI into the NACS. To upgrade the status and influence of the NACS, the chief commissioner of the CSPTC was appointed president of the NACS. This restructuring and empowerment of the NACS is expected to shrink the wide disparity in training capacity between top officials in the Executive and Examination yuans.

Not all civil servants are trained by the NACS or DGPA. As shown in Figure 10.1, in addition to the centralised training provided to senior civil servants by the NACS and DGPA, many ministries and agencies have their own training institutions that cater to their specific portfolio needs and design training curricula that are closely aligned with the ministries' or agencies' goals and responsibilities. For example, judges and prosecutors, police investigators, tax officers, foreign service personnel, auditing officers and others have their own designated training centres that offer agency-based courses. Nevertheless, these agency-based training centres offer numerous and varied training courses, making it difficult to make meaningful comparisons across agencies. Moreover, they usually focus more on elementary- and junior-rank training and give less attention to the training of high-level civil servants. In consideration of these factors, agency-based training will be excluded from discussion in this chapter.

Training by the DGPA of the Executive Yuan

Before the Examination Yuan established the NACS, most training for senior civil servants in Taiwan was conducted by the DGPA under the Executive Yuan. This section summarises the training programs provided to senior civil servants by the DGPA in recent years. These programs can be grouped into three categories:

- domestic training
- overseas training
- policy workshops.

DGPA domestic training programs

Table 10.2 lists the major domestic training programs organised regularly by the DGPA, including the National Affairs Workshop, Visionary Workshop, Senior Leadership Workshop and Management Excellence Workshop. Each workshop accepts up to 40 trainees—a slightly larger number of participants than the workshops offered by the NACS, where class sizes average 20–30 trainees.

While the NACS of the Examination Yuan restricts its senior service training programs to public officials ranked G10 or higher, the DGPA targets a wider trainee group for the development of executive leadership. The DGPA allows mid-level civil servants about to enter the senior ranks to sit in the same workshop as senior-ranked personnel. As shown in Table 10.2, the Management Excellence Workshop provided by the DGPA accepts trainees ranked G9 or higher. The Management Excellence Workshop is a large training program, with 3,400 mid- to high-level civil servants completing the program in 2009 alone. Civil servants ranked G9 have to pass a rank-promotion civil service exam before reaching G10 grade and being officially counted as senior-ranked civil servants. Allowing G9 personnel likely to enter the senior rank to exchange ideas with their senior colleagues is supposed to benefit both groups. Civil servants ranked G9 are also allowed to participate in overseas training programs offered by the DGPA; this will be discussed later in this chapter. By including G9 personnel in the target group of senior civil service training, the DGPA substantially increases its scope of potential trainees.

Table 10.2: Training programs provided by the DGPA

Trainee's rank	Training programs	Number of trainees	Training duration
G12 or above	National Affairs Workshop	Two workshops per year and 40 trainees per workshop	Every Thursday to Saturday for six weeks
G12 or above	Visionary Leadership Workshop	One workshop every two years	Two days
G11 or above	Senior Leadership Workshop	One workshop each year; 40 trainees each workshop, with a minimum of 10 female trainees	Every Thursday to Saturday for five weeks
G9 or above	Management Excellence Workshop	One workshop every two years	Two days

Source: Fang (2009).

DGPA overseas training programs

Overseas training for high-level officials has existed for a long time, but it was not until 2008 that the budget allocated for it was substantially increased. In an effort to better connect the knowledge and capacity of high-level civil servants to those on the international scene, the DGPA decided to invest more financial resources in overseas training. A total of 15 groups with more than 500 participants ranked G9 or higher were sent abroad between 2008 and 2010 (Fang 2010: 61–2). Target institutions for overseas cooperation include the John F. Kennedy School of Government at Harvard University, George Washington University, University of Cambridge, London School of Economics and Political Science, Royal Institute of Public Administration in the United Kingdom, Waseda University and the Lee Kuan Yew School of Public Policy at the National University of Singapore. Since 2011, the overseas training program has expanded to accommodate more G9–G14 civil servants for short-term studies. Not only have more foreign institutions been selected as training partners (for instance, the College of Europe in Bruges), but also the DGPA has relaunched a program to send mid- to high-level civil servants to study masters or doctoral degrees abroad (the original program was abolished 18 years ago before being restarted in 2011).

DGPA policy workshops

In addition to regular domestic programs and various overseas training programs, the DGPA occasionally arranges policy workshops to build necessary competencies for senior civil servants to increase their effectiveness in implementing important policy initiatives. For example, in 2010, 759 trainees ranked G12 and serving as department heads or in higher positions attended the Workshop of Contemporary National Policies (Examination Yuan 2012: 38).

In its early years, the DGPA's training for senior civil servants was not organised in a systematic way; instead most programs were arranged freely or even randomly in accordance with the political and economic needs of the moment. They were mostly conducted under the direction of the Executive Yuan or through proactive planning by the DGPA. The number of workshops for each year was neither fixed nor pre-planned, and some often faced the possibility of discontinuation after a few years of operation. However, the types and number of training programs designed for senior officials have been increasingly streamlined in recent years, revealing the DGPA's intention to continue its lead and influence in training senior civil service members under the current dual-track training system.

Training by the CSPTC of the Examination Yuan

In addition to the DGPA of the Executive Yuan, the CSPTC of the Examination Yuan is another important authority in charge of civil service training. The senior civil service training provided by the CSPTC can be divided into two stages. The first stage started in 1996 when the CSPTC was established. During that period the CSPTC was responsible for training senior civil servants affiliated with non-executive branches only—namely, the Examination Yuan, Legislative Yuan, Judicial Yuan and Control Yuan. It administered a Senior Executive Training Program designed for G12 and G13 civil servants between 1999 and 2004. In total, 131 trainees attended this program, which required weekly attendance of three days for five weeks.

The CSPTC also carried out six Core Competency Seminars each year for G11–G13 bureaucrats from 2005 to 2008. A total of 376 bureaucrats were trained in this program. The six seminars focused on six different core management competencies: innovative vision, strategic analysis, administrative reform, crisis management, interagency coordination and performance management. Each seminar focused on one core competency and took two days to complete. Trainees had to complete all six seminars to receive a certificate. While both programs were well received by high-ranking trainees, a survey indicated that trainees preferred Core Competency Seminars to the Senior Executive Training Program due to the former's shorter training period (Yao 2009: 28). This corroborates the results of other studies that have found that there is little incentive for senior officials to attend training sessions due to their heavy workload (Lai 2011: 44).

The second training stage began in 2010 when the CSPTC assumed responsibility for senior civil servants' medium- and long-term development training and set up the NACS in accordance with the revised Organisational Law. The CSPTC first conducted a survey of the core abilities of senior civil servants, the results of which provided a clearer picture of the core competencies that senior civil servants with different grades needed to function properly. Then the CSPTC invited scholars and experts to develop course modules and came up with its major training program, the Take-Off Program for Senior Civil Service 100 (or 'TOP 100').[9] The TOP 100 program is arranged into three classes (see Table 10.3). The Management Development Training class is offered to civil servants ranked G10 or G11, and emphasises the enrichment of management capabilities. The course designed for officials ranked G12 to G13 is the Leadership Development Training class, which mainly reinforces leadership capabilities. Civil servants ranked G13 to G14 join the Strategy Development Training class, which focuses on cultivating strategic planning capabilities. The TOP 100 was piloted in 2010 and officially established in 2011. Table 10.3 provides the numbers of program trainees for 2010 and 2011. Acknowledging a low representation of female participants in the first year, efforts were made to increase female participation. Table 10.3 indicates that the percentage of female trainees increased from 19 per cent (11 of 58 trainees) in 2010 to 39 per cent (22 of 56 trainees) in 2012.

Table 10.3: Number of TOP 100 trainees by sex, 2010–11

	Management Development Training (G10–G11)			Leadership Development Training (G12–G13)			Strategy Development Training (G13–G14)		
	Total	Male	Female	Total	Male	Female	Total	Male	Female
2010	25	20	5	24	20	4	9	7	2
2011	33	22	11	16	10	6	7	2	5
Total	58	42	16	40	30	10	16	9	7

Source: Internal data provided by the NACS.

The TOP 100 training program adopts the approach of assessment centres and provides trainees with comprehensive feedback—the first time such an approach has been systematically adopted in the nation's civil service training. The objective of this time-consuming

9 For more details of the TOP 100 program, see nacs.gov.tw/english/02_projects/02_details.asp?ID=JNOOIRDMONE (accessed 3 July 2012).

approach is to help trainees understand the gaps in their proficiencies and to recognise the improvements needed through feedback from supervisors, subordinates and peers.

Specifically, the TOP 100 consists of three stages: *pre-training*, *in-training* and *post-training*. During the *pre-training* period, camp activities are designed to help trainees understand the purpose of training and build the consensus crucial for successful training. *In-training*—the second stage and the core of the TOP 100 programs—covers 150 hours of courses offered domestically and internationally.[10] Specifically, it contains 100 hours of core competency courses divided evenly between domestic and foreign study programs, with the remaining 50 hours assigned to general courses. Additionally, depending on need, there may be a customised course of up to 30 hours for individual trainees. *In-training* in either core competency or general courses relies heavily on case studies, role-play and simulation, field trips and workshops. The last stage of the TOP 100 program is *post-training*, which is based on recurring training to strengthen the effectiveness of *in-training*. After completing *in-training*, trainees are periodically invited to attend keynote speeches and experience-sharing meetings to stay up-to-date on changes in society and international affairs.

Recent developments

With such a variety of training programs in place, the current quality of senior civil service training in Taiwan is unprecedented in the nation's history. This section summarises the characteristics of the developments observed in Taiwanese senior civil service training in recent years.

First, in designing training curricula for top officials, training authorities, including the Examination and the Executive yuans, have placed a high priority on the acquisition of global vision and knowledge of international affairs. Not only have overseas training

---

10 The overseas training locations feature notable institutes such as the École Nationale d'Administration (National School of Administration) in France, the National School of Government (NSG) in the United Kingdom, the International Institute for Management Development in Switzerland and the Bundesakademie für öffentliche Verwaltung (BAköV) (Federal Academy of Public Administration) in Germany.

programs blossomed, but also domestic training courses emphasise brainstorming ideas and cultivating experience under a globalisation framework.

Taiwanese civil servants have encountered difficulties in the global arena in the past few decades due to two significant setbacks in Taiwan's diplomatic history. The first was Taiwan's expulsion from the United Nations, while the second was the end of its formal diplomatic relationship with the United States in 1979, both of which led to diplomatic isolation. In many official meetings and activities with international society and organisations, civil servants from Taiwan are excluded from participation. As a result, Taiwanese civil servants are comparatively lacking in knowledge of and experience in handling international affairs. Although Taiwan's government strives to overcome this limitation through economic and trade relationships, cultural exchanges and other non-official activities, this international reality has negatively influenced the international vision and ability of Taiwanese civil servants. Therefore, investing more resources and manpower is necessary and timely to enhance top officials' connection with the international community through effective training.

Another observation is the active development of diverse training modes and methods. Traditional training courses for senior civil servants are lecture based and do not contain diverse teaching methods. Presently, both the NACS and the DGPA closely follow new trends in training methods. In addition to focused lectures, methods such as group discussions, case analysis, benchmark learning, role-playing, simulations and digital learning are all actively employed in training. Although trainees perceive greater learning pressures, they generally support the diversification of training methods.

The third recent development in training Taiwan's top-level officials is that there have been more scientific methods used to evaluate and assess training demand and effectiveness. Previously, there was no demand assessment whatsoever to understand the needs of trainees. Although training institutions made efforts to evaluate the effectiveness of their programs, they relied solely on customer satisfaction surveys. Thus, the types and amounts of feedback data that could be gathered were limited. Even though the results of surveys usually showed good levels of satisfaction, concerns regarding ineffective training remained widespread. Additionally, satisfaction surveys were generally administered immediately after the training, whereas the effectiveness of training may be perceived or may emerge after some time has passed. For instance, Warr et al. (1970) propose that outcome evaluation of training should focus on the achievements gained from the activity, to be assessed at three levels: a) immediate; b) intermediate; and c) ultimate evaluation. Therefore, post-training tracking assessments are necessary to overcome the limitations of gathering information through satisfaction surveys. In response, the NACS established the Assessment and Development Centre as one of its key internal organisations. The centre attempts to conduct working capability assessments of trainees after training. Analysis reports on their capabilities before and after training are then provided to trainees and a customised individual follow-up program is offered to reinforce the effectiveness of training.[11]

The more active use of the public–private partnership (PPP) model is another notable development of the current training system. From the outset, both the NACS and the DGPA have relied substantially on individuals from universities and the business sector to serve as instructors of training courses. Visits to comparable private enterprise organisations are also frequently arranged for trainees. Nevertheless, exchanges with private enterprises, think tanks and universities have grown even more important in recent years. Both the NACS and the DGPA emphasise making strategic alliances with domestic and foreign training institutes, universities, non-profit organisations and enterprises for greater interchange with and connection to the outside world. In addition to jointly organising or sponsoring a wide range of conferences, seminars and workshops with universities and foundations, training institutions have started several other public–private collaborations. For example, the DGPA has outsourced many activities, including contracting the management of its CSDI facilities to a private corporation and outsourcing to universities evening classes for civil servants' advanced studies. Another example is in the TOP 100 program designed by the NACS, which regularly invites university professors and leaders of non-profit organisations or businesses to attend training sessions with civil servants, with the aim of establishing a platform for public–private interchanges.

---

11   The Assessment and Development Centre is a new organisation. It is too early to conclude whether it is well equipped to successfully design and implement customised individual follow-up programs.

Apart from the above-mentioned PPP models employed in the training of high-ranking officials, the government also encourages senior civil servants to study for course credits or academic degrees in universities by offering tuition subsidies and official study leave. As a result, there has been a surge in the number of academic organisations offering masters programs for public employees. For example, more than 80 per cent of the students enrolled in the Executive Master of Public Administration program of the National Taiwan University in the past 12 years have been civil servants; of these, more than one-third have been senior-ranked civil servants. It is expected that the wide adoption of PPP models by centralised training authorities will not only save money and manpower for the government, but also, more importantly, result in more flexibility and greater effectiveness in civil service training.

The fifth characteristic of recent developments in senior civil service training is an increase in female trainees. Though the increase is not significant, it is nonetheless encouraging. Studies show that it takes much more effort for female civil servants to be promoted in the public sector due to the well-known 'glass ceiling' that subtly blocks their advancement (Naff 1994). Official civil service statistics from 2011 revealed that although female civil servants outnumbered male civil servants in administrative agencies, with females comprising 50.4 per cent and males 49.6 per cent, the ratio of females who reached senior rank was only 26.9 per cent to the 73.1 per cent of male senior civil servants (MOCS 2012). Nevertheless, as the gender gap in educational achievements continues to shrink and awareness of women's rights increases in Taiwan, we are optimistic that the current gender inequality in the civil service will gradually improve (Su 2010: 612). In fact, this change is already reflected in the training of senior civil servants. In the past few years, the government has intensified efforts to train and develop high-ranking female officials. For instance, the Executive Yuan offered a leadership development workshop exclusively for female senior civil servants. The TOP 100 program is also attentive to the ratio of female to male trainees during its selection process.

The final development worth mentioning is the repeated emphasis on enhancing top officials' communication skills with the mass media through government training. For decades before the end of martial law, Taiwan's authoritarian government controlled the media.

However, since the 1990s, aggressive growth in the media industry, along with the dynamic development of political and societal forces, has resulted in rapid changes in Taiwan's media environment (Hong 1999; Rawnsley 2007; Kao 2010). The rapid expansion of the media has led to oversupply, excessive competition and aggressiveness in industry practices. It seems that a lack of journalistic ethics and standards sometimes triggers unnecessary tensions between the bureaucracy, the media and the public. There have been many instances in which, due to poor or improper communication with the media, crucial public policy initiatives have failed to win public support and public officials have been forced to step down from their positions. Hence, training institutions have begun to invite experts who specialise in dealing with the media to offer tips and share experiences with senior civil servants. Thus, communicating with the media has become a new type of core competency for senior civil servants, a skill that was not previously considered important in the old insulated bureaucratic environment.

Future challenges and prospects

Although favourable improvements have been made to training senior civil servants in Taiwan under the active efforts of the NACS and DGPA, three important challenges remain. The first results from the competition and cooperation of the unique dual-track training system. Before the CSPTC of the Examination Yuan amended its *Organisation Act* in 2009, the jurisdiction of senior civil servants who could be trained by the CSPTC did not include subordinate organisations under the Executive Yuan. Instead, its training jurisdiction was restricted to personnel employed by the Examination, Legislative, Judicial and Control yuans. Therefore, its supply of potential trainees was rather limited, creating an obstacle in the establishment of a systematic training mechanism for senior civil servants. After the Act was amended, the CSPTC acquired a legal basis for taking charge of the medium- to long-term development training of senior civil servants, which caused an overlap in training targets with the Executive Yuan. Since the cohort of senior civil servants in Taiwan is small, the overlap in training targets has generated some subtle competition between the two training authorities.

Therefore, the imminent challenge is how to effectively coordinate training activities offered by the two institutions. Presently, senior civil servants are trained separately by the Executive and Examination yuans, which by constitutional authority are independent of each other and have fixed boundaries. Thus, an effective mechanism of coordination and communication between the two training institutions—whether formal or informal—is not easily established. The goal of reducing the costs of negotiation and coordination to ensure that the training programs provided by both institutions are mutually complementary and effective is sometimes difficult to achieve. In fact, the mechanism in place is currently claimed to be ineffective (Examination Yuan 2012: 24).

There is no denying that the dual-track system in Taiwan has created a number of benefits due to healthy competition, and institutions being more active and engaged in training endeavours. Nevertheless, in the future, because of the intrinsic departmental rivalry and possibly poor coordination, the dual-track system may lead to resource wastage in the form of duplicated courses or repetitive personnel training. In particular, the budgetary resources allocated to training are unlikely to increase significantly due to the huge fiscal pressures the government faces. When the dual-track system divides these limited resources between the two institutions, it may hinder the utilisation of the advantages of the economies of scale. As such, it will be an important, though challenging, task for the Examination and Executive yuans to break through each other's boundaries and reduce coordination costs to better integrate training resources and maximise the effectiveness of senior civil servant training.

The second challenge faced by the Taiwanese Government is strengthening the connection between training performance and career advancement. Studies indicate that, if successful completion of a training program has minimal correlation with work incentives such as recognition, pay scale and job promotion, civil servants' motivation to participate in training decreases (Noe 1986; Clark et al. 1993; Huque and Vyas 2008). In Taiwan, promotion-related training for elementary to junior ranks and junior to senior ranks offers a strong incentive for bureaucrats in the elementary and junior ranks to participate in training. By law, they cannot advance further in the bureaucratic system without completing promotion-related training programs. However, for senior civil servants, training is almost entirely unrelated to future job assignment or promotion. Apart from applying newly acquired skills in the work setting, their good performance in training programs leads to little desirable reward. Therefore, the likelihood that senior civil servants will be willing to squeeze time out of their busy work schedules to voluntarily attend training programs is low.

In response to top officials' unwillingness to participate in training, the Examination Yuan has formulated a plan to integrate the TOP 100 program into future job assignments. According to the plan, top officials ranked G10 and G11 can be recommended to participate in Management Development Training. On successful completion of training, participants will be included in the talent pool for future G12-rank promotions. Similarly, civil servants ranked G12 and G13 who have completed Leadership Development Training and civil servants ranked G13 and G14 who have completed Strategy Development Training will qualify for the Senior Civil Service Special Management System (SCSSMS), giving them priority for promotion into top positions in ministries or agencies.

However, the SCSSMS planned by the Examination Yuan involves the right of appointment by the leaders of the ministry or agency. Presently, more than 98 per cent of senior civil servants serve in the Executive Yuan and its constituent organisations, which are outside the scope of authority of the Examination Yuan. To put the idea of the SCSSMS into practice requires the consent and cooperation of the Executive Yuan. It may take some time before a consensus is reached and the plan implemented. This once again illustrates the unavoidable coordination costs involved in the current dual-track system of civil servant training.

The final challenge is the question of how to ensure value for money in the training system. This is undoubtedly an issue facing training institutions all over the world. As indicated earlier, increasingly more scientific methods have attempted to evaluate the effectiveness of training for senior civil servants in Taiwan. However, these attempts are still in their early stages. Since civil servants are trained to answer to the public and be accountable for their behaviour and decisions, training institutions must also have the responsibility to demonstrate that their services offer value for money. For instance, the overseas learning emphasised by both the NACS and the DGPA is costly. Is there a systematic tracking system in place to objectively compare the costs and benefits of domestic and overseas programs? It is clear that only when value for money is proved can concerns about the legitimacy of the current dual-track training system be put to rest.

Conclusion

The democratisation and globalisation experienced in Taiwan in past years have produced bureaucratic passivity and a decline in executive leadership. As a result, better and more effective training for senior public servants has become essential for improving national competitiveness. Through competition between two training authorities—the NACS of the Examination Yuan and the DGPA of the Executive Yuan—the scale of top civil service training in Taiwan has risen to unprecedented levels in recent years. A variety of training programs, both domestic and overseas, is offered. While global perspective, strategic management and policy innovation are the most essential themes for training courses, communicating effectively with a media industry that is particularly hard to deal with is considered a new core competency for top-ranking officials in this newly democratised society.

In addition to two common challenges often encountered by other countries—creating a stronger link between training and job assignment and demonstrating value for money for training programs—Taiwan has faced a unique challenge in the form of its dual-track training system, coordination of which must be improved. As argued by Landau (1991), a two-organisation arrangement does not necessarily produce waste or duplication. Instead, it may bring more reliability into a system. So far, we have witnessed healthy competition between the NACS and the DGPA, resulting in:

1. the provision of more systemised training programs
2. an emphasis on global vision and international connection
3. the adoption of diverse training modes and methods
4. the use of scientific methods in the assessment of demand and training effectiveness
5. the inclusion of different resources in broader Taiwanese society to form public–private partnerships in training
6. the participation of more female trainees.

Nevertheless, as an exploratory study, this chapter does not conclude that the current dual-track training system is the best institutional choice for training Taiwanese senior civil servants. How significant are the communication and coordination costs incurred under this dual-track system? Will it save more money if the training authority has the power to combine all budgetary resources so as to fully utilise the benefits of an economy of scale? These types of questions await further study. In the meantime, given the reality that the five-power constitution will continue for years to come in Taiwan and that its accompanying dual-track civil service training system is also unlikely to change in the foreseeable future, it is essential to build an effective mechanism for responsibility sharing and better coordination between the two training authorities.

References

Berman, E. M., Chen, D.-Y. and Huang, T.-Y. 2012. Public agency leadership: The impact of informal understandings with political appointees on perceived agency innovation in Taiwan. *Journal of Public Administration*: 1–22.

Cheung, A. B. 2005. The politics of administrative reforms in Asia: Paradigms and legacies, paths and diversities. *Governance* 18(2): 257–82.

Civil Service Protection and Training Commission (CSPTC) 2000. *Special Report on the Establishment of CSPTC*. [In Chinese]. Taipei: Civil Service Protection and Training Commission.

Clark, C. 2000. Democracy, bureaucracy, and state capacity in Taiwan. *International Journal of Public Administration* 23(10): 1833–53.

Clark, C. S., Dobbins, G. H. and Ladd, R. T. 1993. Exploratory field study of training motivation: Influence of involvement, credibility, and transfer climate. *Group & Organisation Management* 18: 292–307.

Examination Yuan 2012. *The Examination Yuan's Plan for the Improvement of Civil Service Training*. [In Chinese]. Taipei: The Examination Yuan.

Fang, S.-W. 2009. The training of mid to high level civil servants in the Executive Yuan: Current status and future prospects. [In Chinese]. *Personnel Monthly* 49(4): 15–22.

Fang, S.-W. 2010. The Executive Yuan's plan of civil service training. [In Chinese]. *Personnel Monthly* 51(3): 58–64.

Felsenthal, D. S. 1980. Applying the redundancy concept to administrative organisations. *Public Administration Review* 40: 247–52.

Hong, J. 1999. Globalization and change in Taiwan's media: The Interplay of political and economic forces. *Asian Journal of Communication* 9(2): 39–59.

Huque, A. and Vyas, L. 2008. Expectations and performance: Assessment of public service training in Hong Kong. *International Journal of Human Resource Management* 19(1): 188–204.

Kao, S.-C. 2010. Media culture in Taiwan: The case of Taiwanese nationalism. Paper presented at the 18th Biennial Conference of the Asian Studies Association of Australia, Adelaide, 5–8 July.

Knott, J. H. and Miller, G. J. 1987. *Reforming Bureaucracy: The politics of institutional choice*. Englewood Cliffs, NJ: Prentice-Hall.

Lai, F.-Y. 2011. The transformation of senior civil service training in a globalized world. [In Chinese]. *Forum on Training and Development* 130: 40–58.

Landau, M. 1969. Redundancy, rationality and the problem of duplication and overlap. *Public Administration Review* 29(4): 346–58.

Landau, M. 1991. On multi-organisational systems in public administration. *Journal of Public Administration* 1(January): 5–18.

Lerner, A. W. 1987. There is more than one way to be redundant. *Administration and Society* 18(3): 334–59.

Ministry of Civil Service of the Republic of China (Taiwan) (MOCS) 2012. Table 19: Number of civil servants of administration agency (end of 2011). *All Civil Services Database*. Taipei: MOCS. Available from: mocs.gov.tw/pages/detail.aspx?Node=1038&Page=3620&Index=4 (accessed 3 July 2012) (site discontinued).

Naff, K. C. 1994. Through the glass ceiling: Prospects for the advancement of women in the federal civil service. *Public Administration Review* 54(6): 507–14.

Noe, R. A. 1986. Trainees' attributes and attitudes: Neglected influences on training effectiveness. *Academy of Management Review* 11(4): 736–49.

Painter, M. 2004. The politics of administrative reform in East and Southeast Asia: From gridlock to continuous self-improvement? *Governance* 17(3): 361–86.

Rawnsley, G. D. 2007. The media and democracy in China and Taiwan. *Taiwan Journal of Democracy* 3(1): 63–78.

Shiau, J.-Y. 2006. A comparative study of civil service recruitment systems in Taiwan and China. Masters thesis [In Chinese]. National Chengchi University, Taipei.

Shih, J. N. 2006. Capacity of civil service system and government competitiveness: Strategic human resource management perspective. [In Chinese]. *Soochow Journal of Political Science* 22: 1–46.

Su, T.-T. 2010. Civil service reforms in Taiwan. In E. Berman, M. J. Moon and H. Choi (eds), *Public Administration in East Asia: Mainland China, Japan, South Korea and Taiwan*, 609–26. New York: CRC Press.

Tan, Q. 2000. Democratization and bureaucratic restructuring in Taiwan. *Studies in Comparative International Development* 35(2): 48–64.

Tang, C.-P. 2004. When new public management runs into democratization: Taiwan's public administration in transition. *Issues & Studies* 40(3–4): 59–100.

Wade, R. 1990. *Governing the Market: Economic theory and the role of government in East Asian industrialization.* Princeton, NJ: Princeton University Press.

Warr, P. B., Bird, M. and Rackham, N. 1970. *The Evaluation of Management Training.* London: Gower Press.

Yao, S.-Q. 2009. The impact of senior civil service training in Taiwan: A case study of CSPTC's training programs. [In Chinese]. *T&D Fashion* 83: 1–29.

www.ingramcontent.com/pod-product-compliance
Lightning Source LLC
Chambersburg PA
CBHW040153270326
41928CB00040B/3314